PARIS

Welcome to Paris

Anne-Marie Corbierre

Collins
Glasgow and London

Cover Photograph
ZEFA

Photographs
All photographs, Van Phillips
except p.119 (bottom) J. Allan Cash

Illustrations
pp.4–9 Peter Joyce

Maps
pp.38–9 by kind permission of RATP
pp.14, 41–57 adapted by kind permission of Hallwag,
from their city map series
pp.66–77 M. and R. Piggott

First published 1981
Revised edition 1984, 1988
Copyright © Anne-Marie Corbierre 1981
Published by William Collins Sons and Company Limited
Printed in Great Britain

ISBN 0·00 44 7553 4

CONTENTS

The Romans conquer the Parisii.   *Lutetia renamed Paris.*   *Attila captures Paris.*

PARIS

Paris Sans Pair – Paris Unequalled. The reputation of Paris as the leading city in France was not confined to the inhabitants of the town and the surrounding Ile de France in the 13th century. At the same time, in the language of the South of France the following proverb could be heard: *Digas les qu'en un jorn Paris non fo obrat* – tell him that Paris was not built in a day. The South had its own capitals to be proud of – Marseille, Pau and Toulouse – but such was the prestige of Paris, the seat of French royal power, that at a period when French national entity meant very little, Paris was regarded as the centre of France.

Historic events are not alone in having contributed to make Paris what she is today. Her geographical situation had much to attract and retain a thriving population, and there was a river, bordered on either side by wooded hills, with easily defensible islands in the centre – the Gallic tribe of the Parisii settled on one of them over 2000 years ago. Conquered by the Romans, the Parisii burnt their huts and bridges, leaving only their dead and a mass of cinders for the new colonizers who took over the island and rebuilt it as Lutetia which thrived for several centuries. Although there is little evidence to show

that the Right Bank was inhabited, the Gallo-Roman arena by the Jardin des Plantes, the baths under the Museum of Cluny and the discovery, in 1878, of a Roman burial ground at the upper end of the Rue St Jacques all attest to the considerable development of the Left Bank of the Seine. In AD292 Lutetia became an Imperial residence and in 360, after the election of Julian the Apostate, Prefect of the Gauls, as Emperor of Rome, the town, which had by then become one of the principal cities of Gaul, was renamed Paris after the tribe who had founded it.

The arrival of Christianity and the martyrdom of St Denis in 250 did much to fortify the resistance of the inhabitants against the Germanic invasions which began around this period. Sacked in 280, the town was rebuilt and by 451 such was the impact of the religion that Ste Geneviève was able to save Paris from destruction by opening the gates to Attila. In 497, Clovis, converted to Christianity, became king and made Paris his capital in 508. Under the Merovingian dynasty Paris became a thriving monastic city whose abbeys grew in power and wealth as they extended their protection to the inhabitants grouped around them. This religious growth, however, was not synonymous with political stability and, due to the division of Clovis' kingdom among his

City walls built with 24 gates.   *The English capture Paris.*

heirs, Paris remained the centre of conflicting Frankish rivalries and warfare for over 200 years, and her decline was only accentuated when Charlemagne established his capital at Aix-la-Chapelle. This left the way open for the Normans, who devastated the banks of the Seine five times before their decisive defeat in 885 by Count Eudes. As always, after every disaster throughout their history, the inhabitants patiently rebuilt the city.

Despite the approaching millennium and the fear of the unknown after the prophetic date of 1000, a new era of activity began around the middle of the 10th century. It was at about this time that the Right Bank began to develop, probably due to the Nautes, river merchants who were installed around the market on the site of La Grève (the present Hôtel de Ville). Trade by water continued to develop steadily and, in 1141, Louis VI sold the site to the merchants for 70 livres. In the same year another royal charter established a new market on the site of les Halles, where it was to remain for 800 years until its removal to the suburb of Rungis in 1969. By the end of the 12th century the Right Bank was firmly established as the commercial centre of Paris, leaving the Left Bank for the building of religious and educational institutions.

The urban development of medieval Paris owes much to Philippe Auguste who, not content with building the fortress of the Louvre to defend commerce on the Right Bank and to house his archives and treasure, enclosed the cemetery of the Innocents, paved the main streets, and constructed the great wall round the perimeter of his city, guarded by towers and drawbridges at each of its 24 gateways. Although St Louis (IX) spent a large part of his reign on the Crusades, he still found time to order the construction of the Sainte Chapelle to house the relics of Christ's Passion, and to complete the South Porch of Notre Dame in 1257. In the same year, he gave Robert de Sorbon the land adjoining the Palais des Thermes and the buildings necessary for the founding of the University. From the point of view of municipal administration, however, he took a decision which was to have grave consequences for Paris. By that time the corporation, led by the water merchants, had virtually seized the reins of municipal power, meeting together in what was known as the Parloir des Bourgeois to defend their interests and run the city's affairs. Justice was dealt out in the king's name by an officer nominated by the Parloir. Foreseeing the danger to royal authority in such a system, St Louis, assisted by a royal officer, dispensed justice himself.

Hot air balloon ascends from Tuileries, 1783.

Revolution sweeps away the Ancien Régime.

The idea was sound, but from then on endemic rivalry was to poison relations between the town and the monarchy for over five centuries. The first real crisis arose in 1358, when Etienne Marcel, Provost of the Merchants, taking advantage of the political instability, led the people's revolt against the future Charles V. Charles, once he became king, restored order to the city, built the Bastille and a new wall round the north side of the city to protect it from the English, and embellished the Louvre. He also reorganized the city into 16 areas administered by an officer known as *quartinier* whose functions corresponded with those of a mayor or police officer, and he was assisted by 20 sub-officers who dealt with day-to-day affairs. The office of *quartinier* was highly sought after, since it also carried the right to take part in the elections of the merchants' Provost. Under the weak-minded Charles VI, Paris again became the centre of political strife due to the rival Armagnac and Burgundy factions and the ambitions of the English kings Henry V and VI (Henry VI was crowned king of France in Notre Dame in 1430). But the town continued to develop and when Charles VII was at last able to enter Paris in 1437, it was to take possession of a thriving commercial city whose university attracted students from all over Europe.

Although the wars in Italy brought to France the artistic and literary influence of the Renaissance, Paris had already begun to evolve its own architectural style. The Hôtels de Cluny and Sens, built during the last quarter of the 15th century can be considered the precursors of the French Renaissance, which was to reach its culmination during the reigns of François I, who rebuilt the Louvre as a palace, and Henri II, with architects and sculptors such as Jean Bullant, Philibert Delorme, Pierre Lescot and Jean Goujon. The Louvre and the Tuileries Palace, the Hôtel Carnavalet, begun in 1544, and the Fountain of the Innocents, erected in 1548, are due to them. The end of the 16th century saw the beginning of the construction of the Pont Neuf, now the oldest bridge in Paris, ordered by Henri III in 1577 so that he could cross from the Louvre to St Germain des Prés without having to make a long detour. During the religious wars of this period, Paris suffered cruelly, 20,000 died of hunger during the long siege (1589-94), and its gates were opened to Henri IV only after his conversion to Catholicism (and cynical declaration *Paris vaut bien Une Messe* – Paris is well worth a mass). Peace restored, Henri had very definite ideas concerning his capital, which he did not live long enough to realize. However, plans for a

Napoleon Buonaparte restores order and becomes Emperor.

new quarter south of the Temple were partially achieved in his reign when the Rues de Bretagne, Beauce, Perche and Picardie, in the 3rd *arrondissement*, were laid out and the building of the Place Royale begun.

Under Louis XIII and Cardinal de Richelieu, Paris became an Archbishopric and the Académie Française and the Imprimerie Royale were founded. Henri IV's new quarter continued to take shape with the building of the Marais and the joining together of the Ile Notre Dame and the Ile des Vaches to form the Ile St Louis. At the same time, the Left Bank saw the building of the Palais du Luxembourg for Henri's widow, Marie de Médicis, and the construction of a whole series of convents, one of which was the Val de Grâce, on the orders of the pious Anne of Austria.

If Louis XIV was more concerned with Versailles and perpetuating his own glory rather than that of his capital, the Colonnade of the Louvre, Les Invalides and the Place Vendôme are nevertheless worthy monuments of his reign. In practical vein, his minister Colbert built the Observatory, founded the royal tapestry works at Gobelins and re-organized the French merchant navy, thereby considerably developing the port of Paris. Culturally, the city became one of the centres of Europe. Corneille, Molière

and Racine lived there as did such musicians as Lully and Couperin, and the philosopher Pascal. Madame de Sévigné wittily described events in Paris and the court at Versailles in her letters and, together with other members of the aristocracy and writers, was entertained in the salons of the capital.

Building continued under Louis XV with the erection of the Panthéon, and the founding of the Ecole Militaire, whose architect Gabriel laid out the Place de la Concorde. In 1784, the Farmers General (tax officers) obtained permission to build another wall round Paris not only to prevent the illegal entry of goods into the city but also to enlarge the taxable area. Highly unpopular, the wall only added to the rapidly growing discontent of the people who, with their usual wit said: *Le Mur murant rend Paris murmurant* – the Wall walling in Paris makes her wail.

Although the Revolution of 1789 spread throughout France, it could be said that it was above all Paris' revolution, since the main events took place in the capital, from the taking of the Bastille on 14 July 1789 to Bonaparte's 'whiff of grapeshot', marking its end on 5 October 1795. If, during this period of upheaval, construction was reversed with the destruction of many convents and churches, on the other hand several important institutions were foun-

Napoleon I returns to France.

Paris in turmoil, 1839, 1848, 1871.

The World Fair and Eiffel Tower, 1889.

ded, including the two great higher education colleges of the Ecole Polytechnique and the Ecole Normale Supérieure, the Institut, incorporating the Académie Française and three other academies, and the Natural History Museum. Napoleon, once he became Emperor, drew up a new civil code, created the offices of Prefect of the Seine and of the Police, completed the Cour Carrée in the Louvre and began building the wing along the Rue de Rivoli, and started the Arc de Triomphe. Under the Restoration, the convents were reopened and new churches built, but in July 1830, as a result of Charles X's laws reducing the electorate and suppressing the freedom of the Press, Paris was the scene of fierce fighting behind hastily constructed barricades. Under Louis Philippe, the first railway line was opened in 1837 between Paris and St Germain, and new fortifications were built round the town. The people, however, influenced by the ideas of socialists such as Prudhon and Auguste Blanqui, were more interested in the extension of their liberty and better living conditions and, in February 1848, the barricades were rebuilt on the boulevards and street fighting again marked a change of régime. A few months later, the suppression of national workshops caused fresh outbursts of fighting in the Faubourg St Antoine.

The Emperor Louis Napoleon's foreign policy has been justly criticized, but it would be doing him and Baron Haussmann a grave injustice by failing to give them credit for the changes made to Paris in the 1850s. Up till then, Paris was a maze of narrow, tortuous streets, stinking with refuse and crowded with an ever-increasing population. Thousands died every year of disease – the great outbreak of cholera in 1832 carried off 19,000 inhabitants. A vast sewage system to cleanse the streets and improve public health was laid out by Belgrand, new wide boulevards – easy to attack, difficult to defend – were cut through the city, the parks of the Buttes Chaumont and Montsouris were created and, to facilitate administration, Paris was reorganized into 20 *arrondissements* (districts). At the same time, the limits were extended to incorporate the villages of Auteuil and Passy in the west, Montmartre, La Chapelle and La Villette in the north and Belleville, Bercy and Charonne in the east.

The Franco-Prussian War and the Siege of Paris by the Prussians led to the Commune in 1871, the burning of the Hôtel de Ville, the Palais Royal and the Tuileries, another brief siege and a bloody suppression by the French army. Under the 3rd Republic restoration took place in rather questionable taste, but the period is

Paris occupied, 1940–4.

Modern Paris develops.

more notable for the incredible artistic explosion which took place, first with the Impressionists and then, at the beginning of the 20th century, with the birth of the Cubist and Fauvist movements. During the 1914-18 War Paris literally trembled during artillery bombardments of the front lines, but thanks to the victory on the Marne, remained virtually untouched. Building began again after the war and artists, musicians, poets and writers flocked to Paris to live and work in the city and meet together in the cafés of Montmartre and Montparnasse. 1940 was the year of the débâcle and the beginning of the German occupation. For the next four years, Parisians lived by expediency, their meagre rations eked out by food parcels from the country, their apartments heated by stoves filled with sawdust. The city escaped large-scale damage when the Liberation forces arrived in 1944, due to the German commander of the city, Von Choltitz, who refused to obey Hitler's orders to blow up the principal buildings and bridges. Throughout this sombre period, however, the inhabitants never lost their wit or humour, satirical newspapers flourished and in the theatres and cabarets, artistic and cultural life continued.

An 18th-or 19th-century inhabitant returning with the Liberation Army would have recognized Paris; not so today. With modern buildings, skyscraper towers, ring road and expressways along the banks of the Seine, the town has changed considerably over the last 25 years. Chemical and metallurgical industries are established in the suburbs, to the Port of Paris has been added the vast new Port of Gennevilliers in the north west, new satellite towns have grown up on the periphery and a whole new business quarter, La Défense, has been built at the western limit of the town. For many, however, Paris still retains its essential characteristics, vivid and gay, full of beautiful buildings and wide tree-lined avenues. Although the chronic housing shortage is forcing families to leave the centre for the suburbs, new inhabitants arrive daily from the provinces and abroad to take their place, bringing with them their culture and vitality to add to the already colourful character of the Parisians. Charming but cynical, witty, ready to protest or burst into song on the slightest pretext, they are proud of their city and, provided tourists do not upset their daily habits too much, are willing to share it with the thousands who arrive every year. For its people, Paris is not just a city; as the Emperor Charles V said, it is a whole world, and despite its inconveniences and periodic upheavals, many would never live anywhere else.

Paris telephone numbers have been reorganised. Dial 4 before seven-digit numbers and check all numbers given before dialling.

PAPERWORK

Passports A valid passport (or Visitor's Card for UK citizens), bearing the photograph and current address of the holder, is all that is necessary for visitors entering France – and it should be carried with you at all times. **UK citizens** should apply to the passport offices in London, Liverpool, Peterborough, Glasgow, Newport or Gwent; residents of Northern Ireland should apply to the Foreign and Commonwealth Passport Agency, 30 Victoria St., Belfast. **US citizens** should apply to the US passport agencies in Boston, Chicago, Miami, New Orleans, New York, San Francisco or Washington. **Canadian citizens** by post: Passport Office, 125 Sussex Drive, Ottawa, Ontario K1A 0G2; in person: the passport offices in Edmonton, Halifax, Montreal, Toronto, Vancouver or Winnipeg.

Health certificates are necessary only for those arriving from certain African, Asian and South American countries, which have notified the World Health Organization of infection or epidemics. Medical authorities at sea ports, airports and frontiers are empowered to insist on immediate vaccination for those nationals arriving without valid health certificates.

Length of stay Visitors can remain in France for up to three months, after which period they should either contact the local police station or the Préfecture de Police (Service des Etrangers, immigration service), 7–9 Bd du Palais, Paris 4 (tel: 329 21 55 enquiries, or 260 33 22).

Insurance

Health insurance Once it happens, an accident or illness is one of the surest ways to ruin a holiday abroad, and travellers are strongly advised to take the relevant precautions before they leave home. **UK citizens** France and Britain operate a reciprocal health care agreement, but first you must obtain Form E111. A month before departure, if possible, apply to your local social security office where you fill in Form CM1 in order to obtain Form E111. Those intending to stay for more than three months, or to live or work in Paris, should apply to the Department of Health and Social Security Overseas Branch, Newcastle upon Tyne NE98 1YX. Once in France, you will be charged for any medical or dental treatment and for medicines prescribed, and reimbursed later. *Commissariats de Police* (police stations) and *pharmacies* (chemist shops) supply a list of doctors, dentists (*médecins, dentistes conventionnés*) and hospitals affiliated to the French social security service. On production of Form E111, the doctor or dentist will give you a sickness form (*feuille de maladie*) on which he enters his fee. The pharmacist also enters the price of any medicine on this form and affixes stamps (*vignettes*), after which you should sign and date it. Pharmacists and Commissariats de Police also supply the addresses of the nearest social security office to which you should repair with forms and prescriptions in order to be reimbursed. Medical and dental fees are refunded at approx. 75% of the cost; medicines 70%. **Hospital treatment** The patient must pay for treatment received in the out patients' department and then claim a refund as detailed above. If you have to be admitted to hospital, inform social security at once and show your Form E111 to the hospital authorities. Further information can be obtained from: Caisse Primaire Centrale et Assurance Maladie de la Région Parisienne, Service des Relations Internationales, 173 / 175 Rue de Bercy, 75586 Paris Cedex 12. (Tel: 4346 7253). Métro Gare de Lyon. **US citizens** As there is no reciprocal health agreement between France and the USA, visitors should take out private health insurance covering their stay abroad before they leave home. Insurance brokers and travel agents can usually suggest the best type of insurance cover according to length of stay. **Canadian citizens** As with the USA, no reciprocal agreement exists. Before leaving home, contact your federal or provincial health and medical authorities who will advise on whether production of written justification (*feuilles de maladie, prescriptions, etc*) will entitle you to reimbursement on return home or whether you should take out private health insurance cover.

Lost property: Bureau des Objets Trouvés, 36 Rue des Morillons, Paris 15 (tel: 4531 1480). Open Mon-Fri 0830–1700.

Car insurance Green Card (international) insurance and a valid international or national driving licence are necessary for drivers in France. Third party insurance cover is compulsory but, for those new or unused to driving abroad, 'all risks' cover is recommended.

CURRENCY

The French unit of currency is the Franc (F), divided into 100 centimes. Bank notes in circulation: 500, 200, 100, 50 and 20 Francs; silver coins: 5, 2, 1 franc and 50 centime pieces; bronze coins: 10 Franc, 20, 10 and 5 centime pieces.

There are banks with exchange facilities for travellers' checks and bank notes in every quarter of Paris, and some of the larger hotels also change currency, though at a lower rate than the banks. In addition, exchange offices (bureaux de change) in main-line stations are open daily as follows: Gare de Lyon (CIC) 0630–2300, Daily; Gare de l'Est (Credit Lyonnais) 0730–2300; Gare d'Austerlitz (Credit Lyonnais) 0700–2100; Gare St Lazare (Credit Lyonnais) 0700–2000. There are six branches of the Société Génerale at Roissy-Charles De Gaulle airport and two at Orly airport, all of which are open 0630–2330. Roissy 1: on the arrivals and departure floors, by the Air France desk. Roissy 2: Modules A and B. A valid passport or identity card is the only document necessary for those wishing to change money.

Banking hours Banks are open 0900–1645 Mondays to Fridays, and a few close for lunch 1230–1400. All banks close at weekends and on public holidays (p.34), but American Express, 11 Rue Scribe, Paris 9; Thomas Cook, 2 Place de la Madeleine, Paris 8; Banque Nationale de Paris, 2 Place de l'Opera, Paris 2, 49 Ave des Champs-Elysées, Paris 8 and 2 Bd des Italiens, Paris 9 are open on Saturday mornings and will change money. No 154 Champs Elysées (UPB) is open Mon-Fri 0845–1715, Sat & Sun 1030–1300 and 1400–1600; no 117 Champs Elysées

(CCF) Mon–Sat 0900–2000. (The Paris Tourist Information Office, tel: 723 61 72, can supply details.)

Credit cards International arrangements exist at certain banks for the cashing of personal checks accompanied by American Express, Visa, Blue and Eurocards. A moderate fee is charged for the service.

Currency restrictions No restrictions for foreign tourists entering France. It is advisable to bring a small amount of francs, particularly at weekends.

British banks Barclays Bank: (head office) 33 Rue du Quatre Septembre, Paris 2. (Branches) 24 Ave Kléber, Paris 16; 6 Rond Point des Champs-Elysées, Paris 8; 157 Bd St Germain, Paris 6. International Westminster Bank, 18 Place Vendôme, Paris 1. Lloyds Bank International, 43 Bd des Capucines, Paris 2.

American banks American Express, 11 Rue Scribe, Paris 9; 85 bis Rue de Courcelles, Paris 17; 1 Rue du Boccador, Paris 8. Bank of America, 43 Ave de la Grande Armée, Paris 16. Chase Manhattan Bank, 41 Rue Cambon, Paris 1. Bank of Boston, 104 Ave des Champs-Elysées, Paris 8; City Bank, 17-19 Ave Montaigne, Paris 8.

Canadian banks Bank of Montreal, 10 Place Vendôme, Paris 1. Canadian Imperial Bank of Commerce, 49 Rue Hoche, Paris 8. Canadian National Bank, 47 Ave George V, Paris 8. Royal Bank of Canada, 3 Rue Scribe, Paris 9.

CUSTOMS

Travellers arriving by air or sea must pass through customs posts at airports and sea ports; those arriving by rail will have their baggage examined either in the train or in the customs building situated at the end of the arrivals platform.

Narcotics France has redoubled the campaign against the import of narcotics, which is strictly illegal. Penalties are severe and almost invariably involve heavy fines and imprisonment.

Duty-free allowances for UK citizens (*subject to change*) *Tobacco*: 200 cigarettes or 100 small cigars or 50 large cigars or 250gm pipe tobacco (bought in duty-free shop); 300 cigarettes or 150 small cigars or 75 large cigars or 400gm pipe tobacco (bought in EEC). *Alcohol* 1 litre spirits over 38.8 proof or two litres fortified or sparkling wine *plus* 2 litres table wine (bought in duty-free shop; 1½ litres spirits over 38.8 proof or 3 litres fortified or sparkling wine *plus* 4 litres table wine (bought in EEC). 50gm perfume, 250cc toilet water, £28 other goods (bought in duty-free shop); 75gm perfume, 375gm toilet water, £120 other goods (bought in EEC). US customs permit duty-free $300 retail value of purchases per person, 1 quart of liquor per person over 21, and 100 cigars per person.

On return home, importation of certain items – such as animals (see Rabies p.34), uncooked foodstuffs, plants and seeds, firearms and knives, fur products, *etc* – is either prohibited or subject to strict control in individual countries, and visitors are advised to check, before their departure, with customs authorities in their own countries. Further information on customs regulations can be obtained in France from the American, British and Canadian consulates (adresses on p.36) who supply the following leaflets on request: (US citizens) *Know Before You Go*, *Customs Hints for Returning US Residents*; (UK citizens) Customs Notices nos 1 and 12; (Canadian citizens) *Customs and Excise I Declare/Douanes et Accise Je Déclare.*

HOW TO GET THERE

By Air
From the UK Air France and British Airways operate several direct daily scheduled flights to Paris from London (Heathrow), Birmingham, Manchester and Glasgow. British Caledonian operates daily scheduled flights to Paris from Gatwick. These companies also offer a range of cheaper excursion fares which must be booked and paid for in advance.

From Canada There are direct flights to Paris from Montreal and Toronto by Air Canada and Air France. APEX (Advance Purchase Excursion) offers special terms on scheduled flights if reservation and payment are made at least 30 days in advance – length of stay is limited to between 14 and 60 days. There is also a variety of special charter and excursion rates, *eg* La Bonne Aubaine (Windfall), with a wide range of different tariffs – high and low season, tourists and young people under 23 years. It pays to shop around.

From the US Air France, Braniff, National Airlines and TWA operate daily scheduled flights to Paris, with direct flights departing from Boston, Chicago, Dallas, Houston, Los Angeles, Miami, New York and Washington. Pan American also operates daily flights to Paris. Lively competition vying for passengers on transatlantic flights ensures a wide range of tariffs to suit most purses – APEX, charter, economy and excursion rates.

Airports Paris has three airports – to the north east are Charles de Gaulle, at Roissy (27km/16mi) and Le Bourget (17km/10mi), to the south lies Orly South and West (14km/8mi). Airport services include banking and exchange facilities, medical service and vaccinations, postal service, identity photographs, photocopiers, car rental and a secretarial service (known as 2a Service). In addition there are special facilities for babies and for the disabled (wheelchairs, *etc*). Information desks are staffed by competent multilingual hostesses.

As well as taxis, buses carry passengers from Charles de Gaulle to the air terminal at Porte Maillot (departures every 15 mins, approx. time taken 35 mins); from Orly South and West to the Gare des Invalides on the Left Bank (departures every 15 minutes, approx. time taken 35 mins). A combined bus and train service (Roissy Rail) takes passengers from Charles de Gaulle to the Gare du Nord (departures every 15 minutes, approx. time taken 30 mins); and from Orly (Orly Rail) a similar service operates with stops at the Gare d'Austerlitz, Pont St Michel, Gare d'Orsay, Gare des Invalides and Pont de l'Alma (departures every 15 mins, approx. time taken 40 mins). Charles de Gaulle at Roissy has two terminals and if visitors are being met by friends they should specify at which terminal they disembark.

By Rail

Trains depart daily from Charing Cross and Victoria stations in London and arrive in Paris, at the Gare du Nord, approximately 5½ hours later (the channel crossing is made by ferry or hovercraft). The night boat train, with sleeping accommodation, leaves Victoria station between 2100–2130 and arrives in Paris the following morning between 0730–0800.

Main-line stations All main-line stations (listed below) are served by several métro lines and also provide currency exchange and postal facilities as well as the usual services associated with rail terminals – left luggage, lockers, porters, trolleys, *etc.* In addition, there are tourist information offices at the Gare du Nord (tel: 526 94 82) open 0800–2200 (2000 out of season); Gare d'Austerlitz (tel: 584 91 70) open 0800–2200 (1500 out of season); Gare de l'Est (tel: 607 17 73) open 0800–1300 and 1700–2200 (2000 out of season); Gare de Lyon (tel: 343 33 24) open 0800–1300 and 1700–2200 (2000 out of season). All these offices close at 2000 out of season. Paris main-line stations:

Gare d'Austerlitz (journeys to south-west France)

Gare de l'Est (to the east)

Gare de Lyon (to south east and the south)

Gare Montparnasse (to Brittany and the west)

Gare du Nord (to the north)

Gare St Lazare (to Normandy and the north west, and for boat trains from Dieppe, Le Havre and Cherbourg)

By Car/Ferry

There are numerous car-ferry crossings to France from Britain: Dover and Folkestone to Boulogne, Dunkerque and Calais; Newhaven to Dieppe; Southampton to Le Havre; Plymouth to Roscoff and Weymouth to Cherbourg, although the last two are not recommended for Paris in view of distance. Hovercraft services operate from Dover and Ramsgate to Calais for passengers with or without cars. These crossings are considerably quicker than by boat (approx. 35 mins) but may be subject to delay or cancellation in bad weather.

The quickest route to Paris from Dunkerque (292km/182mi) and Calais (305km/191mi) is via the A1 autoroute. (There are toll charges on all autoroutes.) From Dunkerque take the N225 and then the A25 to join the A1 at Lille. From Calais, the A26 leads to the A1 at Arras. Travellers from Boulogne (242km/151mi) should take the N1 to Amiens, then the D934 to Roye where the A1 can be joined, or, if preferred, continue on the N1 to Paris via Beauvais. Motorists arriving from Dieppe (167km/104mi) should take the N27 to Rouen from where they can join the A13 to Paris, and for those arriving from Le Havre (204km/128mi) the N 182 across the Tancarville Bridge leads to the A13 for Paris.

The only documents required of visitors entering France by car are a valid national or international driving licence and the international Green Card insurance, which must be signed by the policy holder. Other compulsory requirements are a nationality plate or sticker, warning lights and/or a red warning triangle and seat belts for front passengers. Motorists should also have their head lamps properly adjusted and either fitted with yellow disks or painted yellow.

Minor breakdowns and the lack of basic spare parts cause loss of valuable travelling time apart from considerable irritation, and the following is a brief list of parts which, even if the driver cannot fit himself, will be easily fitted when taken along to a local garage in France: coil (*condensateur*); distributor cap (*tête de delco*); sparking plug (*bougie d'allumage*); fan belt (*courroie de ventilator*); head and side light bulbs (*ampoules*) – a spare set of these is obligatory for every car in France; brake lights (*feux de stop*); fuses (*fusibles*); temporary windscreen (*pare-brise gonflable*). If you cannot speak the language, it is a good idea to carry the handbook for your vehicle as the pictures may do the vital job of communication for you.

By Coach

Individual travel agents and tour operators – Brittours, Thomas Cook, Republic Tours, *etc* – provide imformation and bookings for coach trips to Paris. Magic Bus departs Thurs–Sun. (01 836 7799). Europabus departs several days a week from Victoria Coach Station in London for Gare St Lazare in Paris – the bus can be joined in Canterbury or at Dover. Normandy Ferries also organizes trips from Birmingham, Swansea, London and Plymouth, with the possibility of joining the bus at certain towns between those terminals and ferry departure at Southampton.

GETTING AROUND PARIS

Paris is divided into 20 *arrondissements* (administrative areas) each of which has its own town hall, or Mairie. These *ar-*

rondissements make up the municipality of Paris, administered by the Mayor whose offices are at the Hôtel de Ville (town hall). Starting from the centre (area of Louvre, Palais Royal and west half of Ile de la Cité) the sequence of *arrondissements* is arranged in a spiral working outwards and covering both sides of the Seine.

Métro (See map pp. 38–9)

The Paris underground is run by the RATP (Régie Autonome des Transports Parisiens) and is made up of 13 lines crossing from north to south, east to west and diagonally, plus two short supplementary lines. Large maps are posted in every station and the terminals of each line are shown in the centre of every platform. Connections with other lines are indicated by the orange sign *Correspondance*.

valid on buses and métro: unlimited travel in Paris up to Zone 3 for one day. Tourist Passes (*Carte Sesame*), valid for an unlimited number of journeys for 2, 4 and 7 days can also be obtained from ticket offices in métros and bus terminals. Children under 4 travel free. *Carte Vermeil* (Senior Citizen's Card), discount card for women over 60 and men over 65 years. To obtain it, go with your passport as proof of age to the Abonnement Office in any of the main railway stations or to the SNCF office in the basement of the Bureau de Tourism, 127 Ave des Champs-Elysées, Paris 8. The fee for the card is moderate and entitles the holder to travel, entertainment and museum discounts, $\frac{1}{2}$ price in some cases. Details from French Government Tourist Offices, addresses see p.36.

The métro service starts at around 0530

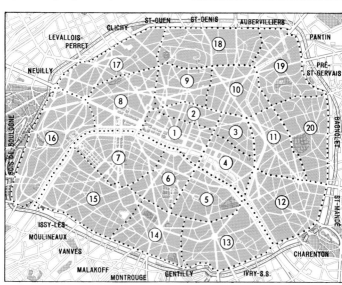

The service operates on a flat-rate basis, and it is much more economical to buy a book of 10 tickets (*carnet* price for children under 10), available for 1st and 2nd class travel, at ticket offices in métro stations or at tobacco kiosks in *Café Tabacs* — the tickets are valid for use on both bus and métro. The *Carte Orange* is valid for a month, available at ticket offices and bus terminals from the 20th day of the preceding month, valid on both bus and métro. There is also a weekly version of this, the *Carte Jaune Hebdomadaire*, valid from Monday to the following Sunday. *Formule 1* ticket

and continues to approx. 0030 at night, and is both frequent and regular. Although constant modernization is underway, with escalators and travellators, visitors should know that access to platforms is often via numerous staircases and long corridors. No part of the city is more than 400m/440yd from a métro station. RATP information booths exist on platforms or in the halls of several stations. The RER (Réseau Express Régional) is a fast service composed of the Métro linked up with the SNCF lines to the suburbs. It crosses Paris from north to south and east to west (lines

A, B and C).
the suburbs. It crosses Paris from north to south and east to west (lines A, B and C).

Buses

Buses in Paris are dark green, with their number on the front and itinerary on the sides. Start and finish times vary according to individual lines, but all buses are in service between 0700 and 2030. In addition, the following run until at least midnight: 21, 26, 27, 31, 38, 52, 62, 63, 80, 91, 92, 95, 96 and the PC (Petite Ceinture – the Ring Road Bus) which goes all the way round Paris on the Boulevards Extérieurs, stopping at all the *Portes*. Frequency of buses is between 7 and 10 minutes Mondays to Saturdays, with reduced services on Sundays and holidays.

Night Service (*Noctambus*) 10 buses leave at hourly intervals from the Chatelet between 0130 and 0530 for the nearest suburbs. The Carte Orange is valid for these buses otherwise fares vary according to distance travelled on the buses which are named NA, NB, NC, ND, NE, NF, NG, NH, NJ and NR (which goes to the markets at Rungis and leaves every half hour from 0100 Tuesdays–Saturdays).

Bus stops (many with shelters) are painted yellow and red, and list the bus route concerned and indicate how many tickets are required for the journey, since, unlike the métro, buses do not operate on a flat-rate system. Tickets are punched in the machine on entering the vehicle.

Buses can be one of the best ways of sightseeing in an unfamiliar town, and the following routes may be of interest: **21** Saint Lazare–Opéra–Palais Royal–Louvre–Châtelet–Cité (Palais de Justice and Sainte Chapelle)–Saint Michel–Luxembourg–Port Royal–Parc Montsouris–Cité Universitaire. **63**: Halle aux Vins (University Paris VI)–Cluny–Saint Germain–Odéon–Saint Sulpice–Palais Bourbon–Gare des Invalides–Place de l'Alma–Trocadéro–Palais de Chaillot–Porte de la Muette (Bois de Boulogne). **82**: Luxembourg–Notre Dame des Champs–Saint François Xavier–Ecole Militaire–Champ de Mars–Tour Eiffel–Palais de Chaillot–Porte Maillot–Neuilly (American Hospital).

Montmartre Bus A minibus from the Place Pigalle via Moulin de la Galette, Place des Abbesses, Place du Tertre, Sacré Cœur and the vineyard. A good way to see Montmartre.

General information on public transport can be obtained from the RATP tourist offices at 53 bis Quai des Grands Augustins, Paris 6 (tel: 346 14 14/42 03) or Place de la Madeleine (by the flower market) Paris 8 (tel: 265 31 18). They also publish métro and bus route schedules and organize bus tours of Paris (Paris Vision) and day and half-day trips outside Paris. Details of tours and the schedules are obtainable from the tourist offices which also accept bookings.

Trains

The main-line stations run services to the suburbs and the Gare d'Orsay operates a service out to Versailles. Details of rail routes, fares and schedules can be obtained from the central railway information office (tel: 260 51 51) and from SNCF tourist offices or stations.

Taxis

Paris is plentifully supplied with taxis which are found in ranks signposted *Tête de Station*. Prices appear on the meter below the dashboard. It is usual to add 15%, as a tip to the charge, which is increased at night, for journeys to the suburbs, for baggage and for trips from railway stations, air terminals and race courses. Taxis can also be ordered by telephone from the following numbers: 200 67 89; 203 33 33; 656 94 00; 657 11 12; 735 22 22; 739 33 33.

Car Rental

International car rental firms such as Avis, Hertz, Europcar and Inter Rent all have various offices in Paris. The system of charging is based on a daily rate plus mileage and payment is accepted by credit card. Documents required are a valid passport and driving licence and, for those without credit cards, some kind of residential proof corresponding to the address on passport or identity card, *eg* telephone or electricity bill or Paris address. Cash deposits are required from those without credit cards.

For young people, the minimum age varies between 21 and 25 years, and a driving licence must be at least one year old. Reservation in advance and payment on return home may be arranged through the offices of the above firms in Britain, Canada and the United States. Disabled persons *Intertouring*. Tel: 4588 5237.

Motoring Organizations

Motorists who are members of the Automobile Association, the Royal Automobile Club and the Royal Scottish Automobile Club in Britain, the American Automobile Association and the Automobile Club and Touring Club of Canada can benefit from reciprocal services offered by the Automobile Club de France, 6 Place de la Concorde (tel: 265 34 70/65 99) and the Touring Club de France, 14 Avenue de la Grande Armée (tel: 502 14 00/14 50). In addition, the Royal Automobile Club of Britain has offices in Paris at 8 Place Vendôme (tel: 260 62 12) and the AA is represented in Boulogne (tel: code 21, 302222). Lists of emergency breakdown points with telephone numbers and other facilities in France and Paris can be obtained on request from the clubs in Britain, Canada and the United States.

Rules of the Road

France drives on the right and overtakes on the left; priority is given to those arriving from the right at intersections, T junctions and on roundabouts.

Roads are divided into Autoroutes (A), Expressways, National (N) and Departmental (D) roads. All roads are well marked and signs conform to the regulations laid down by the EEC. Directional signing on autoroutes is dark blue with white lettering but is gradually being changed from blue to green with white lettering on N and D roads.

Speed limits 130kph/80mph on autoroutes and 110kph/68mph in rainy weather; 90kph/56mph on national and departmental roads except where marked 110kph/68mph; 60kph/37mph in towns and built-up areas. On the Boulevard Périphérique round Paris, speed is limited to 80kph/50mph.

Documents Motorists must carry their driving licence and insurance cards (the international Green Card for tourists) at all times.

Safety regulations Seat belts are compulsory for front-seat passengers and strongly recommended for back-seat passengers; children must travel in the back. For motorcyclists, crash helmets with reflectors are compulsory. Vehicles equipped to carry more than nine passengers should be fitted with a tachograph in proper working order.

Road conditions and holiday routes The Touring Club de France (address above), and the Road Information Centre at Rosny Sous Bois (tel: 858 33 33) give information on the best holiday routes, roads to be avoided, *etc.* In the summer season, the radio station, France Inter, provides an English-language news flash, with occasional tips on conditions and routes, at 0900 and 1600. Information can also be obtained in the larger newspapers during holiday periods (Easter, Whitsun, the first days of July, 14 July, the last weekend in July and August) when the Ministry of Transport publishes tables giving the best departure hours and dates from large towns and seaside resorts. In addition, *Bison Futé* (the Red Indian character created by the Ministry of Transport) issues a map with holiday routes marked in green, obtainable at ports of entry and at many toll posts on autoroutes during the summer holiday season. If you want to find out weather conditions in Paris and Normandy, telephone 555 95 90.

Parking There are now parking meters in most of the main streets of Paris and there is parking at almost all of the *Portes* and in the centre – Right Bank: Concorde, Étoile, Ave George V, Madeleine, Opéra and Hôtel de Ville near the Louvre, Bd Haussmann, St Augustin and at Galeries Lafayette, Place Vendôme, Les Halles, Centre Georges Pompidou; Left Bank and Ile de la Cité: Notre Dame, St Germain des Prés, Odéon, Invalides, Ecole Militaire and Panthéon, Bd Montparnasse, Place Saint-Sulpice. Beware of the blue-uniformed 'meter maids' patrolling the streets in search of illegally-parked cars. Fines can be substantial and parking in a bus lane, on a pedestrian crossing or on a street with a red and blue disk (no parking sign) can lead to your car being towed away or your front wheels being locked – in either case you should report to the nearest police station.

Fuel and oil Paris is well equipped with service stations and many of the parking areas and Périphérique exits have filling stations. It is an offence to run out of fuel on the autoroutes and expressways.

Horns It is an offence to sound a horn in towns other than as a warning.

Lights Dipped headlights are recommended in towns after dusk: all rear and brake lights should be in proper working order.

Mirrors A rear mirror in the car, and a wing mirror on the left-hand side, by the window, are compulsory.

Tyres Driving with poorly inflated or worn tyres is a finable offence in France. The tread pattern must have a depth of at least 1mm throughout three-quarters of the breadth and round the entire outer circumference. Police are often on the lookout for worn tyres at toll posts and the entries to autoroutes.

Accidents If there is no bodily injury, French motorists fill up a form known as a *Constat à l'Amiable* giving details of the accident, which is then signed by both parties each of whom sends a copy to his insurance company. These forms are supplied by insurance companies and those intending to drive in France are advised to ask their own insurance companies or automobile clubs whether similar forms are obtainable before beginning their journey. In the case of injury, contact the police at once. In the country the Gendarmerie or nearest police station should be informed (telephones every 2km/1¼mi on autoroutes); in Paris telephone Police-Secours or the Firemen (Pompiers) by dialling 17 and 18 respectively.

Driving offences As long as common sense prevails, driving is straightforward, *but*: exceeding the speed limit, reckless, dangerous or drunken driving, crossing the white centre line and failing to stop at a red light are offences which can lead to imprisonment in serious cases, and fines which can go up to ₣6000 and over.

Bicycle Rental

Bicycles and mopeds can be rented from Autothèque: 80 Rue de Montmartre, Paris 2 (tel: 236 87 90). Minimum age for mopeds, 18. Refundable deposit system, daily and weekly charges. Formalities: passport or identity card and address in Paris, plus (for mopeds) a crash helmet as these are not rented out. Open Mondays-Fridays 0900–1230, 1400–1830. Paris Vélo: 2 Rue du Fer à Moulin, Paris 5 (tel: 337 59 22) rent bicycles only. Refundable deposit system, daily, weekend, weekly and monthly charges. Formalities: passport or identity card and, for minors, written parental authority. Open Mondays–Saturdays 0900–1900.

Waterborne Travel

Seine There are four sightseeing services offering taped commentaries in English and floodlit tours at night (May to 15 Oct).
Bateaux Mouches Pont de l'Alma, Paris 8 (tel: 225 96 10). Departures every 30 mins every day 1000–1200 and 1400–1900. Restaurant for lunch 1300 and for dinner 2030 (jacket and tie, booking advisable.

Vedettes Paris Tour Eiffel Pont d'Iéna, Paris 7 (tel: 551 33 08/705 50 00). Daily departures every 30 mins 1000–1700.

Vedettes Pont Neuf Pont Neuf, Paris 1 (tel: 633 98 38). Every day, departures 1030, 1115 and 1200, and every 30 mins 1330–1800.

Vedettes de Paris & Ile de France Port de Suffren, Paris 7 (between the Pont d'Iéna and Pont Bir Hakeim, Left Bank (tel: 705 71 29/550 23 79). Departures every 30 mins daily 1000–1200 and 1330–1900.

Canal and Seine *Canauxrama*, (tel: 4624 8616). Canal St. Martin: from the Bassin de la Villette (métro Jean Jaurès) to the Porte de l'Arsenale (métro Bastille) mornings, vice-versa afternoons. *Paris Canal* (tel: 4874 8616). Seine and the Canal St. Martin. From the Quai Anatole France (métro Solferino) to the Bassin de la Villette (métro Jean Jaurès) in the mornings, vice-versa afternoons, May–

Nov. Bookings required for both the above.

Helicopter Tours

Hélicap – tel: 4557 7551.
Hélifrance – Héliport de Paris, 4 Ave de la Porte de Sèvres, Paris 15. Métro Balard. Tel: 4557 5367.

Chauffeurs and Guides

The large international car rental firms (Avis, Hertz, Inter Rent, *etc*) rent out cars with chauffeurs many of whom act as guides. Rates are quoted by the day and tipping is at the discretion of the client. The following firm provides interpreter-guides (on an individual or party basis) qualified to accompany tourists to museums, show them round Paris, transport them from one airport to another and help with restaurant and theatre bookings, *etc*. Minimum charge half a day, tipping at the discretion of the client. The firm advises réservations well in advance over the Christmas, Easter and Whitsun periods and during September and October (the high season for trade fairs and conventions). The firm is Troismil France, 35 Rue La Boétie, Paris 8 (tel: 563 78 36, telex: 640360).

Secretarial and Interpreting Services (in English) Many of the larger hotels provide this service. Other addresses include: Eclair Courrier, 25 Avenue Franklin Roosevelt, Paris 8 (tel: 225 86 10) and Office Central de Traducteurs-Interprètes, 116 Avenue des Champs-Elysées, Paris 8 (tel: 225 44 57).

ACCOMMODATION

Paris offers more than 1000 hotels, with categories, prices and sizes to meet all tastes and to suit most budgets. Hotel categories are officially fixed by the Tourist board according to amenities, comfort and type of establishment and are indicated by stars at the entrance to the hotel: L with 4 stars – luxury hotel (Palace); 4 stars – first class; 3 stars – very comfortable; 2 stars – good average hotel, often with private bath or shower; 1 star – small plain hotel (it is often prudent to inspect the room first, especially on the outer areas of the town).

Generally speaking, most of the luxury and 4-star hotels are situated on the Right Bank in the 1st, 2nd and 8th *arrondissements*, areas which are both central and fashionable, and parts of the 16th and 17th *arrondissements*, near the Etoile, the Trocadéro and Porte Maillot. However, this need not deter the visitor wishing to stay on this side of the Seine, since there is also a number of comfortable, relatively inexpensive hotels in these areas, and the residential quarters of the 16th and 17th *arrondissements* offer fairly peaceful surroundings. Hotels to the north and east of the areas mentioned tend to be cheaper but offer less in the way of comfort (1 and 2 stars).

Prices and categories of hotels on the Left Bank, with the exception of a few top class and 3-star hotels, are often lower. The Latin Quarter and Montparnasse, however, can be noisy due to the animated café and night life. The 7th and part of the 15th *arrondissements* are mainly residential areas and, provided the hotel is not on a main artery, are generally quieter.

By law the price of a hotel room, with taxes and service charges, must be displayed in the room and is usually posted on, or just next to, the door. Advertised charges usually show the price per night for a single or double room, with or without bath or shower, and indicate whether breakfast is included in the price and whether dogs are allowed in the hotel. Weekly or monthly terms are arranged individually with the management. Prices for children under 8 are sometimes slightly reduced, while a cot or crib in the parents' room can usually be arranged for young children. A sign showing a crossed knife and fork and wine glass indicates that the hotel has a restaurant, but apart from top international hotels and some others with well-known restaurants, many hotels do not provide this service.

Tipping In most cases the 15% service charge and taxes are automatically included in the bill, shown by the letters s.t.c. (service and taxes included), and if this is so, there is no necessity for the customer to leave an additional gratuity.

Facilities for the disabled A fair number of hotels can provide wheelchairs for the disabled. And the Association des Paralysés de France, 17 Bd Blanqui, Paris 13 (tel: 580 82 40) publishes a booklet called *Où Ferons Nous Etape?* (Where shall we stay); their Paris branch, 22 Rué Père Guerin, Paris 13 (same telephone number) provides useful advice and lists of cinemas, museums, theatres and restaurants with facilities for the disabled.

Self-catering accommodation For anyone intending to stay under a month in Paris, this is not recommended in view of the expense involved (agents' fees, deposits, *etc*) and the fact that bookings are invariably made on a monthly basis. If intent on self-catering, the following may be contacted: Inter Urbis, 1 Rue Mollien, Paris 8 (tel: 563 17 77); Paris Acceuil, 23 Rue Marignan, Paris 8 (tel: 296 14 26/ 256 37 47) for bed and breakfast in private apartments.

Hotel reservation Visitors to Paris are strongly advised to reserve hotel accommodation in advance, especially over the Easter and Whitsun periods, in June, September and October, when many conventions, trade fairs and important exhibitions are held. International hotel chains have centralized booking facilities and the following will also make reservations in advance, or on the spot should anyone arrive without a prior reservation.

Concordia, 108 Rue St Lazare, Paris 8 (tel: 293 46 19, telex 641803); agency in Britain: 52 Grosvenor Gdns, Victoria SW1W 0AU (tel: 01 730 3467). New York: 801 West Beach St, Long Beach NY11561 (tel: 516 889 8889).

UI Utell International, 2 Rue du Colonel Driant, Paris 1 (tel: 261 83 28, telex 240545); agencies in Britain: Bomba House, Cambridge Grove, London W6 (tel: 741 15 88); United States: 119 West 55th St, New York (tel: 212 397 2449); Canada: *Toronto* 950 Yonge St, Suite 405, Toronto, Ontario M4W 2J4 (tel: 416 967 3442). *Quebec* Wats (800) 268 7041, telex: 06 217634. *Vancouver* Suite 1107, 805 West Broadway, Vancouver, BC V52 1K1 (tel: 604 873 4661). *Alberta* and BC Wats (800) 663 9582, telex: 04 51565.

Office du Tourisme de Paris – Bureaux d'Acceuil (The welcome offices of Paris) Central Office: 127 Avenue des Champs-Elysées, Paris 8 (tel: 723 61 72/720 16 78).

Invalides Air Terminal office (tel: 705 82 81).

Gare d'Austerlitz, in the arrivals hall of the main-line terminal (tel: 584 91 70).

Gare du Nord, in the arrivals hall of the main-line terminal, or 18 Rue de Dunkerque (tel: 526 94 82).

Gare de l'Est, in arrivals hall (tel: 607 17 73).

Gare de Lyon, at the exit of the main-line terminal (tel: 343 33 24).

The above offices do not make reservations more than a week in advance.

Accommodation outside Paris For those arriving by air, there are hotels near the airports of Roissy-Charles de Gaulle and Orly. Tourists with cars, who prefer to stay outside Paris, should consult the list provided by the Office du Tourisme de Paris (address above). For those without cars staying outside Paris is not recommended unless they can be sure of a good public transport service into town.

Babysitters Babysitting services can sometimes be arranged by the management or with staff in the hotel, but if not contact: Kid Service, 17 Rue Molière,

Paris 1 (tel: 296 04 16 / 17 / 26 / 27) open 0830—2030 Mondays — Fridays, 1030—2030 Saturdays. American College in Paris, 31 Ave Bosquet, Paris 7 (tel: 555 91 73) open 9—5pm Mondays—Fridays; Centre Universitaire, Bd Jourdan, Paris 14 (tel: 4589 6852) from 0930—1330 and 1430—1730 except Saturday and Sunday; Institut Catholique, 21 Rue d'Assas, Paris 6 (tel: 4548 3170) from 0930—1130 and 1430—1730; Baby Sitting Actif, 34 Rue Delambre, Paris 14 (tel: 4327 8238).

FOOD AND DRINK

To do justice to this vast, even controversial, subject, the section following would need to be extended to encyclopedic proportions. Indications given below, therefore, are of a general nature only and do not claim to rival the knowledgeable comments of specialist writers on this topic in the press and in food and wine guides.

Restaurants of every type and size abound in Paris, ranging from gastronomic 'temples' to small local bistros, brasseries and cafés.

For those interested in tasting French regional cookery, there are restaurants specializing in: the white wine and cream, and fish dishes of Normandy; garlic and saffron flavoured bouillabaisses and bourrides (fish stews) and herb scented dishes of Provence; rustic dishes based on pork products of the Auvergne; and the foie gras (liver of fattened ducks and geese), confit (preserved duck and goose) and cassoulet (casserole of beans with a variety of meats and sausage) of the South West. Brasseries serving sauerkraut and pork specialities from Alsace are to be found in the 10th *arrondissement*, near the Gares de l'Est and du Nord, and Montparnasse still has numerous small pancake houses, *crêperies*.

Foreign restaurants have proliferated in recent years in Paris. There are Chinese and Vietnamese restaurants everywhere, small restaurants serving kebabs have sprung up in the Quartier St Sèverin, at the north-east end of the Boulevard Saint Michel, and there are many restaurants serving Italian, Japanese, Lebanese, North African, Russian and South American dishes.

In recent years, many leading chefs have moved away from the classic traditional French cooking with rich food in heavy sauces, and are concentrating on newly invented, lighter dishes composed of fresh but unexpected ingredients and flavours. This *nouvelle cuisine* 'new cookery' when carefully thought out and

well prepared is delicious but can also be the excuse for unhappy mixtures and insufficient cooking, particularly where fish and poultry are concerned, served up in very small portions but at great expense. Many of the more serious minded chefs and restaurant owners, however, while still inventing new dishes, have come to re-appreciate the virtues of some of the lighter classical dishes and are combining these and the *nouvelle cuisine* on their menus.

Restaurants for lunch, particularly the smaller ones in the central and business quarters, begin to fill up from about 1215 onwards and it is not unusual for them to be full by 1300. In the evenings, when it is always prudent to reserve in advance, Parisians tend to dine fairly late, often arriving around 2100.

Menus are posted up outside restaurants and must include a recommended fixed price menu, *Menu Conseillé*, as well as the items à la carte. Despite the increasing cost of overheads and of market produce both of which contribute to the high prices charged in restaurants, many owners still manage to provide at least two reasonable, fixed price menus and, in some cases, a *menu dégustation* composed of a selection of four or five specialities offering very good value. Wine is not usually included in the price, but house or carafe wines (cheaper than those on the wine list, which are expensive) are often available. A service charge of 15% is generally added to the bill when it is brought to the table, and there is no need to leave an additional gratuity unless it is small change.

Moderately priced meals in rather noisy surroundings are available in the Drugstore restaurants on the Champs Elysées, the Boulevard des Capucines and St Germain. At lunchtime, the *brasseries* and little restaurants in the small streets in the centre and business quarters offer good value. In the evenings, visitors exploring the Beaubourg, Halles and Le Marais quarters on the Right Bank, and the Latin Quarter and the St Germain des Prés on the Left Bank can find small, reasonably priced restaurants. For those with not much money to spend, pizza houses, *crêperies*, self-service establishments and fast-food chains all offer low-priced fare. Kiosks outside certain cafés and on some street corners sell pancakes, but standards of hygiene vary.

As there are no licensing laws in France, alcoholic drinks are served at all hours in the cafés and bars. Wines and spirits can also be bought, along with mineral water, beer and soft drinks, in small shops, supermarkets and grocery stores.

Coffee and other drinks consumed at the zinc counters in cafés are cheaper than when taken at the surrounding tables or on the terraces. Cafés also sell sandwiches and snacks and bottled and light draught beers (*bière pression*). A wider variety of light and dark beers is found in the imitation English pubs which also sell food. Scotch has become a fashionable drink over the past ten years, and threatens to overtake the traditional French *apéritif*, but it is expensive. The water in Paris is subject to extremely strict rules of hygiene and is tested regularly. It is therefore perfectly safe to drink and no café or restaurant can refuse to supply it on request (ask for a *carafe d'eau*). The fashion for drinking tea is spreading in Paris, and there is a number of small places serving teas, pastries, light lunches and snacks.

Anything other than a small but representative list of restaurants in Paris would be impractical. Those wishing to consult fuller lists should refer to the following guides, obtainable in bookshops and in some small newsagents: *Guide des Restaurants*, published by and obtainable at the Office du Tourisme de Paris, 127 Avenue des Champs-Elysées, Paris 8; *Le Guide des Restaurants Auto-Journal*; *Le Guide Gault et Millau*. For a list of reasonably priced restaurants, consult *Le Guide Paris Pas Cher*.

The **restaurants** on the list below are all very expensive, in most cases luxurious, and they offer some of the finest food, wine and service in Paris. It is imperative to reserve your table in advance.

Le Duc 243 Bd Raspail, Paris 14 (tel: 320 96 30). Closed Saturdays, Sundays and Mondays. Fish.

Le Grand Vefour 17 Rue de Beaujolais, Paris 1 (tel: 296 56 27). Closed Saturday evenings, Sundays and August.

Jacques Cagna 14 Rue des Grands Augustins, Paris 6 (tel: 326 49 39). Closed August, 24 Dec. − 12 Jan., Saturdays and Sundays.

Jamin 32 Rue de Longchamps, Paris 16. Closed July, Saturdays and Sundays.

Lasserre 17 Ave Franklin Roosevelt, Paris 8 (tel: 359 53 43). Closed Sundays and August.

Laurent 41 Ave Gabriel, Paris 8 (tel: 225 00 39). Closed Saturdays and Sundays.

Ledoyen Carré des Champs-Elysées, Paris 8 (tel: 266 54 77). Closed Sundays and August.

La Marée 1 Rue Daru, Paris 8 (tel: 763 52 42). Closed Sat.−Sun., August. Fish.

Maxim's 3 Rue Royale, Paris 8 (tel: 265 27 94). Closed Sundays.

Taillevent 15 Rue Lamennais, Paris 8 (tel: 563 39 94). Closed August, mid Feb., Saturdays, Sundays, public holidays.

La Tour d'Argent 15−17 Quai de la Tournelle, Paris 5 (tel: 354 23 31). Closed Mondays. On the 6th floor overlooking Notre Dame and the Seine.

Le Vivarois 192 Ave Victor Hugo, Paris 16 (tel: 504 04 31). Closed Saturdays, Sundays and August. Nouvelle cuisine.

The following lists select **restaurants by area** in all price ranges. Prices change so rapidly that it is impossible to give anything but a very loose classification: inexpensive (under F120 per head), moderate (F120−180) and expensive (over F180). It is, however, possible to find restaurants serving meals at prices varying between F50−80, and remember too, it is often the wine prices which increase the bill at the end. Many restaurants close in August and on certain days either at the weekend or at the beginning of the week and it is wise to telephone and reserve in advance.

Right Bank

1 & 2 Arr. (Halles, Bourse, Opéra, Palais Royal)

L'Absinthe 24 Place du Marché St Honoré, Paris 1 (tel: 260 02 45) moderate to expensive.

André Faure 40 Rue du Mont-Thabor, Paris 1 (tel: 260 74 28) inexpensive.

Au Petit Ramoneur 74 Rue St Denis, Paris 1, inexpensive.

L'Atelier Bleu 7 Rue des Prouvaires, Paris 1 (tel: 733 74 47) inexpensive.

Gerard Besson 5 Rue Coq Heron, Paris 1 (tel: 233 14 74) expensive.

Bistro de la Gare 38 Bd des Italiens, Paris 2 (tel: 828 46 91); 30 Rue St Denis, Paris 1 (angle Square des Innocents) (tel: 260 84 92) inexpensive.

Chez Clovis 33 Rue Berger, Paris 1 (tel: 233 97 07) moderate.

Drouant 18 Place Gaillon, Paris 2 (tel: 742 55 61) (see Gazetteer p.83) expensive.

L'Escargot de Montorgueil 38 Rue Montorgueil, Paris 1, moderate to expensive.

Pierrot 18 Rue Etienne Marcel, Paris 2, moderate to expensive.

Joe Allen 30 Rue Pierre Lescot, Paris 1 (tel: 286 70 13) American, moderate.

Pile ou Face 52 Rue Notre Dame des Victoires, Paris 2, expensive.

Chez Roger 97 Rue Quincampoix, Paris 1, inexpensive.

3 & 4 Arr. (Beaubourg, Le Marais, Ile St Louis)

L'Ambassade d'Auvergne 22 Rue du Grenier St Lazare, Paris 3 (tel: 272 31 22) regional cookery, moderate.

Auberge de la Jarente 7 Rue de Jarente, Paris 4, moderate.

Bofinger 5 Rue de la Bastille, Paris 4 (tel:

272 87 82) an old fashioned brasserie, moderate to expensive.

La Calanque 2 Rue de la Coutellerie, Paris 4, inexpensive to moderate.

Le Domarais 53 Bis Rue des Francs Bourgeois, Paris 4, expensive.

L'Excuse 14 Rue Charles V, Paris 4 (tel: 277 98 97) moderate to expensive.

Le Menestrel 51 Rue St Louis en L'Ile, Paris 4 (tel: 354 78 62) inexpensive.

L'Orangerie 28 Rue St Louis en L'Ile, Paris 4 (tel: 633 93 98) fashionable and expensive.

Le Trumilou 84 Quai de l'Hôtel de Ville, Paris 4 (tel: 277 63 98) inexpensive.

8 Arr. (Champs-Elysées, St Lazare)

Androuet 41 Rue d'Amsterdam (tel: 874 26 93) cheese specialities, expensive.

Bistro de la Gare 73 Champs-Elysées (tel: 359 67 83) inexpensive.

La Capricorne 81 Rue Rocher (tel: 522 64 99) inexpensive.

Chiberta 3 Rue Arsène Houssaye (tel: 563 77 90) expensive.

Chez Germain 19 Rue Jean Mermoz, inexpensive.

Fermette Marbeuf 5 Rue Marbeuf (tel: 720 63 53) moderate to expensive.

L'Artois 13 Rue d'Artois, moderate.

Lamazère 23 Rue de Ponthieu (tel: 359 66 66) expensive.

Le Sarladais 2 Rue de Vienne, moderate to expensive.

Savy 23 Rue Bayard (tel: 225 41 47) moderate.

Velentin 19 Rue Marbeuf (tel: 359 80 11) inexpensive.

9 & 10 Arr. (Opéra, Gares de l'Est and du Nord, Grands Boulevards)

Auberge Landaise 23 Rue Clauzel, Paris 9 (tel: 878 74 40) moderate to expensive.

Au Petit Riche 23 Rue Le Pelletier, Paris 9 (tel: 770 68 68) expensive.

Auberge du Clou Ave Trudaine, Paris 9 (tel: 878 22 48) moderate.

Bistro de St Cécile 15 Rue St Cecile, Paris 9 (tel: 246 48 14) inexpensive

Brasserie Flo 6 Cour des Petites Ecuries, Paris 10 (tel: 770 13 59) moderate.

Charlot 12 Place Clichy, Paris 9 (tel: 874 49 64) seafood, expensive.

Chartier 7 Rue du Faubourg Montmartre, inexpensive.

Chez Michel 10 Rue de Belzunce, Paris 10 (tel: 878 4410) nouvelle cuisine, expensive.

Aux 2 Canards 8 Rue du Faubourg Poissonnière, moderate.

Louis XIV 6 Bd St Denis, Paris 10 (tel: 208 56 56) seafood, expensive.

La Moutardière 12 Ave Richerand, Paris 10 (tel: 205 96 80) inexpensive.

Le Quercy 36 Rue Condorcet, Paris 9 (tel: 878 30 61) regional cookery, moderate.

11, 19 & 20 Arr. (Bastille, Eastern Paris)

Astier 44 Rue Jean-Pierre Timbaud, Paris 11 (tel: 357 16 35) moderate.

Au Boeuf Couronné 188 Ave Jean Jaurès, Paris 19 (tel: 607 13 55) moderate.

Anjou-Normande 13 Rue de la Folie Mericourt, Paris 11, moderate to expensive.

Au Cochon d'Or 192 Ave Jean Jaurès, Paris 19, expensive.

Cartet 62 Rue de Mâlte, Paris 11 (tel: 805 27 56) expensive.

Au Rendez-vous de la Marine 14 Quai de la Loire, Paris 19, inexpensive.

Le Pavillon du Lac Parc des Buttes Chaumont, Paris 19 (tel: 202 08 97) moderate.

Le Picotin 13 Rue de la Pierre Levée, Paris 11, inexpensive.

La Table Richelieu 276 Boulevard Voltaire, Paris 11, moderate.

12 & 13 Arr. (Gare de Lyon, Nation, Gare d'Austerlitz, Place d'Italie)

Auberge Etchegorroy 41 Rue Croulebarbe, Paris 13 (tel: 331 63 05) Basque cookery, moderate to expensive.

La Connivence 1 Rue de Cotte, Paris 12 (tel: 628 16 47) inexpensive.

La Gourmandise 271 Avenue Daumesnil, Paris 12, moderate to expensive.

Le Menestrel 10 Rue de l'Esperance, Paris 13, moderate.

La Popotière 35 Rue du Banquier, Paris 12, moderate.

Le Pressoir 257 Ave Daumesnil, Paris 12 (tel: 344 38 21) expensive.

Le Temps des Cerise 18 Rue de la Butte aux Cailles, Paris 13 (tel: 589 69 48) inexpensive.

Le Train Bleu 1st Floor Gare de Lyon (tel: 343 09 06) moderate to expensive.

Au Trou Gascon 40 Rue Taine, Paris 12 (tel: 344 34 26) expensive.

16 & 17 Arr. (Passy, Western Paris)

Apicius 122 Avenue Villiers, Paris 17, expensive.

Le Bernardin 18 Rue Troyon, Paris 17, expensive.

Le Beaujolais d'Auteuil 99 Bd de Montmorency, Paris 16 (tel: 743 03 56) moderate to expensive.

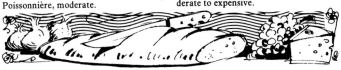

Brasserie Stella 133 Ave Victor Hugo, Paris 16 (tel: 727 60 54) moderate.

Charlot 128 bis Bd Clichy, Paris 17 (tel: 522 47 08) seafood, expensive.

Faugeron 52 Rue de Longchamp, Paris 16 (tel: 704 24 53) luxury, expensive.

La Ficotière 17 Rue Jean Giraudoux, Paris 16, moderate.

Hameau d'Auteuil 5 Place de Barcelone, Paris 16 (tel: 525 74 21) moderate.

Le Lory 56 Rue Poussin, Paris 16, moderate.

La Toque 16 Rue de Tocqueville, Paris 17, moderate.

Paul Chène 123 Rue Lauriston, Paris 16, expensive.

Au Tournant de la Butte 46 Rue Caulaincourt, Paris 18 (tel: 606 39 86) inexpensive.

18 Arr. (Montmartre)

Les Copains d'Abord 62 Rue de Caulaincourt (tel: 606 29 83) inexpensive.

Chez Ginette 101 Rue Caulaincourt, moderate.

La Maison Rose 2 Rue de l'Abreuvoir, Paris 18, inexpensive.

La Pomponette 42 Rue Lepic, Paris 18, moderate.

Left Bank

5 & 6 Arr. (Latin Quarter, Luxembourg)

Allard 41 Rue St André des Arts, Paris 6 (tel: 326 48 23) moderate to expensive.

Atelier Maître Albert 1 Rue Maître Albert, Paris 5 (tel: 633 17 78) inexpensive to moderate.

Auberge des Deux Signes 46 Rue Galande, Paris 5 (tel: 325 46 56) moderate to expensive.

La Bûcherie 41 Rue de la Bûcherie, Paris 5 (tel: 354 78 06) moderate to expensive.

Dodin Bouffant 25 Rue Frédérick-Sauton, Paris 5 (tel: 325 25 14) expensive.

Les Fêtes Gourmandes 17 Rue de l'École Polytechnique, Paris 5, moderate.

Josephine 117 Rue du Cherche-Midi, Paris 6 (tel: 548 52 40) expensive.

Moisonnier 28 Rue des Fossés-St-Bernard, Paris 5 (tel: 329 87 65) Lyonnaise cookery, moderate.

Le Petit Navire 13 Rue des Fossés-St-Bernard, Paris 5 (tel: 354 22 52) fish, inexpensive to moderate.

Le Petit Zinc 25 Rue de Buci, Paris 6 (tel: 354 79 34) moderate.

La Procope 13 Rue de l'Ancienne Comédie, Paris 6 (tel: 326 99 20) (see Gazetteer p.109) inexpensive.

Restaurant des Saints Pères 175 Bd St Germain, Paris 6 (tel: 548 56 85) inexpensive.

6, 14 (Montparnasse) **& Arr.**

L'Aquitaine 54 Rue De Dantzig, Paris 15

(tel: 828 67 38) moderate to expensive.

Le Bar a Huitres 112 Bd Montparnasse, Paris 6 (tel: 320 71 01) seafood, inexpensive to moderate.

Bistro de la Gare 59 Bd Montparnasse, Paris 6 (tel: 548 38 01) inexpensive.

Chez Albert 122 Ave du Maine, Paris 14 (tel: 326 61 69) expensive.

Le Chat Grippé 87 Rue d'Assas, Paris 6, moderate to expensive.

La Maison Blanche 82 Boulevard Lefebvre, Paris 15, moderate to expensive.

Olympe 8 Rue Nicolas-Charlet, Paris 15 (tel: 734 86 08) nouvelle cuisine, expensive.

La Petite Bretonnière 2 Rue de Cadix, Paris 15 (tel: 828 34 39) moderate.

Pierre Vedel 50 Rue des Morillons, Paris 15 (tel: 828 04 37) nouvelle cuisine, moderate.

La Porte Fausse 72 Rue du Cherche Midi, Paris 6 (tel: 222 20 17) inexpensive.

La Route du Beaujolais 17 Rue de Lourmel, Paris 15, inexpensive.

7 Arr. (Champs de Mars, Ecole Militaire, Faubourg St Germain)

La Belle France 1st Floor, Eiffel Tower. Reservation essential, moderate to expensive.

La Boule d'Or 13 Bd Latour Maubourg (tel: 705 50 18) expensive.

La Bourgogne 6 Ave Bosquet (tel: 705 96 78) expensive.

D'Chez Eux 2 Ave de Lowendal (tel: 705 52 55) regional cookery, moderate to expensive.

Le Divellec 107 Rue de l'Université, expensive.

Au Fins Gourmets 213 Boulevard Saint-Germain, expensive.

La Fontaine de Mars 129 Rue St Dominique (tel: 705 46 44) inexpensive.

Le Galant Verre 12 Rue de Verneuil (tel: 260 84 56) nouvelle cuisine, moderate.

Le Petite Chaise 36/38 Rue de Grenelle (tel: 222 13 35) inexpensive.

Le Pied de Fouet 45 Rue Babylone (tel: 705 12 27) inexpensive.

Thoumieux 79 Rue St Dominique (tel: 705 49 75) inexpensive to moderate.

La Vert Bocage 96 Bd Latour Maubourg (tel: 551 48 64) expensive.

Night Spots

Although the list below represents an aspect of Paris night life it must be admitted that such establishments exist for, and are mainly frequented by, tourists. Prices vary, but allow between F150 and F300 per head.

Alcazar 62 Rue Mazarine, Paris 6 (tel: 329

02 02) dinner, revue, disco dancing.
La Belle Epoque 36 Rue des Petits champs, Paris 2 (tel: 296 33 33) dinner, dancing and cabaret.
Le Bilboquet 13 Rue St Benoit, Paris 6 (tel: 222 51 09/548 81 84) dinner and good jazz in the Club St Germain.
Don Camillo 10 Rue des Sts Pères, Paris 6 (tel: 260 29 42) dinner, cabaret.
L'Eléphant Bleu 49 Rue de Ponthieu, Paris 8 (tel: 359 58 64) cabaret, dinner dancing.
Folies Bergère 32 Rue Richer, Paris 9 (tel: 4246 7711).
Le Lido (Cabaret Normandie) 116 bis Ave des Champs-Elysées, Paris 8 (tel: 359 11 61) dinner, dancing, revue with Bluebell Girls.
Le Milliardaire 64 Rue Pierre Charron, Paris 8 (tel: 225 25 17) cabaret – music hall.
Moulin Rouge Place Blanche, Paris 9 (tel: 606 00 19) dinner dancing, revue.
Paradise Latin 28 Rue Cardinal Lemoine, Paris 5 (tel: 325 28 28) (closed Tuesdays) dinner and revue.
La Rotisserie de l'Abbaye 22 Rue Jacob, Paris 6 (tel: 326 36 26) dinner and revue.
Les Trois Maillets 56 Rue Galande, Paris 5 (tel: 354 00 79) dinner and revue.
Villa d'Este Rue Arsène Houssay, Paris 8 (tel: 359 78 44/563 61 03) dinner, revue.

SHOPPING

Without doubt Paris is the world capital for women's clothes, chic accessories, jewellery and perfumes, and for food and wine. It is also an important centre for antiques and a major art market, and there are shops selling the finest furniture, glass and porcelain.

As well as large department stores, there are myriad boutiques selling clothes, leather goods, curios, decorative items, furniture, carpets, *etc*, on both sides of the river. Many boutiques close on Mondays but open until at least 1900 in the evenings, and some open on Sunday mornings. Food shops generally open 0830–1300 and 1400–1930 Tuesdays–Saturdays, 0830–1300 on Sundays, and often close all day on Mondays, although one can usually find at least one butcher (*charcuterie*) or grocer (*épicerie*) open in each quarter on Monday. Bakeries operate a similar system.

All the big **department stores** have some English-speaking members of staff, and many list their departments in English.
Au Bon Marché 38 Rue de Sèvres, Paris 7. Open Mon–Sat 0930–1845. Specialities

of this Left Bank store include household linen and carpets; good self-service food hall.
Aux Trois Quartiers 17 Bd de la Madeleine, Paris 1. Open Mon–Sat 0940–1830. Good table linen, gloves and men's department, Madelios, in annex next door.
Bazar de l'Hôtel de Ville 55 Rue de la Verrerie, Paris 4. Open Mon–Fri 0900–1830 (1900 Sat, 2200 Wed). All the do-it-yourself fans in Paris flock to the magnificent hardware store in the basement. Good kitchen utensils, electrical equipment, book and record departments.
FNAC (Fédération Nationale d'Achat des Cadres). This buying centre has four main shops, each with its own speciality, often selling at prices considerably lower than elsewhere:
Forum 1–7 Rue Pierre Lescot, (first floor), Paris 1. Open Mon 1300–2000, Tues–Sat 1000–2000. Photographic, audio-visual and mini-computer equipment, records and books. Auditorium for discussion groups, film shows and other cultural activities.
Sports Forum (same address as above, third floor). Sports items and equipment, especially for camping and water sports.
Etoile 26 Ave de Wagram, Paris 8. Open Tues–Sat 1000–2000. Records and small items of electrical household equipment.
Montparnasse 136 Rue de Rennes, Paris 6. Open Tues–sat 1000–2000 (2130 Wed). Books, records, and audio-visual equipment.
Galeries Lafayette 40 Bd Haussmann, Paris 9. Open Mon–Sat 0930–1830. Large china, glass and kitchen utensils departments; fashion on the first and third floors, with boutiques selling models by famous dress designers. There is also a smaller branch of this store in Montparnasse at 22 Rue du Départ, Paris 14, open Mon–Sat 1000–1730.
Magasins Réunis Place de la République, Paris 11, and 30 Ave des Ternes, Paris 17. Open Tues–Sat 0940–1830. The branch in the 17th *arrondissement* is specially notable for food hall, carpets and well-equipped gymnasium and saunas.
Printemps 64 Bd Haussmann, Paris 9. Open Mon–Sat 0935–1830. Largest perfumery department in France; noted for lingerie, de luxe ready-to-wear range, toys, and for Brummel, the men's department (just behind at 112 Rue de Provence). There are branches in the 11th *arrondissement* at the Place de la Republique and also in the 17th *arrondissement* at 30 Avenue des Ternes.
Samaritaine Pont Neuf, Paris 1. Open

Mon–Fri 0930–1830 (1900 Sat). Like Harrods of London, this vast store with its four shops, each containing different departments, boasts of its ability to supply anything and everything on demand. Excellent selection of professional and working clothes which are bought up by the young as trendy gear; good food, kitchen and hardware departments.

Many **supermarkets** are situated on the outskirts of the town, but among those in the centre or easily accessible are:

Euromarché Auteuil 1 Ave Général Sarrail (near Porte Molitor), Paris 16. Open Mon–Sat 1000–2200.

Gem 16 Rue des Belles-Feuilles, Paris 16. Open Mon–Sat 0900–2000.

Inno-Maine 31 Rue du Départ, Paris 14. Open Mon–Sat 0915–1900 (2100 Fri).

Inno-Passy 53 Rue de Passy, Paris 16. Opening hours as Inno-Maine, above.

In addition, the **Monoprix** and **Prisunic** chains, situated all over Paris, are open Mon–Sat 0930–1930.

A very useful service is provided by the **drugstores** which stay open late and have well-stocked bookshops, newspaper and magazine stands and tobacconists; nearly all have pharmacies, grocery departments and areas selling records, watches, small radios, calculators and other gadgets. All have restaurants on the premises.

Drugstore Champs-Elysées 133 Ave des Champs-Elysées, Paris 8. Open every day 0830–0200.

Drugstore Matignon 1 Ave Matignon, Paris 8. Open every day 0900–0200.

Drugstore Opéra 6 Bd, des Capucines, Paris 9. Open every day 0930–0200.

Drugstore St Germain 149 Bd St Germain, Paris 6. Open every day 0900–2000.

The following are among the best-known **shopping areas** and **streets** in Paris:

Capucines Bd des, Paris 1. Women's clothes, shoes.

Champs-Elysées Ave des, Paris 8. Accessories, women's clothes, perfumes.

Du Four Rue, Paris 6. Women's clothes, boots and shoes.

Forum des Halles Paris 1. Opened in 1979 on the site of the old market, Les Halles. (180 boutiques on six floors.) Boutiques, accessories, jewellery, food shops, furniture, leather goods. A good place to look for small presents.

Haussmann Bd, Paris 9. Department stores, Marks and Spencers; you can find ivory and tortoiseshell items at 55, Aux Tortues.

Madeleine Bd de la, Paris 8. Women's clothes, shoes and jewellery. Place de la Madeleine: luxury food shops.

Maine-Montparnasse Commercial Centre, Paris 14. Women's and men's clothes, accessories; furniture (Habitat and Galeries Lafayette).

Paradis Rue de, Paris 10. Porcelain, glass and table ware.

Passy Rue de, Paris 16. Fashion boutiques, cosmetics; food shops.

Porte Maillot, Place de la. Ground floor and basement of the Palais des Congrès (Rue Haute and Rue Basse). Accessories, jewellery, women's and men's boutiques (including haute couture boutiques: Courrèges, Lanvin and Louis Feraud) shoes, antiques and interior decoration.

Rennes Rue de, Paris 6. Books and records at the FNAC (p.23); clothes for men and women, shoes, haute couture boutiques.

Royale Rue, Paris 8. Gold- and silver-smiths, jewellery.

St Germain Bd, Paris 6 and 7. Books, interior decorators, men's and women's clothes.

St Honoré Faubourg, Paris 8. Luxury goods, cosmetics, hairdressers (Carita at No. 11), jewellery, haute couture and other fashion boutiques.

Seine Carré de la, Paris 6 and 7. Group of streets on Left Bank comprising Rues du Bac, Bonaparte, Dauphine, Jacob, Lille and Seine. Antiques and paintings.

Sèvres Rue de, Paris 7 and 15. Women's clothes, department store Au bon Marché.

Tournon Rue de, Paris 6. Antiques, interior decorators, fashion boutiques.

Tronchet Rue, Paris 8 and 9. Men's and women's clothes, accessories, shoes.

Vendôme Place, Paris 1. Jewellery.

Victoires Place des, Paris 1. Fashion boutiques with big names in ready to wear.

Victor Hugo Rue, Paris 16. Men and women's clothes, jewellery, shoes, interior decorators, furniture.

In addition there are stamp and curio shops in the arcades of the **Palais Royal**, Paris 1. Fashion and curio shops in the **Beaubourg** and **Marais**, Paris 1, 3 and 4, and in the **Ave Victor Hugo**, Paris 16. No shopper should overlook the **Boulevard St Michel** and the **Quais** by the Seine, selling second-hand books and prints.

Paris **haute couture** houses are to be found in the following streets:

Cambon Rue. Chanel is at No 31.

Champs-Elysées, Rond Point des, Carven is at No 6.

François 1er Rue. Courrèges is at No. 40, Balmain at 44, Philippe Venet at 62.

George V Ave. Givenchy is at No. 3, Per Spook at No. 18.

Marceau Ave, Paris 16. Yves St Laurent is at No. 5.

Marigny Ave. Pierre Cardin is at No. 27.
Montaigne Ave. Ungaro is at No. 2,
Hanae Mori at 17, Guy Laroche at 29,
Dior at 30, Nina Ricci at 39, Jean-Louis
Scherrer at 51.
Pierre 1er de Serbie Ave. Ted Lapidus
is at No. 37.
St Florentin Rue Jean Patou is at No. 7.
St Honoré Faubourg. Lanvin is at No.
22, Louis Feraud at 88.
Many of the houses above, Cardin, Courrèges and St Laurent in particular, have
opened boutiques in various streets on
both sides of the river, in the big department stores and shopping centres. Prices
are much cheaper than those charged in
the haute couture houses and it is quite all
right to go in and look round without
necessarily buying.

Markets

Every *arrondissement* in Paris has at least
two or three weekly street markets which
generally open early in the morning and
continue until lunchtime – a few markets
also take place on Sundays. As well as
stalls offering charcuterie (delicatessen
wares), cheeses, fish, meat, fruit and ve-
getables, many markets have stands selling clothes and an assortment of bric-à-
brac.
Antique markets Le Louvre des Anti-
quaires, 2 Place du Palais Royal, Paris 1.
Open Tues–Sun 1100–1900. Some 250
dealers selling antiques in the renovated
premises of the former Louvre department store. The authenticity of all items is
guaranteed. Village Suisse (behind the
junction of the Ave de la Motte Picquet
and Ave de Suffren, Paris 7). Open
Thurs–Mon 1030–1230 and 1400–1900.
Antiques and curios.
Flea markets (selling second-hand everything imaginable) Marché aux Puces,
Porte de Clignancourt, see p.115. Marché
Didot, Paris 14. (Situated between the
Porte de Vanves and the Porte de Chatillon in the south of Paris.) Open Saturday
afternoons and Sundays. Place d'Aligre,
Paris 12 (Metro Ledru Rollin) open every
day till 1300.
Flower markets Place Louis Lépine, Ile
de la Cité. Open every day, but on Sundays
it becomes a bird market. Place de la
Madeleine, Paris 8. Open Tues, Wed, Fri,
Sat. Place des Ternes, Paris 17. Open
Tues–Sun.
Stamp market Marché aux Timbres (on
the corner of Ave Gabriel and Ave Marigny). Open Sundays and public holidays
0800–1900, Thursday afternoons.
Auction rooms Sales held daily, some-
times in the evening, at the Hôtel Drouot,
Rue Drouot, Paris 9 (tel: 544 38 72).

English and American Bookshops

Attica 34 Rue des Ecoles, Paris 5.
Specializes in American books.
Brentano's 37 Ave de l'Opéra, Paris 2.
Also sells American and English news-
papers and magazines.
Galignani 224 Rue de Rivoli, Paris 1.
Specializes in modern literature, the arts
and sciences.
MacDougall's 8 Rue Casimir Delavigne,
Paris 6. American literature.
Marshall's Bookshop 26 Rue Brey,
Paris 17. English bookshop and tearoom.
Nouveau Quartier Latin 78 Bd St
Michel, Paris 6. English-language paper-
backs, American art books and English
books for children.
Shakespeare and Company 37 Rue de
la Bûcherie, Paris 5. One of the largest
selections of second-hand books in
English in Europe.
Smith & Son 248 Rue de Rivoli, Paris 1.
Also sells American and English news-
papers and magazines and has a tea shop
on the first floor.
The Village Voice 6 Rue de Princesse,
Paris 6. American and English books and
magazines. Sells snacks: fruit juice, coffee,
tea.

Shopping Terms

Shop names *alimentation*, general term
for food shops; *boucherie*, butcher; *boulan-
gerie*, bakery; *cave*, wine and spirits shop;
Charcuterie, delicatessen; *coiffeur*, hairdressers; *confiserie*, confectioners; *crémerie*,
dairy; *droguerie*, shop selling household
goods, cleaning products and paints; *épicerie*, grocers; *librairie*, bookshop; *magasin*, shop; *maroquinerie*, shop selling
leather goods; *mercerie*, haberdashers; *pa-
peterie*, stationers; *pâtisserie*, pastry shop;
quincaillerie, hardware store.
Services and items *bibliothèque*, library;
ceinture, belt; *chaussures*, shoes; *confection*,
ready-to-wear clothes; *coupe*, haircut;
électro-ménager, electrical household
equipment; *meubles*, furniture; *mis en plis*,
hair set; *panne*, breakdown; (*dépannage*,
breakdown service); *pointure*, shoe size;
taille, dress size; *tapis*, carpet; *sac à main*,
handbag; *valise*, suitcase.

ENTERTAINMENT

No one need fear boredom, Paris is well
known for concerts, opera and theatre and
for its varied and very lively night life.
Whatever your interests you will find
something to do or see by day or night. the
time-honoured way of really getting to
know any city is to walk its streets and

breathe its special atmosphere. If you want to stroll around at night, the main buildings and monuments are floodlit from dusk till midnight (an hour later in summer). There are also floodlit river trips and Son et Lumière, in French and English, in the Invalides from April to October, although visitors should check times of English performances with Paris Tourist Office, 127 Champs-Elysées.

Theatre

There are theatres all over the town, ranging from those in the centre and on the Grands Boulevards, specializing in light comedy, to the fringe and experimental theatres, mainly in the Marais, Montparnasse and the Latin Quarter, and the national and state-subsidized theatres. the Comédie Française, Place André Malraux, lives up to its name as the House of Molière, staging first-class productions of his works as well as other great French classics. Its annexes, Théâtre National de l'Odéon and Petit Odéon, Place de l'Odéon, accommodate visiting companies such as the Royal Shakespeare Company, or specialize in more modern plays.

Programmes are more varied at the Théâtre de la Ville, Place du Châtelet, the Théâtre de Chaillot, Place du Trocadéro, and in the experimental theatre at the Centre Georges Pompidou, which stages modern plays, concerts and ballets.

There are also the theatrical companies, the best-known being: the Compagnie Jean-Louis Barrault-Madeleine Renault, which has a wide repertoire and also sponsored concerts and ballet; the company run by Robert Hossein, which specializes in huge productions, often based on historical themes and the classics; the productions staged by Jean Desailly and Simone Valère; Peter Brooke's productions at the Bouffes du Nord theatre; the comic *Branquignols* run by Robert Dhéry.

Curtain up is between 2000 and 2100, and matinées are held on Sunday afternoons and sometimes on Wednesdays. Tickets are either bought at the box office or reserved by telephone, and there are a few agencies in central Paris, which will reserve seats for a fee. Subscription to the state theatres and some of the fringe and experimental theatres (*eg* Théâtre de la Grande Cartoucherie, Rue du Champ du Manœuvres, Paris 12; Théâtre de la Bastille, 76 Rue de la Roquette, Paris 11. Lucernaire Forum, 53 Rue Notre Dame des Champs; Théâtre Oblique, 78 Rue de la Roquette) provides advantageous booking conditions and price reductions.

Smoking is not permitted in French theatres and you should tip the usherette about a Franc.

A speciality of Paris is the *café-théâtre*, a small theatre, serving drinks and sometimes snacks, which stages one-man shows, satirical and comic sketches and revues. Performances begin late, between 2130 and 2230, and often two different shows are given each evening. Examples of this form of entertainment are the Café Edgar, 58 Bd Edgar Quinet; Cithea, 112 Rue Oberkampf, Paris 11; Point Virgile, 7 Rue Saint-Croix-de-la Bretonnerie, Paris 4; Les Blancs-Manteaux, 15 Rue des Blancs-Manteaux; Gaîté Montparnasse, 26 Rue de la Gaîté. A similar form of entertainment, popular with Parisians, is found in the *Cabarets de Chansonniers* where satirical sketches and parodies of French political life are performed. Two well-known ones are the Caveau de la République, 1 Bd St Martin, and Les Deux Anes, 100 Bd Clichy. Performances begin around 2100, with matinées on Sundays. Prices at *chansonniers* and *café-théâtres* are often much lower than at other theatres, and there are reductions for students and, in some cases, subscription rates are offered. Tickets may be reserved by telephone or bought direct at the box office. It should be noted that, in order to appreciate this type of theatre, a reasonable knowledge of French is essential.

Music hall is very popular in Paris and internationally acclaimed artists perform at the Olympia, 28 Bd des Capucines; Palais des Congrès, Place de la Porte Maillot; Le Zenith, 211 Avenue Jean Jaurès, Paris 19. Metro: Porte de Pantin, Palais Omnisports Bercy.

Cinemas

Performances begin from 1400 onwards and continue until late at night – the last showing starts at 2200 and at midnight on Friday and Saturday. Prices are on display above the box office and seats are expensive due to the fact that, except for some of the smaller private cinemas, all prices are officially fixed.

Many large cinemas have been converted into a complex housing three or four smaller theatres. Most major first runs are shown on the Champs-Elysées, the Grands Boulevards, particularly the Bd des Italiens, and in at least one or two of the larger cinemas in each *arrondissement*. Foreign films are dubbed or subtitled, but when you see the letters 'v.o.' in an advertisement, it means that the film is shown in the original language version (look out for this, especially in the films shown in the 6th and 8th *arrondissements*). There are also numerous cinemas showing previous runs (*reprises*) or holding festivals based on a particular actor, director or theme. National Film Theatres (*Cinémathèques*) are at the Palais de Chaillot and in the Centre Georges Pompidou. As in theatres, smoking is not permitted in cinemas, and you should tip the usherette a Franc.

Opera and Ballet

The Opera House, Place de l'Opéra, is justly considered to be one of the world's greatest operatic and ballet centres, ranking with La Scala in Milan, Covent Garden in London, or the Metropolitan in New York. It can be extremely difficult to get a seat, due to great demand, the prices, and a system of subscription, which often results in seats being sold out well in advance of performances. For enthusiasts, however, willing to turn up early in the morning, there are a few seats available for the same evening. Light opera is performed, though not always regularly, at the Opéra Comique, 5 Rue Favard; Théâtre Musical de Paris, Place du Châtelet (the old theatre du Châtelet); Théâtre de Boulogne, 60 Rue de la Belle Feuille, Boulogne Billancourt (Métro Marcel Sambat).

Modern ballet, performed by French and international companies, can be seen at Théâtre de la Ville, Place du Châtelet, Odéon, Espace Cardin, 1 Ave Gabriel, the Palais des Congrès, Place de la Porte Maillot, and in some of the larger suburban theatres such as the Théâtre de Boulogne.

Concerts

The French reputation for not being a nation of music lovers is ill-deserved, since not a day goes by without a concert or recital being given in one or other of Paris' main concert halls: Salle Pleyel, 252 Faubourg St Honoré; Salle Cortot, 78 Rue Cardinet; Salle Gaveau, 23 Rue de la Boétie; Théâtre des Champs-Elysées, 15 Ave Montaigne; Palais des Congrès, Place de la Porte Maillot; concert hall of the Maison de la Radio, 116 Ave du Président Kennedy; Théâtre Musical de Paris (see above).

Concerts are also given in churches, including Notre Dame, La Sainte Chapelle and St Eustache, in some colleges and in certain theatres. Music lovers can listen to international orchestras and virtuosi, and the home-produced Orchestre de Paris, the Philharmonic Orchestra of Radio France and national and provincial orchestras, many of which are internationally renowned. Paris also runs its own summer music festivals between June and September.

Jazz and Rock

Top-line national and international performers appear in the Salle Pleyel and the Palais des Congrès (addresses above); the Palace, 8 Rue du Faubourg Montmartre; the Bataclan, 50 Bd Voltaire; the Palais des Sports, Porte de Versailles; Le Zenith, 211 Ave Jean Jaurès. Metro: *Pte de Pantin* and at Omnisports Bercy. Among established clubs dedicated to 'le jazz hot' are the Caveau de la Huchette, 5 Rue de la Huchette, the Club St Germain (underneath the Bilboquet restaurant), 15 Rue St Benoit, and Le Furstenberg, 27 Rue de Buci, on the Left Bank, and the Slow Club on the Right Bank at 130 Rue de Rivoli.

The recent jazz and folk revival has led to the establishment of many new clubs and sessions are held in a number of places including the American Centre, 261 Bd Raspail; Le Petit Journal St Michel, 71 Bd St Michel, Paris 5; Le Petit Opportun, 15 Rue des Lavandières-Ste-Opportune, Paris 1; Le Petit Journal Montparnasse, 13 Rue Commandant Mouchotte, Paris 14; Dunois, 28 Rue Dunois, Paris 13; Hotel Méridien-Bar Lionel Hampton, 81 Boulevard Gouvion-St-Cyr, Paris 17; New Morning, 7-9 Rue des Petites Ecuries, Paris 10; in the basement of Dreher, 1 Rue St Denis (Place du Châtelet); Most performances begin around 2230 and tickets are available at the entrance.

Cabaret

(Some of the larger cabarets are mentioned on p.22.) Cabaret abounds on both sides of the river and, among others, there are the Crazy Horse Saloon, 12 Ave George V, whose striptease and nude revues are world famous for the standard of the productions and the beauty of the girls; the Cotton Club, 6 Rue Caumartin; the West Indian Canne à Sucre, 4 Rue St Beuve; the Folies Bergère, 32 Rue Richer; Peanuts, 51 Rue Lucien Sampaix. Smaller, more intimate cabarets include Caveau des Oubliettes, 11 Rue St Julien-le-Pauvre, which specializes in old French songs; Club des Poètes, 30 Rue de Bourgogne, (songs and poetry); Port du Salut, 163 Rue St Jacques.

Most cabarets in Montmartre are tourist traps but for those who don't mind risking an evening among the ghosts of Bruant, Picasso and Max Jacob, the Lapin Agile, 4 Rue des Saules, is perhaps the best; also worthwhile is Au Tire Bouchon, 9 Rue Norvins, Paris 18. Dinner or snacks are served at many cabarets, but you can go in just for the show (best to check on the times in the specialized press, see below).

Clubs and Discos

Discothèques and clubs have proliferated all over the town in the past few years. A fair number are clubs, some of which, like Régine's, 49 Rue de Ponthieu, or Chez Castel, 15 Rue Princesse, are exclusive and, in order to get in, you need a recommendation from a friend, or they have to like your face, or you have to book a table for dinner, *etc.* Other clubs, after a little persuasion or perseverance at the entrance, admit you quite easily.

A well known disco is the Palace, 8 Rue du Faubourg Montmartre (once a theatre). People from all walks gyrate under laser beams (roller skating in the basement). Other discos include the Bus Palladium, 6 Rue Fontaine, Paris 9; Le Memphis, 3 Impasse Bonne-Nouvelle, Paris 10; Le Milliardaire, 68 Rue Pierre-Charvon, Paris 8; La Scala, 188 Bis Rue de Rivoli, Paris 1; Le Tango, 11 Rue Au Maire, Paris 3; Les Bains Douches, 7 Rue du Bourg l'Abbé (in a converted bath house); L'Écume des Nuits, 1 Bd Gouvion-St-Cyr, Paris 17 (basement of the Hôtel Meridien); Elysées Matignon, 2 Ave Matignon, Paris 8 (tel: 225 73 13 / 359 81 10); the Navy Club, 58 Bd de l'Hôpital, Paris 13; La Main Jaune, Place de la Porte Champerret, Paris 17 (roller skating); the Riverside, 7 Rue Grégoire des Tours, Paris 6; Club 79, 79 Avenue des Champs-Elysées, Paris 8; Whisky a Gogo, 57 Rue de Seine, Paris 6.

Information

English-language publications giving details of entertainment and night life in Paris are either elusive (*Paris Metro*) or snapped up almost immediately e.g. *Paris Free Voice* which is distributed free at the American Centre 261 Bd Raspail and the American Church 65 Quai d'Orsay. Two of the best sources are the monthly magazine *Passion* available at most of the bookshops listed on p.25 and in the newspaper kiosks, which deals with all aspects of life in Paris, and *Time Out*. The best French sources are *Allo Paris*, distributed free in large hotels and airline offices, *Pariscope* and *l'Officiel du Spectacle*, all of which are published on Wednesdays. Film and the theatre programmes are advertised in the daily press on the pages headed *Programme Spectacles*. *Le Monde des Arts et Spectacles* in the Thursday edition of Le Monde (buy it on Wednesday afternoon) is another useful source of information. You can also telephone *France Information Loisirs* (FIL) English speaking service 720 88 98 for information on concerts, cinemas and theatres.

SPORTS AND ACTIVITIES

Athletics Meetings are held at: Stade Charlety, 83 Bd Kellermann, Paris 13; Stade Jean Bouin, Ave du Général Sarrail, Paris 16; and outside Paris in the stadiums at St Maure (94) and Viry Chatillon (91). Details of programmes appear in the national press and are also available from Fédération Française d'Athlétisme, 10 Faubourg Poissonnière, Paris 10 (tel: 770 90 61).

Bowling A very popular pastime in France. Prices are reasonable and vary according to the day and time – allow for rental of special shoes. Bowling is played at: Bowling Etoile/Foch, entrance RER métro, Ave Foch Parking Station, Paris 16 (tel: 500 00 13); Bowling Front de Seine, Hôtel Nikko, 1ʳ Rue Gaston de Caillavet, Paris 15 (tel: 579 21 71); Bowling de Montparnasse, 27 Rue de Commandant Mouchotte, Paris 14 (tel: 321 61 32); bowling de Paris, Jardin d'Acclimatation, Bois de Boulogne (tel: 747 77 55).

Curling at 27 Rue du Commandant Mouchotte, Paris 14 (tel: 260 18 77).

Cycling The French have always been a nation of cyclists and important races, such as the Tour de France in July, are always well covered in the press and on TV. Bicycles can be rented from addresses on p.17, and from Bicy-Club de France. 7 Rue Ambroise-Thomas, Paris 9 (tel: 523 36 62), where, on payment of entrance fee, you can participate in organized trips (1 day and weekend). If you want to cycle outside Paris, bicycles can be put on the train and the SNCF (national railway) runs its own rental service whereby you pick up the bicycle on arrival at your destination. Details and lists of the stations are available at the enquiry desks of main-line stations (p.13). Reservations should be made at least three days in advance to the relevant station.

Football (soccer) The Paris club is Paris St Germain. Big games are played at Parc des Princes, 24 Rue du Commandant Guilbaud, Paris 16 (tel: 288 02 76).

Golf There are public courses in the suburbs at: Chevry II, 91190 Gif Sur Yvette (tel: 012 25 26); St Aubin, 91190 St Aubin (tel: 941 25 19); St Pierre du Perray, 91100 Corbeil (tel: 075 17 47). Private clubs sometimes allow visitors, who are members of a club at home, to use their course on payment of a green fee (cheaper during the week than at weekends). Clubs and other equipment may be rented out. Telephone to check on entry conditions with the following clubs, many of whom have English-speaking staff: Golf d'Ormesson, Bélvedère du Parc, 94 Ormesson Sur Marne (tel: 933 02 26) closed Tues; Golf du Racing Club de France, La Boulie, 78 Versailles (tel: 950 59 41); Golf de St Cloud, Parc de Buzenval, 60 Rue du 19 Janvier, 92 Garches (tel: 979 01 85) closed Mon; Golf de St Nom La Bretèche, 78 St Nom de Bretèche (tel: 460 90 80).

Horse racing Flat race meetings are held at: Longchamp, Bois de Boulogne; Evry (27km/17mi); Maisons-Laffitte (20km/12mi); St Cloud. Steeplechase and trotting races take place at Auteuil in the Bois de Boulogne, at Enghien (16km/10mi) and at Vicennes, on the south-east edge of the Bois de Vincennes. Bets may be placed at any café marked PMU, and must be in before the day's racing starts. In order to win the famous Sunday *Tiercé*, which is televised, you have to try and pick the first three winners in or out of order.

Horse riding Most of the clubs are expensive and exclusive, but you can ride at the Manège Howine, 19 bis Rue d'Orléans, 92 Neuilly (tel: 624 06 41) and Centre Hippique de Bailly near Versailles (tel: 460 91 85). Fees depend on whether you ride alone or in a group, and half-yearly membership is possible. Details from Allo Sports 4276 5454.

Ice skating Paris has several ice rinks (*patinoires*). Prices are around F15 for adults, with reductions for children, and skates may be rented. As many rinks close in summer, it is advisable to check by telephone: Buttes-Chaumont, 30 Rue Edouard Pailleron, Paris 19 (tel: 208 72 26); Gaieté Montparnasse, 16 Rue Vercingetorix, Paris 14 (tel: 321 60 60); Molitor, 8 Ave de la Porte Molitor, Paris 16 (tel: 527 01 04); Olympique, Gaîté Montparnasse, 27 Rue du Commandant Mouchotte, Paris 14 (tel: 260 15 90).

Rugby This is the speciality of South-West France, but big international matches (Triple Crown) take place at the Parc des Princes (see Football).

Soccer (see Football).

Squash This sport has become very fashionable, and is developing rapidly. Most players are catered for by private clubs, but the following courts are open. Telephone for opening hours and entry conditions: Squash Club Quartier Latin, 19 Rue de Pontoise, Paris 5, tel: 4334 8245; Squash Club de Saint Cloud, 4338 Bureaux de la Colline, Rue Royale, 92 St Cloud, tel: 4602 1412; Squash du Marais, 15 Rue des Lions St-Paul, Paris 4, tel: 4277 6737; Voie des Sables, 94800 Villejuif, tel: 4726 0606 (also tennis, golf, swimming).

Swimming (*natation*) The following is not an exhaustive list of pools (*piscines*) as practically every *arrondissement* has municipal baths: Blomet (covered) 17 Rue Blomet, Paris 15 (tel: 783 35 05); Deligny (open) opposite 25 Quai Anatole France, Paris 7 (tel: 551 72 15); Etoile (covered) 32 Rue de Tilsitt, Paris 17 (tel: 380 50 99); Keller (sliding roof, open July and Aug) 14 Rue de l'Ingénieur Keller, Paris 15 (tel: 5771212); Lannes, 32 Bd Lannes, Paris 16 (tel: 4503 0328); Hotel Nikko, 61 Quai de Grenelles, Paris 5 (tel: 4575 2545) covered; Pontoise, 19 Rue Pontoise, Paris 5; Jean Taris, 16 Rue Thovin, Paris 5 (tel: 4325 5403) facilities for the disabled.

Tennis The French International Championships are held in June at the Stade Roland Garros, 2 Ave Gordon Bennet, Paris 16 (tel: 743 96 81). Other championships are held at the Stade Pierre Coubertin, 84 Ave Georges Lafont, Paris 16 (tel: 527 79 12). Tennis is now a major and extremely popular sport in France and, quite apart from the various private clubs which are usually very expensive, the many municipal courts in Paris are often reserved for school use or for use by Sports clubs. They are, however, usually open to the public during certain periods. You will be able to obtain the details of the opening hours of these clubs and their addresses from Allo Sports (tel: 4276 5454) (see below).

Allo Sports is an information service, run by the *Mairie* of Paris, which gives general information and details on all sporting activities in Paris and the Paris region.

Information and programmes of sporting events are published in *Les Rendez-Vous de Pariscope* a section of the magazine *Pariscope*, in the sporting paper *l'Equipe* and in the sports pages of the national press.

YOUNG PARIS

Where to Stay

The Office du Tourisme de Paris publishes a list of hotels in all price ranges (available from French Govt. Tourist Offices addresses p.36) and will also make hotel reservations one week in advance of arrival. For those arriving without any previous arrrangements, the best course is to go straight to the Centres d'Accueil (welcome centres) at the main-line stations (on p.13) or the Office du Tourisme at 127 Ave des Champs-Elysées, all of whom make on the spot reservations.

You can also go to either of the following, who guarantee to find accommodation in one of their residences, hostels or in one of the low-priced hotels with which they are in contact: Accueil des Jeunes en France (AJF) 139 Bd St Michel, Paris 5, tel: 4354 9586 (métro: Port Royal) and 119 Rue St Martin, Paris 4, tel: 277 87 80 (opposite the Centre Georges Pompidou); Union des Centres de Rencontres Internationales de France (UCRIF) 20 Rue Jean Jacques Rousseau, Paris 1, tel: 236 88 18 (métro: Les Halles) and at the Gare du Nord opposite platform 32, open from 0800−2100, tel: 874 68 69. Both of these organizations also issue students' cards, arrange reduced fares on the SNCF (national railway) and give useful advice on restaurants, entertainment, *etc*. Try also Maison International de la Jeunesse et des Etudiants (MIJE), 11 Rue du Fauconnier, Paris 4, tel: 4274 2345.

Members of the Youth Hostels Associations (YHA) can stay in hostels in the suburbs of Paris, details of which can be obtained from the Féderation des Auberges de Jeunesse, 6 Rue de Mesnil, Paris 16 (tel: 261 84 03) or from the British YHA, 49 Trevelyan House, 8 St Stephen's Hill, St Albans, Herts (tel: St Albans 55215); The American YHA, National Campus, Delaplane, Virginia 22025 (tel: 703 592 3271); The Canadian Hostelling Association 333 River Road, Vanier City, Ontario K1L 8139 (tel: 613 746 0060).

Rooms in the Cité Universitaire, the residential campus of the University of Paris, are often available in the summer and further details can be obtained by writing direct, or going in person between 1000 and 1200, to the Fondation Nationale de l'Université de Paris, 19 Bd Jourdain, Paris 14, tel: 589 68 52 (métro: Cité Universitaire).

Pitching a tent or sleeping in the parks and open spaces is not permitted in Paris. There are two camping sites in the near suburbs: Parc de Camping du Bois de Boulogne, Allée du bord de l'Eau, Paris 16 (tel: 506 14 98); Camping Paris-Est-Le-Tremblay, Quai des Allies, 94500 Champigny-Sur-Marne (tel: 4397 4397). These sites, which are run by the Touring Club de France, are heavily booked in the summer and it is advisable to reserve well in advance. Members of equivalent associations (AAA, AA or RAC) or international camping associations can benefit from a 10% price reduction. Details from French Govt. Tourist Offices or directly from the Touring Club de France, 14 Ave de la Grande Armée, Paris 16 (tel: 502 14 00), whose guide to camping sites in France is available on written request. Another useful guide is the Guide Officiel Camping Caravaning, published by the Féderation Française de Camping et de Caravaning

(FFCC) 78 Rue de Rivoli, Paris 4. Also from Office de Tourisme de Paris, 127 Champs Elysées, Paris 8.

Food and Drink

Registered students can take advantage of students' restaurants (Resto U) on production of their card or an international student card obtainable from the AJF (see above) or the Council on International Educational Exchange (CIEE) 49 Rue Pierre Charron, Paris 8, tel: 359 23 69 (métro: Alma Marceau). (This organization, which is American, also advises on reductions for entry to museums, cinemas and theatres and arranges for reduced travel on the railway and buses).

Many smaller restaurants have set menus at under F·50 and, in general, it is a good plan to study and compare the menus posted outside restaurants. There are several self-service restaurants, and one of the best is on the 5th floor of Magasin 2 in La Samaritaine, Pont Neuf, where you can admire the view of the Seine while you eat. There are also Chinese restaurants − especially in the 13th *arrondissement* which is the new 'Chinatown' of Paris − and North African restaurants in the Quartier de St Séverin, at the north-east end of the Boulevard St Michel, and in the 10th and 18th *arrondissements*. The fast-food chains on the main thoroughfares sell triple-decker hamburgers and there are also the *Croissanteries* selling hot croissants, quiches and tarts. Tunisian and oriental bakeries exist in the 5th, 10th and 18th *arrondissements* and also in *Le Marais*, and the Turkish cafés and groceries in the Rue de Faubourg St Denis by the Porte St Denis sell doner kebabs. If you like pancakes and cider, the *crêperies* in Montparnasse provide filling, reasonably priced fare. In the evenings, look out for the *café-théâtres*, many of which offer relatively inexpensive menus and entertainment. Don't forget the cafés, most of which serve snacks and the brasseries, which often have a cheap *plat du jour* (dish of the day).

Shopping

Trendy clothes are on sale in the boutiques in the Rue de Rennes and Rue de Sèvres, in the 6th *arrondissement*, in the Rue de Passy (16th), in the Forum des Halles (1st) and surrounding streets. You can buy traditional French overalls, smocks and waiters' jackets in La Samaritaine at Pont Neuf, and this part of the Rue de Rivoli has a C & A and several inexpensive shoe shops. The Monoprix, Prisunic and Unishop stores are useful sources for blouses, jeans and sweaters. The flea markets at the Place d'Aligre and at the Porte Montreuil (open weekends) are good hunting grounds for bargains (see also markets on p.24). Sales (*soldes*) take place in January and June and some shops hold permanent sales (where you see the signs *Braderie*, *Démarques*, *Dégriffes* or *Griffsoldes*). Two addresses worth knowing are: Galeries St Elizabeth, 172 Rue du Temple, and the Comptoir du Sentier, 96 Rue du Cléry, Paris 2.

The FNAC (addresses p.23) in the Forum des Halles and in the Rue de Rennes have the largest selection of books in Paris and also specialize in records and audiovisual equipment. There are numerous second-hand bookshops in the Latin Quarter. Record shops abound all over Paris – on the Champs-Elysées (Lido Musique and Champs Disques) in the FNAC stores, particularly the branch on the Ave de Wagram, in the Bazar de l'Hôtel de Ville, Galeries Lafayette, Le Printemps and in the drugstores (addresses p.23). Paul Beuscher, 23–29 Bd Beaumarchais, stocks the widest variety of musical instruments in town and another source, for guitars and wind instruments, is the ground floor of Hamm, 135 Rue de Rennes, Paris 6. For cameras: Shop Photo, 33 Rue du Commandant Mouchotte, Paris 14 (the largest specialist shop in Europe) and the FNAC stores. If your camera is in need of repair, go to Photo Cine Ms, 3 Rue Charles-Baudelaire, Paris 12 or Phocirep, 14 Boulevard Blanqui, Paris 13 (which also sells second-hand cameras.)

Entertainment

Among the best sources of information (in French) are the magazines *Pariscope* and *l'Officiel du Spectacle*, which give details of programmes, times, prices and reductions for students and the nearest métro. The best guide for students is *Paris en Jeans*, published by Hachette, with information on entertainment, shopping, restaurants and a host of useful addresses. The daily press and *Paris Hebdo* provide up-to-date information and there are posters in the métro and on the round kiosks in the streets, advertising theatres and concerts. (If you read only English, see p.28.) Never go without your student card and always enquire at box offices and entrances to museums whether there are price reductions for students.

Foreign films in their original language (v.o.) are shown chiefly in the 6th and 8th *arrondissements* and several of the Latin Quarter cinemas specialize in showing reruns and old films. The main *cinémathèques* (film theatres) are in the east wing of the Palais de Chaillot and the Centre Georges Pompidou.

National theatres, such as the Théâtre de Chaillot and the Théâtre de la Ville, have some of the least expensive seats as do fringe theatres and *café-théâtres*, many of which are in the Beaubourg, Marais and Montparnasse districts. If you are staying long enough (at least 6 months), it is worth while taking out subscriptions of the national theatres and to some of the others, such as La Cartoucherie in Vincennes.

Many larger pop and rock concerts take place at the CIP, Porte Maillot; the Palace, 8 Rue du Faubourg Montmartre; the Palais des Sports, Porte de Versailles; Le Zenith, Porte de Pantin; Le Bataclan, 50 Bd Voltaire. Big jazz concerts, given by visiting artists and bands, are held at the CIP and in the Salle Pleyel, 252 Faubourg St Honoré, Paris 8. Paris has always been well known for its jazz clubs, caves and small cabarets on the Left Bank and new ones have opened in the Châtelet, Beaubourg and Marais areas. The magazines *Rock Folk*, *Best*, *Jazz Hot*, *Le Monde de la Musique* and *Jazz Magazine* give up-to-date information on these as well as on the 'in' discos. The American and Canadian Centres, and the British Council arrange exhibitions, hold discussion groups, present classical, jazz and pop concerts and give film shows.

Information on sporting activities is given on p.28 and further details can be obtained from the Office du Tourisme, 127 Ave des Champs-Elysées, Paris 8 (tel: 723 72 11) or the Direction des Affaires Scolaires de la Jeunesse et des Sports de la Ville de Paris, 17 Bd Morland, Paris 4 (tel: 277 15 50).

General information Apart from the addresses given in this section, students will also find useful advice on entertainment, sports and all matters of general interest, at the Centre d'Information et de Documentation Jeunesse (CIDJ) 101 Quai Branly, Paris 15 (tel: 566 40 20).

Crisis line If you are feeling lonely or have come up against a crisis, telephone the English-speaking SOS Amitié: 4723 80 80 between 1500 and 2300.

Hitchhiking service When you want to leave Paris contact: Allostop, 85 Passage Bardy, Paris 10 (tel: 246 00 66).

CHILDREN'S PARIS

Getting Around

There are no special reductions for children on buses and métros in Paris, but if you are only staying for a week, you can buy a tourist ticket, valid for 2, 4 or 7 days, with which you can travel anywhere as often as you like. You can also buy a series of 10 tickets (*carnet*), which is useful on the métro as one ticket takes you as far as you like on any given journey and children under ten pay half price if they buy a carnet of 10 tickets. If you plan to stay at least a month, buy a *carte orange* (orange card), a ticket kept in a special plastic cover, which you can use for up to one month on all buses and métros in the city.

Things to See

Many of the buildings and places described in the Gazetteer (pp.78–124) will interest children as much as adults. Below are some museums of special interest (addresses in alphabetical list of museums and galleries (pp.58–65).
Armée You can see all kinds of weapons, including old swords and daggers, firearms, coats of armour and military uniforms and models and plans of battles in bygone days. **Arts Africains et Océaniens** The aquarium in the basement is full of tropical fish, crocodiles and giant turtles. There is also a fine collection of butterflies. **Arts et Traditions Populaires** Household items and tools used by country folk in the old days – spinning wheels, old toys and puppets, costumes and musical instruments. **Découverte** Scientific experiments, models and a planetarium showing the movement of the stars and the solar system. Film shows on a variety of scientific subjects are shown here regularly. **Galliéra** This is now the French costume museum. Exhibitions cover specific subjects, suchs as old hats, balldresses, *etc.* **Grévin** Like Madame Tussaud's in London, there are lifelike waxworks of famous people, past and present, including pop stars and famous sportsmen. This museum has an annex on the first floor of the *Forum des Halles*, Paris 1, with a Son et Lumière show of Paris between 1885 and 1900. Open every day 1100–2200 (last performance 2115); Sundays and public holidays 1300–2000 (last performance 1915). **Histoire Naturelle** Stuffed animals, skeletons of dinosaurs and other prehistoric animals, fossils and minerals are on display in this museum which is in a park with a small zoo and an aquarium. **Marine** has a marvellous display of old boats and ships, including American clippers, an English Royal Yacht and Canadian canoes as well as old French vessels, models of destroyers, torpedoes and submarines. **Musée International de la Machine A Sous**, 23 Rue Beaubourg, Paris (Métro Rambuteau). Open every day 1100–1900. Collection of some of the oldest fruit and slot machines, and other curiosities. **Postal** This museum covers not only stamps, but the whole history of communications from earliest clay tablets (2500BC) to the most modern stamp presses used today. You can

see early telephones and telegraph systems, mail coaches, balloons sent up during the Siege of Paris in 1871, and learn how today's mail is electronically sorted.
Radio France 116 Ave du Président Kennedy, Paris 16. The history of radio and television is described in guided tours 1000–1230 and 1500–1830 every day except Monday. (Métro: Mirabeau, Passy, Ranelagh. Buses 22, 52, 70, 72.)
Techniques If you are interested in machinery and scientific instruments, this is the museum to visit. Steam engines, early motor cars, and the first aeroplane to cross the Channel in 1909 are among the hundreds of fine exhibits, which also include early clocks, microscopes, radio equipment and some of the first electrical machinery ever invented. Also see the **Cité des Sciences** – all the latest technological developments. Amuse yourself in the Inventorium which is specially designed for children. La Géode, next door, shows films on a giant circular screen. Métro: Pte de la Villette.
Shops: Jouets Montparnasse, 35 Bd Edgar Quinet, Paris 14; **Le Train Bleu**, 2 Ave Mozart, Paris 16.
Outside Paris: Jouet, Musée du 2 Enclos de l'Abbaye, Poissy (Yvelines). Open every day, except Mondays, Tuesdays and public holidays, 0930–1200, 1400–1730. A toy museum with all kinds of 19th- and early 20th-century toys including dolls, puppets, early games, model railways and tin soldiers. (SNCF from Gare St Lazare, or by car on the A13 Autoroute.) **Neuilly, Musée de** Château d'Arturo Lopez, 12 Rue du Centre, 92 Neuilly. Open every day, except Tuesdays and public holidays. 1430–1700. Over 60 clockwork figures are on display, including a moon smoking Peirrot's cigar, a poet crying real tears and an angel flapping her wings in time to her harp. Get there before 1500 to see the figures working. (Métro: Pont de Neuilly. Bus 73.)

Out of Doors

The Bois de Boulogne has a lot to offer children, especially the Jardin d'Acclimatation, by the Porte Maillot, which was designed with them in mind, and has a miniature railway running all the way round. Inside the gardens, there is an amusement arcade, a mini car track, a children's museum and hall of mirrors. You can take a trip up the Enchanted River or visit the animals on the farm and ride a pony. On Wednesdays and at the weekends, there are Punch and Judy shows at 1500 and 1600. Elsewhere in the Bois, bicycles and tandems can be rented by the lakes and rowing boats on the larger lake. Or you can just picnic and play handball on the grass in fine weather. Not

Far out of Paris, at the Parc de St Cloud, there is a good sandpit for children, and stilts, bicycles, tandems and pedal cars can also be rented in the park. There are donkey rides in the Jardins du Ranelagh and in the Champ de Mars, which also has swings and merry-go-rounds. You can sail boats on the round ponds in the Luxembourg or Tuileries Gardens. Boats can be rented out on the lakes in the Bois de Vincennes where you can also ride donkeys, go on the swings and merry-go-rounds or roller skate. Gingerbread men are sold here during Easter Week at the Annual Fair, on the Reuilly Lawn. France's largest zoo is set in 17 hectares/42 acres on the edge of the Bois de Vincennes by the Porte Dorée. One of the best ways of seeing the sights of Paris is by river. The boats go round the oldest part of the town on the islands and then upstream to the modern tower blocks on the Left Bank.

Entertainment

Wednesday is a holiday for French children and many special cinema and theatre programmes take place then and at the weekends. The best way to find out what is on, with times and admission prices, is to look in the magazines *Pariscope* and *'Officiel du Spectacle* under the section *Pour Les Jeunes* (for the young). Punch and Judy shows (*Guignol*) and puppet shows (*marionnettes*) take place in the Champ de Mars, the Jardins du Luxembourg, in the Parc Montsouris and in the gardens between the Avenues Marigny and Matignon. There are always at least two circuses in town and most reduce their prices for children. If you are between 4 and 14 and like painting, dancing, playing with puppets or are interested in building models and making your own films, one of the best places to go on Wednesdays and Saturdays is to the children's workshops on the ground floor of the Centre Georges Pompidou. Hours of individual workshops vary and it is best to check (tel: 277 12 33, extension 4907) the exact time in order to avoid disappointment. There is also a special library here for children, where adults (including parents) are not admitted.

Shops

The best-known toy shop is Le Nain Bleu, 406 Rue St Honoré, Paris 8, with every type of toy on its three floors. The big stores, particularly Le Printemps, also have good toy departments. Other shops include Ali Baba, 29 Ave de Tourville, Paris 7; Paris Jouets, 20 Avenue Trudaine, Paris 9; La Maison des Trains, 24 Passage du Havre, Paris 9; Jouets & Cie, 11 Boulevard de Sébastopol, Paris 1; Pain d'Épice (bric-à-brac and replicas of old toys), 29 Passage Jouffroy; Jouets Extraordinaires (educational toys, puzzles and games), 70 Rue d'Auteuil, Paris 16; Jouets Montparnasse (models, electric trains, *etc*), 35 Bd Edgar Quinet, Paris 14. L'Amicale Comptoir des Articles de Fêtes, 32 Rue des Vignoles, Paris 20, is a vast warehouse and the best source of novelties, gewgaws, magic sets, puppets, paper lanterns, hats, masks and everything a child could wish for at a birthday party. All the English bookshops, mentioned on p.25, stock children's books as do the big stores, particularly Au Bon Marché in their Trois Hiboux department, on the ground floor of Magasin 1.

GENERAL INFORMATION

Chemists (Pharmacies) are easily recognized by the green cross sign. Most are open Mon–Sat 0900–1930, but some shops outside the city centre close for lunch 1230–1400. The names of chemists open in each *arrondissement* on Sundays are posted on the door and the local police station also has a list (*Pharmacies de Garde*). Night Service: (all night) Dhéry, Galerie des Champs, 84 Ave des Champs-Elysées; (till 0200) the Drugstores Champs-Elysées, Opéra, St Germain (addresses p.23;) (till 2200) Fau, 10 Place Raoul Dautry, Paris 14; (till 2400) Machelou, 5 Place Pigalle, Paris 9; (till 2400) Pharmacie des Arts, 106 Bd St Germain, Paris 14. Two pharmacies with English speaking staff and some English and American products: Pharmacie Anglaise, 62 Ave des Champs Elysées, Paris 8, Mon–Sat till 2230 (closed Sundays); British American Pharmacie, 1 Rue Auber, Paris 9, Mon–Sat 0830–2000 (closed Sundays). **Closing days and times** National museums and galleries close on Tuesdays, Municipal museums on Mondays. Private museums vary. In general, banks close at weekends (see Banking hours p.11) and at noon the day before and on public holidays. Cinemas open every day, usually from 1400 on; most theatres close on Sunday evenings and either on Tuesday or Wednesday (indicated by *relache* in the press). For shops see p.23–5. **Electricity** 220/240 voltage is becoming standard but 110 still exists in some parts of the city. Most light sockets are bayonet type and power points are two or three pin (earthed). Overseas visitors may need adaptors, available at most good electrical supply stores.

Health For health insurance see p.10. Doctors' and dentists' consulting hours vary according to individuals and payment is by cash. Lists of doctors receiving patients on Sundays and public holidays are posted on chemists' doors and can also be obtained from police stations. If you need a doctor urgently or at night: Association des Urgences Médicales sur Paris (AUMP) tel: 828 40 04 (24-hour service); SOS Médecins tel: 337 77 77/707 77 77 (24-hour service); SOS Dentistes tel: 337 51 00; for severe burns tel: 344 33 33/329 21 21 ext. 403 (adults), 346 13 90 (children); anti-poison unit tel: 205 63 29; De l'Assistance Publique, tel: 4378 2626; SOS Pacemakers, tel: 4250 3308. English-speaking hospitals (see p.36).

Rabies Rabid wild animals, mainly foxes, are at large in some parts of France. Caution is essential when approaching any wild animals, or dogs roaming free from control. There is at present no effective preventive vaccine against rabies. A bite or scratch incurred through contact with a wild or stray animal should be washed immediately with soap and water, and medical advice sought.

The UK totally prohibits importation of animals (including domestic pets) except under licence. One of the conditions of the licence is that the animals are retained in approved quarantine premises for up to six months. No exemptions are made for animals that have been vaccinated against rabies. Penalties for smuggling involve imprisonment, unlimited fines and destruction of the animal.

Any animal being imported into the US must have a valid certificate of vaccination against rabies.

For details apply to the Ministry of Agriculture (Animal Health Division), Hook Rise South, Tolworth, Surbiton, Surrey KT6 7NF.

Lost property Contact the local police station and then your embassy immediately if you lose your passport. Report all stolen items to the police station. Lost property found on buses and métros can sometimes be retrieved within 24 hours at the terminals, otherwise the main office is at 36 Rue des Morillons, Paris 15 (tel: 531 14 80) open weekdays 0830–1700 (till 2000 Thurs) closed Sundays. There are lost property offices at the main railway stations and at Charles de Gaulle and Orly airports.

Newspapers English-language newspapers and magazines are on sale at many of the big kiosks and news stands in the city centre, at Smith's bookshop, in many of the drugstores and at the UNESCO news stand, 9 Place Fontenoy, Paris 7. The best tourist publications are *All Paris*, *Pariscope* and *l'Officiel du Spec tacle*, published on Wednesdays. In addition, *Passion* (bi-monthly) magazine available at big news stands and Smith's and *Paris Free Voice* free from the American Church (address p.36), schools and the American Centre, 261 Bd Raspail provide useful information for English speaking visitors, but they tend to dis appear rapidly.

Police The police or *les flics* ('the cops') ar easy to recognize in their dark blu uniforms and caps (at night in rain or fo they often wear white capes and caps). Yo should address them as '*Bonjour*, *Monsie l'Agent*'. They are there to keep the peace direct the traffic and are usually ver helpful when asked for directions. Th *Gendarmerie* have more specialized duties including motorcycle escorts, and they ar often seen watching out for dangerou driving or speeding on the motorways.

Main **police stations** (*Commissariat de Police*): *Paris 1* 51 Place du Marché S Honoré; *Paris 2* 5 Place des Petits Pères *Paris 3* 5 Rue Perrée; *Paris 4* Plac Baudoyer; *Paris 5* 21 Place du Panthéon *Paris 6* 78 Rue Bonaparte; *Paris 7* 116 Ru de Grenelle; *Paris 8* 1 Ave Gén.-Eisen hower; *Paris 9* 12 Rue Chauchat; *Paris 1* 1 Rue Hittorff; *Paris 11* Place Léon Blum *Paris 12* 3 Rue Bignon; *Paris 13* 144 Bd d l'Hôpital; *Paris 14* 114 Ave du Maine *Paris 15* 154 Rue Lecourbe; *Paris 16* 7: Rue de la Pompe; *Paris 17* 19–21 Ru Truffaut; *Paris 18* 74 Rue de Mont-Cenis *Paris 19* 2 Rue André-Dubois; *Paris 20* (Place Gambetta; *Emergency Police:* Dia 17 (Police-Secours).

Postal Services Post offices are identi fied by the letters PTT or P & T (*Postes Télécommunications*) and the blue an white birdlike sign outside, and are ope Mon–Fri 0800–1900 and 0800–1200 o Sats. The main post office at 52 Rue d Louvre, Paris 1, is open 24 hours all th year round, the branch at 71 Ave de Champs-Elysées is open on Sunda 1000–1200 and 1400–2000. Postag stamps can also be bought at *Tabac* (tobacconists) which always have po boxes (painted yellow) outside. Post rates are available at the post office counter rates abroad vary according to desti nation. Poste Restante: letters should b addressed to Poste Restante, Paris R.P. 52 Rue du Louvre, Paris 1, or Post Restante Paris VIII, 71 Ave des Champs Elysées, Paris 8.

Principal **post offices** (*Bureaux d Postes*): *Central Post Office* 52 Rue d

Louvre Paris 1; *Paris 2* 6–8 Place de la Bourse; *Paris 3* 259 Rue St Martin; *Paris 4* Place de l'Hôtel de Ville; *Paris 5* 10 Rue de l'Epée-de-bois; *Paris 6* 6 Rue St Romain; *Paris 7* 56 Rue Cler; *Paris 8* 49 Rue La Boétie; *Paris 9* 4 Rue Hippolyte-Lebas; *Paris 10* 2 Square Alban-Satragne; *Paris 11* 21 Rue Bréguet; *Paris 12* 30 Rue de Reilly; *Paris 13* 27 Ave d'Italie; *Paris 14* 210 Boulevard Brune; *Paris 15* 19 Rue d'Alleray; *Paris 16* 40 Rue Singer; *Paris 17* 110 Ave Wagram; *Paris 18* 19 Rue Duc; *Paris 19* 12 Ave Laumière; *Paris 20* 248 Rue des Pyrénées.

Public holidays 1 January, Easter Monday (movable date), 1 May, 8 May, Ascension Day (movable), Whit Monday (movable), 14 July, 15 August, 1 November, 11 November, Christmas Day. Banks and post offices, most doctors, pharmacies and social security offices close on these dates.

Telephones and telegrams Phone booths are found in post offices, in cafés, where you often have to buy a special coin (*jeton*), and on busy thoroughfares. Coin (pay) boxes take 20 and 50 centimes and 1 and 5 Franc coins. Since October 1985, all telephone numbers in Paris and neighbouring suburbs making up the Ile de France Region have 8 figures — 7 plus a different pre-fix: For Paris, Departments Hauts de Seine (92), Seine Saint Denis (93) and Val de Marne (94) the 1st number is 4 Ex: 4564 2222. For the Val d'Oise (95) and Les Yvelines (78) the number is 3 Ex: 3951 9536, and L'Essonne (91) and Seine et Marne (77) both begin with 6 Ex: 6424 5563. A useful little booklet *Pour Téléphoner de Paris*, available from post offices, lists all codes in France and abroad and gives the rates based on time, (the same information is given at the beginning of telephone directories). To get the overseas operator for person-to-person, or reversed charge (collect) calls, dial 19, wait for dialling tone, then dial 33 followed by the relevant country code (44 for the UK and 11 for the US). All overseas numbers dialled direct begin with 19 followed, after the buzz, by the country code. Calls from Paris to the provinces begins with 16 followed by the area code. Calls dialled direct to outside Paris and abroad are cheaper after 2000 Mon–Sat, Suns and public holidays.

Telegrams may be sent from the telegram counter in post offices, or by calling 3655 for telegrams in France and 233 44 11 for abroad in English. Call 4233 4411 for telegrams in French.

Time France has adopted Summer and Winter time, and clocks go back one hour during the first week of April and one hour forward on the first or second Sunday in October (dates are well advertised in the press, on radio and TV). UK citizens: 1 hour behind French time, except for short periods in April and October. US and Canadian citizens: East Coast 6 hours behind, West Coast 9 hours behind. Don't forget to adjust your watch on arrival. For French-speaking clock (Horloge Parlante) (tel: 3699).

Tipping Most hotels include service and taxes on the bill, though the maid, if she has done any sewing for you, and the porter in large hotels, should be tipped a few Francs extra. Many restaurants now automatically add 15% to the bill, and on set menus it is often included, but it is customary to leave any small change on the table. Taxi drivers expect a tip of 12–15%, and a little more if they carry a lot of baggage or more than two passengers. However, they have shown a tendancy to greed in recent years, and visitors should beware of being gulled into leaving more than is necessary. In garages, if your oil, water and tyres have been checked and your windscreen cleaned, it is customary to give the attendant a Franc. Porters at railway stations and airports are usually tipped a fixed price, depending on the amount of baggage, however this problem is often solved by the fact that there are very few porters, and baggage is usually wheeled by the passenger himself on caddies or trolleys. Usherettes in cinemas and theatres and lavatory attendants should be tipped a Franc, or two at most.

Public toilets The round public toilets, *vespasiennes* as they were called, have now disappeared from the streets of Paris, and toilets are to be found in some of the larger métro stations, in the railway stations and in cafés. Men's and women's toilets are distinguished by a stylized sign, or *Dames*, *Hommes* or *Messieurs* and they are generally free. The Mairie de Paris is gradually installing modern toilets on many of the busier streets — charge 1 Franc. Toilets in cafes are generally free, although it is customary to order a coffee or drink first, and some cafes are now installing 50cm slot machines in women's toilets.

Weather The weather in Paris can best be described as capricious, especially in winter or spring when cold wet spells often alternate with fine sunny days. Visitors should be warned that it can remain cold until well after Easter with bitterly cold blasts of wind blowing down the avenues and boulevards. At other times, it can be extremely hot and dry. Two of the best months of the year are September and October when the days are often pleasantly warm and sunny.

General tourist information Office du Tourisme de Paris, 127 Ave des

Champs-Elysées Paris 8 (tel: 723 61 72). Open Mon–Sat 0900–2200 (low season till 1800), Suns and holidays 0900–2000. Other branches at: Invalides (tel: 705 82 81) open every day 1200–1900; Gare du Nord (tel: 526 94 82) open Mon–Sat 0800–2200 (low season till 2000); Gare de l'Est (tel: 607 17 73) open 0800–1300, 1700–2200 (low season till 2000); Gare de Lyon, the same hours as Gare de l'Est; Bureau d'Accueil de l'Hotel de Ville, 29 Rue de Rivoli, Paris 4 (tel: 217 15 40) open Mon–Sat 0845–1830 (closed Sundays and holidays).

USEFUL ADDRESSES

American Cultural Centre, 261 Bd Raspail, Paris 4 (4321 4220).
American Express, 11 Rue Scribe, Paris 9 (226 09 99).
American Library, 10 Rue du Général Camou, Paris 7 (551 46 82).
British Council, 9 Rue Constantine, Paris 7 (554 99/705 66 20).
Canadian Cultural Centre, 5 Rue Constantine, Paris 7 (551 35 73).
English-speaking Hospitals: The American Hospital, 63 Bd Victor Hugo, 92 Neuilly (747 53 00). Bus 82. British Hertford Hospital, 3 Rue Barbès, 92 Levallois Perret (4758 1312). Métro: Anatole France. Bus 83.
Pawnshop: Crédit Municipale de Paris, formerly the Mont de Piété and popularly known as *Chez Ma Tante* (At my aunt's), 55 Rue des Francs Bourgeois, Paris 4 (271 25 43) may be able to help if you are staying in Paris long enough. It is a government pawnbroking service, founded in 1777 to combat private usury and hosts of well-known personalities have made use of its services at one time or another.
Public Reference Libraries: Every *arrondissement* in Paris has a municipal library – two of the best are at 124 Rue Lecourbe, Paris 15 (828 77 42) and at 4 Rue Commandant Schloesing, Paris 16 (727 26 47). Métro: Trocadéro. Buses 22, 30, 32, 63. Many museums have libraries and there are other public libraries:
Bibliothèque de l'Institut National de la Statistique et des Divisions Economiques (INSEE), 18 Bd Adolphe Pinard, Paris 14 (540 01 12/12 12); 195 Rue de Bercy, Paris 12 (345 72 31). Econonic history, international agreements, economic publications and information on current affairs. Métro: Porte de Vanves. Buses 58, PC.
Bibliothèque du Conservatoire des Arts et Métiers (CNAM), 292 Rue St Martin, Paris 3 (271 24 14). Science and technology. Non-members of CNAM are charged a small fee. Métro: Arts et Métiers. Buses 38, 47.

Bibliothèque Historique de la Ville de Paris, 24 Rue Pavée, Paris 3 (272 10 18). Métro: St Paul. Buses 69, 76.
Bibliothèque Ste Geneviève, 10 Place du Panthéon, Paris 5 (329 61 00). Reference. Métro: Luxembourg. Buses 84, 89.
Observatoire Economique de Paris (a branch of INSEE above), Tour Gamma, 195 Rue de Bercy, Paris 12 (345 72 31). Métro: Gare de Lyon. Buses 20, 57, 63.

French Govt. Tourist Offices

London 178 Piccadilly, London W1V 0AL (01 493 9232). **New York** 610 Fifth Ave, NY 10020 (212 757 1125). **Chicago** 645 North Michigan Ave, Chicago, Ill. 60611 (312 751 7800). **Beverley Hills** 9401 Wilshire Bd, Beverley Hills, Calif. 90212 (213 272 2661). **San Francisco** 1 Hallidie Plaza, San Francisco, Calif. 94102 (415 986 4161). **Coral Gables** 2121 Ponce de Leon Bd, Coral Gables, Florida 33134 (305 445 8648). **Montreal** 1981 Ave McGill College, Montreal, QCMH3 A2W9 (511 288 4264).

Embassies and Consulates

Australia 4 Rue Jean Rey, Paris 15 (575 62 00). **Britain** (embassy) 35 Rue du Faubourg St Honoré, Paris 8 (266 91 42); (consulate) 2 Gté de Retiro, Paris 8 (4266 9142). **Canada** (embassy) 35 Ave Montaigne, Paris 8 (723 01 01); (consulate) 4 Rue Ventadour, Paris 1 (296 87 19). **New Zealand** 7–9 Rue Léonard-de-Vinci, Paris 16 (500 24 11). **Republic of Ireland** 12 Ave Foch, Paris 16 (500 20 87). **South Africa** 59 Quai d'Orsay, Paris 7 (555 92 37). **United States of America** (embassy) 2 Ave Gabriel, Paris 8 (296 12 02); (consulate) 2 Rue St Florentin, Paris 1 (261 80 75/260 14 88); (visas) 4 Ave Gabriel, Paris 8 (296 14 88); (information services) 2 Rue St Florentin, Paris 1 (261 80 75).

Places of Worship

American Church 65 Quai d'Orsay, Paris 7 (705 07 99). **Anglican** St George's, 7 Rue Auguste Vacquerie, Paris 16 (720 22 51). **Baptist Church** 48 Rue de Lille, Paris 7 (261 24 23/13 96); Eglise du Main, 123 Ave du Maine, Paris 14. **British Embassy Church** St Michael's, 5 Rue d'Aguesseau, Paris 8 (4742 7088). **Christian Scientist** 36 Bd St Jacques, Paris 14; 58 Bd Flandrin, Paris 16; 43 Rue La Boétie, Paris 8. **Church of Scotland** 17 Rue Bayard, Paris 8. **Episcopalian** American Cathedral, 23 Ave George V, Paris 8 (720 17 92). **Greek Orthodox** St Stephen's, 7 Rue Georges Bizet, Paris 16 (720 82 35). **Islam** Grande Mosquée, 19 Rue Geoffroy-St-Hilaire, Paris 5 (535 97 33). **Jewish** Ass. Consistorale Israélite de Paris, 28 Rue Buffault, Paris 9 (526 80 87);

Great Synagogue, 44 Rue de la Victoire, Paris 9 (285 71 09); Liberal Synagogue, 24 Rue Copernic, Paris 16. **Roman Catholic** (services in English) St Joseph's, 50 Ave Hoche, Paris 8 (563 20 61). **Russian Orthodox** 12 Rue Daru, Paris 8 (622 37 34). **Wesleyan Methodist** 5 Rue Rocquepine, Paris 8 (265 43 58).

Telephone Nos

Fire Brigade 18, Police (emergency) 17, Speaking Clock 3699, Weather Forecast (Paris region) 4369 0202 (other regions) 555 91 09.

ANNUAL EVENTS

As some dates given below are subject to change, visitors are advised to check with the Office du Tourisme de Paris, 127 Ave des Champs-Elysées, Paris 8 (tel: 723 61 72), and Bureau d'Accueil de l'Hôtel de Ville, Paris 4 (277 15 40) open Mon–Sat 0845-1830 (closed Sundays and public holidays). As well as the leaflet *La Saison de Paris* these offices also issue a monthly leaflet listing the principal events of the month, *Paris Selection.*

January Winter sales are held in the shops. International Boat Show, CNIT, La Défense (2nd or 3rd week).

February World Tourist and Travel Show (2nd week).

March Agricultural Show, Parc des Expositions, Porte de Versailles, Paris 16 (1st week). Salon des Arts Ménagers (Ideal Homes Exhibition), CNIT, La Défense (2nd week). Foire Nationale à la Ferraille et au Jambon (Antiques, Junk and Ham fair), Parc Floral, Bois de Vincennes (2nd week).

March or April Foire du Trône (Throne and Gingerbread fair), Reuilly Lawn, Bois de Vincennes (Palm Sunday). Salon des Indépendants (art), Grand Palais, Ave Winston Churchill, Paris 8. Azaleas, tulips, hyacinths and other spring flowers in Bagatelle Gardens, Bois de Boulogne.

April Opening of Foire de Paris (Paris Fair), Parc des Expositions, Porte de Versailles, Paris 16 (late Apr/early May).

May Labour Day, lily of the valley sold in the streets (1 May). Celebrations Allied Victory 1945 (8 May). Paris Air Show, Le Bourget (late May/early June).

June Roses in Bagatelle Gardens, Bois de Boulogne. Floralies (flower show), Floral Gardens, Bois de Vincennes. Festival du Marais (music, dancing, theatre), Le Marais, 3rd and 4th *arrondissements* (mid June/mid July).

July National Day: military reviews, fireworks, dancing in the streets (14 July). Paris Summer Music Festival (mid July/mid Sept). Music Festival (mid July/mid

Sept). Music Festival, Orangerie, Château de Sceaux, 92 (mid July/mid Oct). Fête Foraine des Loges (Annual Fair), Forest of St Germain en Laye, (RER to St Germain then bus or taxi).

September Biennale de Paris, Fête à Neu Neu, Bois de Boulogne, children's fun fair. Antiques Fair, Grand Palais, Ave Winston Churchill, Paris 16 (4th week) every two years.

September or October International Contemporary Art Exhibition (FIAC), Grand Palais, Ave Winston Churchill, Paris 16.

October Grape harvest and wine festival of Montmartre, corner of the Rue des Saules and Rue St Vincent, Paris 18 (1st or 2nd week). Salon de l'Automobile (Motor Show), Parc des Expositions, Porte de Versailles, Paris 16. International Contemporary Art Exhibition (FIAC), Grand Palais, Ave Winston Churchill, Paris 16 (early Oct or Dec). Veteran Car Race, Rue Lepic to Place du Tertre, Paris 18 (mid Oct). Salon d'Automne (art), Grand Palais, Ave Winston Churchill, Paris 16 (late Oct/Dec).

November All Saints' Day: cemeteries visited and graves decorated (1 Nov), Armistice Day: military review, Arc de Triomphe, Paris 8 (11 Nov). Antiques Fair, Espace Austerlitz, 24 Quai d'Austerlitz, Paris 13.

December Midnight Mass in the principal churches of Paris (24 Dec).

Sport

February and March Triple Crown International Rugby Tournament, Parc des Princes, Paris 16. President of the Republic Stakes, Auteuil Racecourse, Bois de Boulogne (Palm sunday).

May French Rugby Cup Final, Parc des Princes, Paris 16. International Paris Marathon, Place de la Concorde. French Open Tennis Championships, Stade Rolan Garros, Paris 16 (late May/early June).

June French Football Cup Final, Parc des Princes, Paris 16 (early June). Paris Steeplechase, Auteuil Racecourse, Bois de Boulogne (late June). Paris Grand Prix, Longchamp Racecourse, Paris 16 (last Sun).

July Finish of Tour de France cycle race, Ave des Champs-Elysées, Paris 8 (mid July).

October Grand Prix de l'Arc de Triomphe, Longchamp Racecourse, Paris 16 (1st Sun).

December International Show Jumping Tournament and Horse Show, Parc des Expositions, Porte de Versailles, Paris 16 (mid Dec). Figaro Marathon Race, Bois de Boulogne.

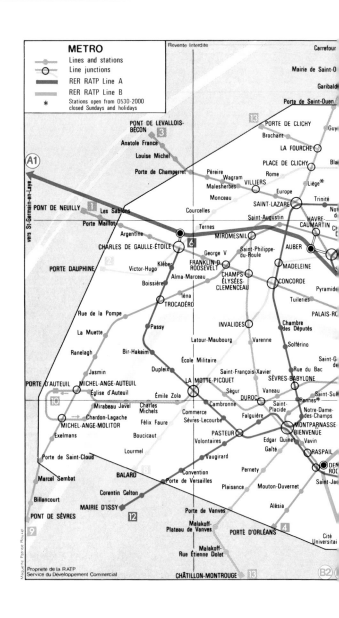

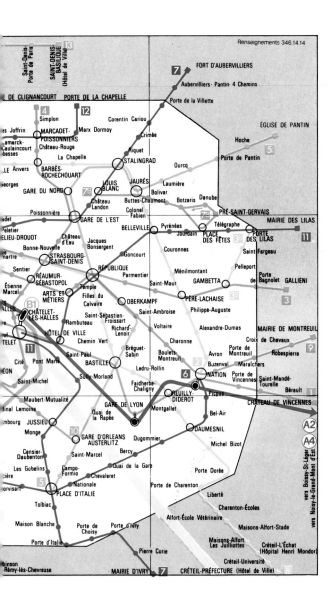

Renseignements 346.14.14

Central Paris Maps

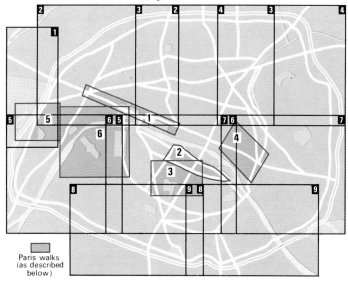

Paris walks
(as described
below)

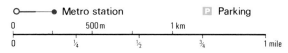

○——● Metro station   P Parking

0   500 m   1 km

0   ¼   ½   ¾   1 mile

PARIS WALKS

1. La Voie Triomphale *pp. 66–7*
From the Louvre to the Arc de Triomphe, this walk takes in fashionable Paris: the Tuileries, Place de la Concorde, Champs-Elysées and the Etoile.
Approx. distance 3½km/2mi.

2. Les Quais *pp. 68–9*
This walk explores riverside quays and the old streets of St Germain des Près, and includes the Mint, the French Institute, and historic churches.
Approx. distance 5km/3mi.

3. Le Quartier Latin *pp. 70–1*
The Left Bank student quarter offers much: the Cluny museum, the Sorbonne, Rue Mouffetard, scene of a lively daily market, and the Val de Grâce monastery with its fine church.
Approx. distance 3½km/2mi; optional return by Bd St Michel 1½km/1mi.

4. Le Marais *pp. 72–3*
Rich in history, this is an area to explore at leisure. Do not miss Place des Vosges, Carnavalet museum, National Archives and the many beautiful period mansions.
Approx. distance 4km/2½mi.

5. Le Bois *pp. 74–5*
A walk through Passy, which retains a village atmosphere, brings you to the Parisians' favourite park, Le Bois de Boulogne, laid out by Napoleon III and Haussmann on the lines of Hyde Park.
Approx. distance 8km/5mi.

6. Military Paris *pp. 76–7*
The military side is reflected in the Invalides, Ecole Militaire and in the streets named after distinguished soldiers; there is also the Eiffel tower.
Approx. distance 5km/3mi.

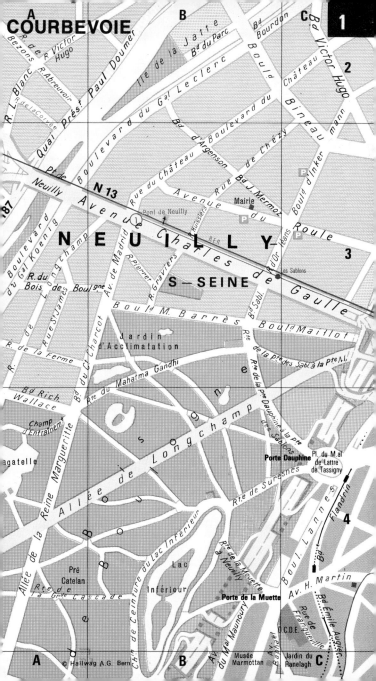

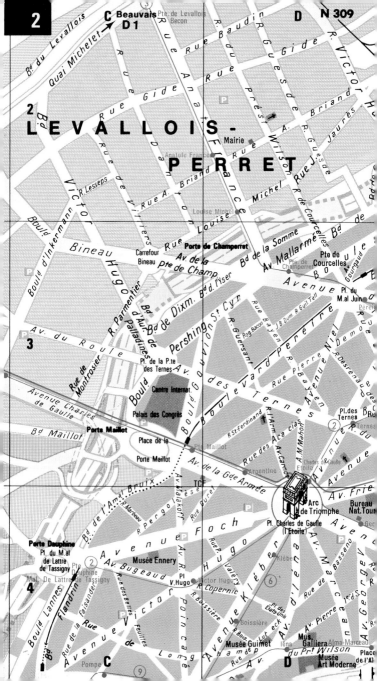

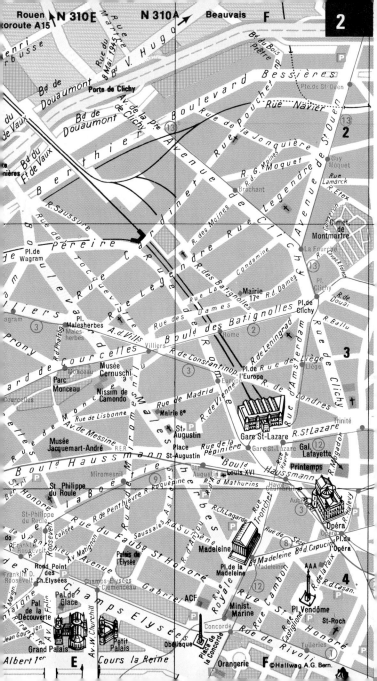

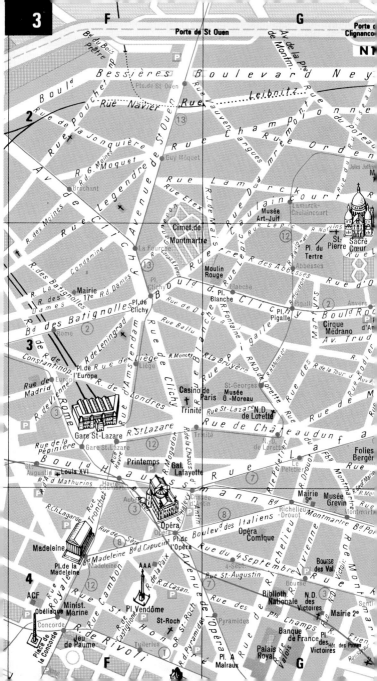

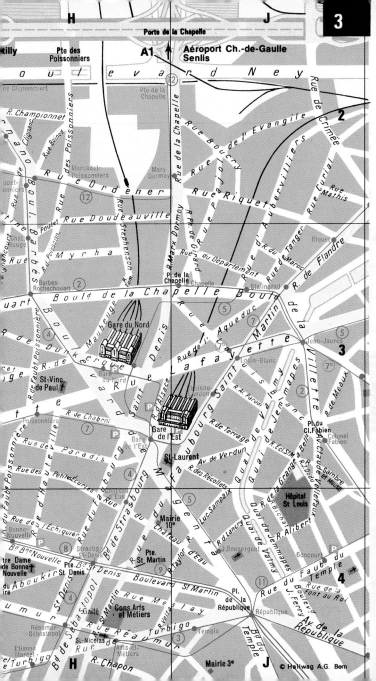

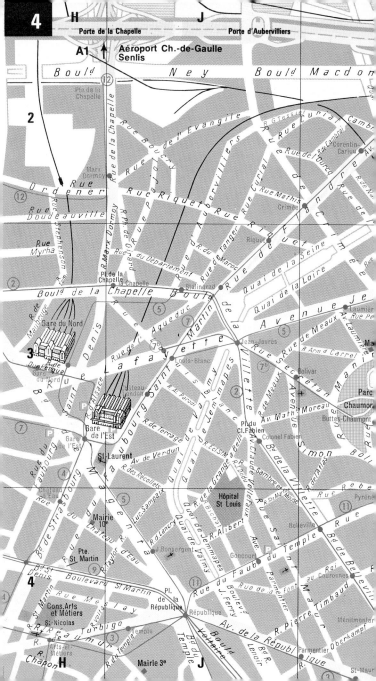

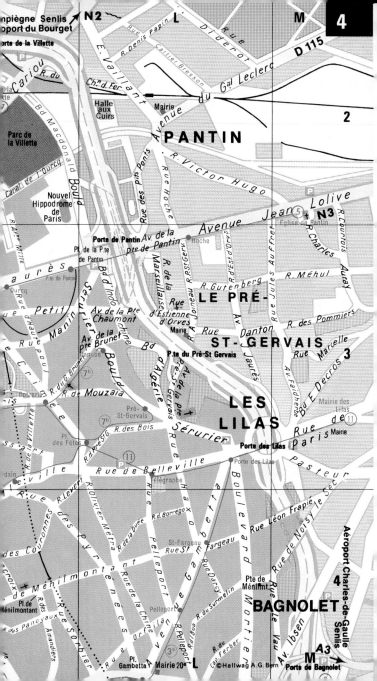

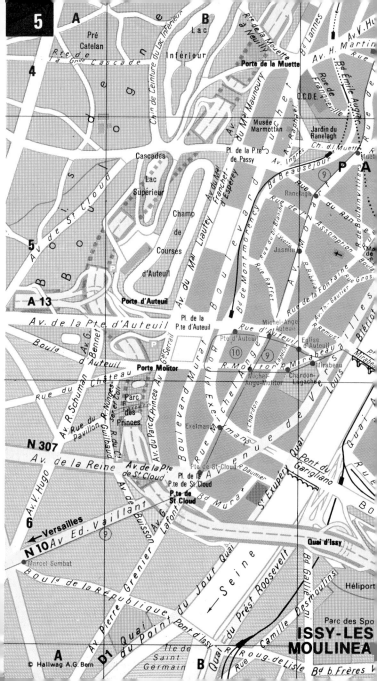

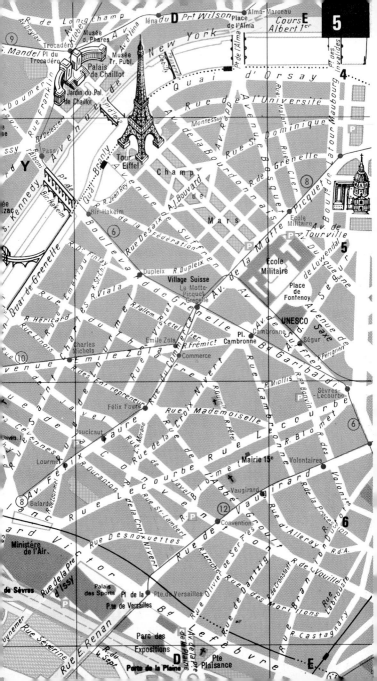

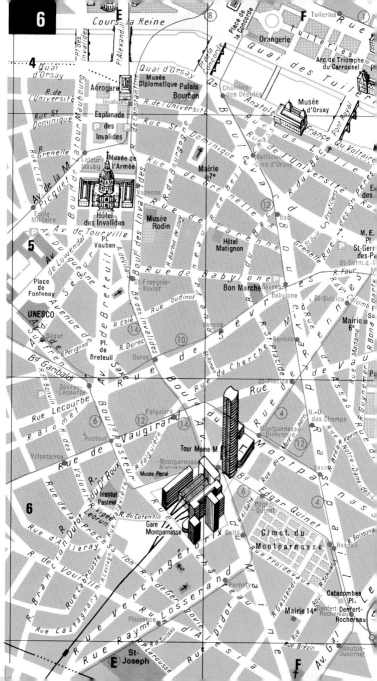

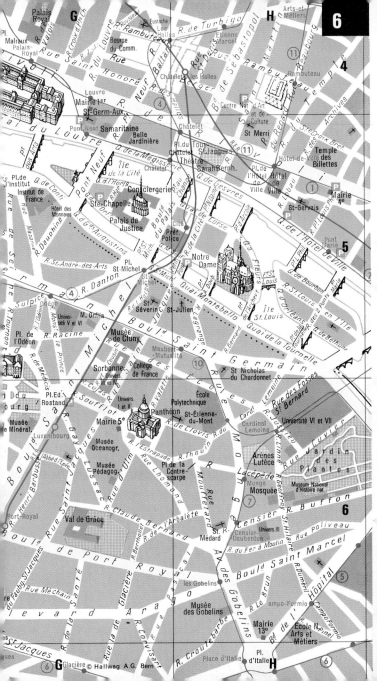

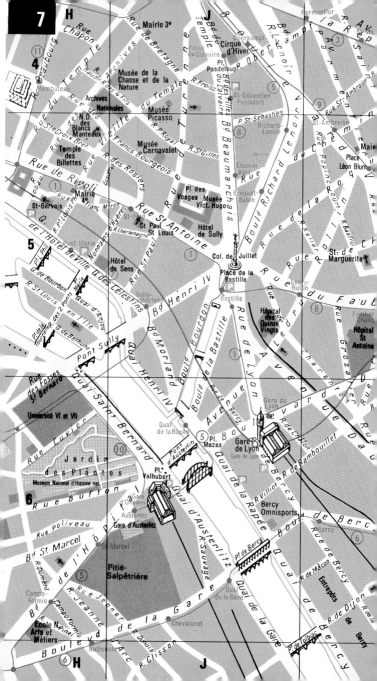

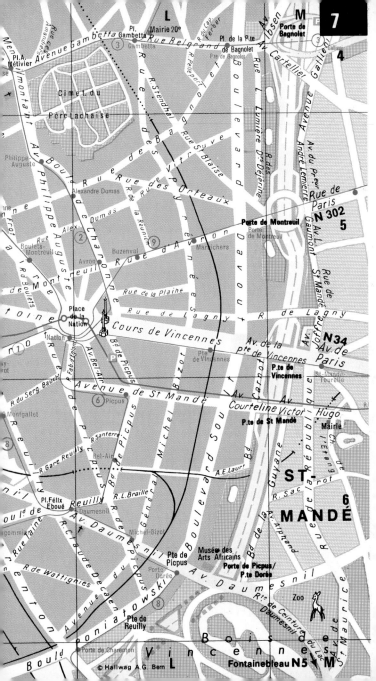

Pl. Mairie 20e
Pl. Gambetta
Rue Belgrand
Pl. de la P.te de Bagnolet
Av. Ibsen
Porte de Bagnolet
Av. Gallieni

Av. Gambetta
R. du Cap. Ferber
Rue Gambetta
P.te de Bagnolet
Av. Cartellier

Menilmontant
Av. Pte St Fargeau
Pl.A. Métivier

Cimet. du Père Lachaise

Boulevard

Rue de Bagnolet

Rue Pelleport

Rue Stendhal

Rue des Maraichers

Rue de la Lumière Drs. Déjerine

P.te des

Av. du Prer André Lemière

Rue de Paris

N 302 5

Philippe Auguste

Av. Philippe Auguste

Boulevard

Alexandre Dumas

Rue des Vignoles

Rue Vitruve

Rue des Orteaux

Rue St Blaise

Porte de Montreuil

Boulevard Davout

Rue de St Mandé

Rue du Lieut Gaumont

Rue Alexandre Dumas

de Charonne

Rue de la Réunion

Porte de Montreuil

Rue de Paris

Boulets-Montreuil

Buzenval

Rue d'Avron

Maraichers

N 34 Av. de Paris

Montreuil

Avron

Rue d'Avron

Rue de la Plaine

Rue de Lagny

R. de Lagny

Antoine

de Boulets

Place de la Nation

Natton

Rue de Lagny

Cours de Vincennes

Av. de la P.te de Vincennes

P.te de Vincennes

Av. Carnot

St-Mandé Tourelle

Av. du Fg. St Antoine

Av. Bel Air

Bd de Picpus

Pte de Vincennes

Av. de la P.te de Vincennes

P.te de Vincennes

Bd Soult

R. du Serg Bauchat

Avenue de St Mandé

Courteline Victor - Hugo

Av.

R. de l'Erang

Picpus

Av. de St Mandé

P.te de St Mandé

Mairie

Montgallet

R. Santerre

Bd de Picpus

A.E. Laur

ST-

Reuilly

R. Gare Reuilly

Bel-Air

Boulevard Soult

R. Sacarot

6 MANDÉ

R.L. Braille

Michel Bizot

Av. Courteline

R. du Niger

Pl. Félix Eboué

Reuilly

Daumesnil

Michel-Bizot

R. de Reuilly

R. de Picpus

Bd de Picpus

Bd Poniatowski

Av. de la P.te Dorée

Av. Daumesnil

R. de Wattignies

Av. Decaen

Rue du Général Michel Bizot

Porte Dorée

Pte de Picpus

Musée des Arts Africains

Porte de Picpus/P.te Dorée

Av. Daumesnil

Bd de la Guyane

Av. Alphand

Rte de Ceinture du Lac

R. Ch. Daumesnil

Zoo

Av. Daumesnil

St Maurice

Av. Poniatowski

Pte de Reuilly

Boul'd Poniatowski

Bois de Vincennes

Boulevard de

Boul'd Poniatowski

Porte de Charenton

© Hallwag A.G. Bern

L

Fontainebleau N 5

M

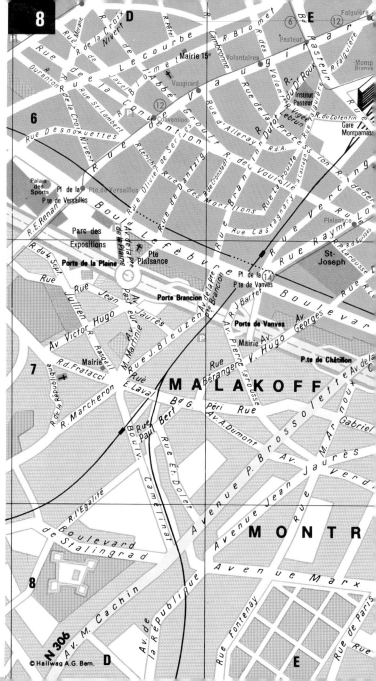

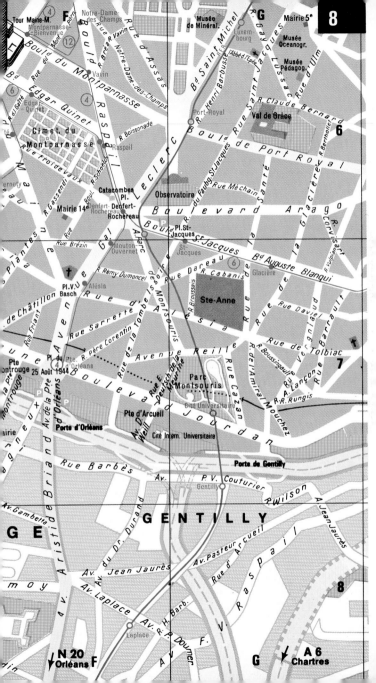

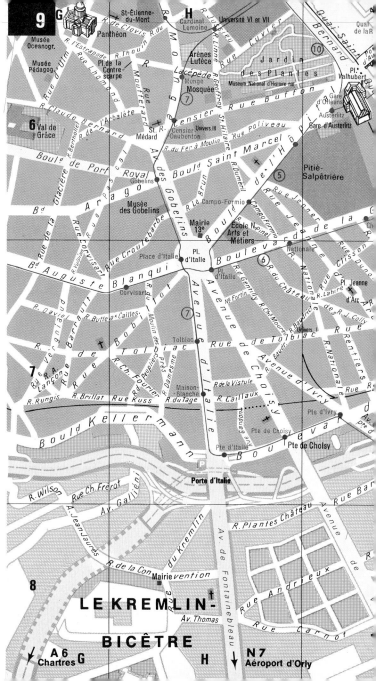

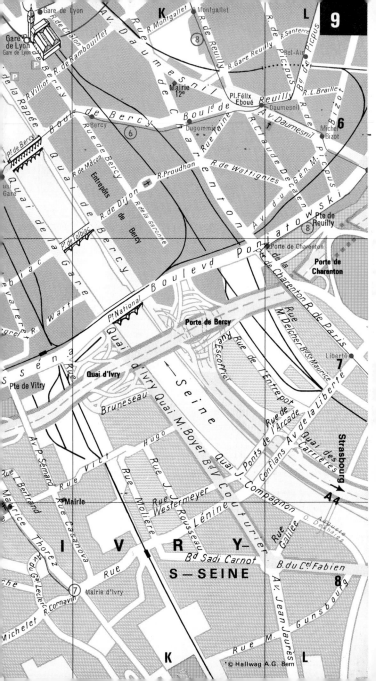

MUSEUMS & GALLERIES

Metro names: *italic*; bus nos **bold**.
Code numbers refer to maps on pp. 41—57.

General Information

Generally speaking, national museums are closed on Tuesdays and municipal museums on Mondays and public holidays (p.34), but there are exceptions. The hours in private museums vary and you should check the hours in the press or with the organizations below.

Entrance fee Most museums in France charge a moderate fee which is often reduced on Sundays.

The following organizations arrange guided tours for groups. Requests should be made 3—4 weeks in advance to:

Action Culturelle de la Ville de Paris Centre d'Information de l'Hôtel de Ville, 75004 Paris (tel: 277 15 40).

Bureau d'Action Culturelle Palais du Louvre, 75401 Paris Cedex 01 (tel: 260 39 26, extensions 3312, 3416, 3012, 3014).

Caisse Nationale des Monuments Historiques et des Sites, Hôtel de Sully, 62 Rue St Antoine, 75004 Paris (tel: 887 24 14/15).

Paris et Son Histoire, 82 Rue Taitbout, Paris 9 (tel: 526 2677).

It should be noted that many collections are in the process of reorganization which, in some cases, involves removal to a different museum. To avoid disappointment, check at the entrance of the museums above.

Archives Nationales (see Histoire de France p.60).

Armée, Musée de l' (see p.101).

Art Juif, 42 Rue des Saules, Paris 18. Open Tuesday, Thursday and Sunday 1500—1800. Situated on the third floor of the Jewish centre in Montmartre, the museum includes paintings by Chagall and Soutine, a 13th-century Hebraic Bible, engravings and models of ancient synagogues and religious items   **3**G2
Lamarck-Caulaincourt. **80.**

Art Moderne de la Ville de Paris 11 Ave du Président Wilson, Paris 16. Open daily except Mondays and public holidays 1000—1730 (2030 Wednesdays). Devoted to 20th century works of art, the museum's collection includes works by the Cubists (Picasso and Braque), examples of the Fauvist artists such as Matisse and Derain, and other early 20th century artists including Chagall, Dufy, notably 'La Fée Electricité' said to be the world's largest painting, Matisse, Modigliani, Utrillo and Vlaminck. The Musée d'Art et d'Essai, where temporary exhibitions on parti-

cular themes are held, has now been moved to the adjoining Palais de Tokyo. There is also a section ARC (Animation, Research, Confrontation) which covers research into all forms of art. The building also houses a creative children's museum and workshop exhibiting works for and by the young.
Alma Marceau. **32, 63, 72, 82, 92.**

Arts Africains et Océaniens 293 Ave Daumensil, Paris 12. Open daily, except Tuesdays, 0945—1200 and 1330—1715. (Some of the rooms are open in rotation.) The museum comprises four sections: an aquarium in the basement with an important collection of tropical fish and reptiles; West and Central African art on the ground and first floors; North African exhibits on the second floor. The rest of the museum has exhibits from the Pacific and Australia.   7L6
Porte Dorée. **46, PC.**

Arts Décoratifs Pavillon du Marsan, Le Louvre, 107—109 Rue de Rivoli, Paris 1. Open daily. This museum contains the most important collection of decorative and ornamental art in France, dating from the Middle Ages to the 20th century, with furniture, religious sculpture and paintings, bronzes, ceramics, silverware and tapestries.   6F4
Palais Royal. **21, 48, 69, 72, 85.**

Arts de la Mode: Pavillon de Marsan, 109 Rue de Rivoli, Paris 1. Open Wed.—Sat. 1230—1830, Sun. 1100—1700. Specialising in Haute Couture exhibits, this newly opened museum in the same building as the Musée des Arts Decoratifs holds temporary and retrospective exhibitions of creations by great designers, such as Chanel, Dior, Poiret and Yves St Laurent.
Palais Royal. **21, 48, 69, 72, 85.**

Bibliothèque Nationale 58 Rue de Richelieu, Paris 2. Open daily 1200–1800. Housed in the 17th-century Hôtel Tubeuf and its annexes, the library was originally formed from the royal collections. The Ordonance of Montpellier, in 1537, decreed that from that date on one copy of every publication should be deposited in the royal libraries. Since then, the collections have been considerably enriched by Mazarin, who lived there for a time, and, later, by private donations and through acquisitions. The present library is divided into various departments: Printed Books, including two Gutenberg Bibles and original editions of works by François Villon, Pascal and Rabelais; Periodicals; Manuscripts, including papyrus scrolls from the Dead Sea, Charlemagne's Gosple and the Saint Louis Psalter, correspondence and manuscripts by writers such as Hugo and

Proust and scientists such as Pasteur and Marie Curie; Prints, engravings and photography; Maps; Musical manuscripts and scores; Records and recordings. 3G4 *Palais Royal, Bourse, Quatre Septembre.* **20, 29, 39, 48, 52, 66, 67, 74, 85.**

Carnavalet 23 Rue de Sévigné, Paris 3. Open daily, except Mondays and public holidays, 1000−1740. This is officially the **Musée Historique de la Ville de Paris** which illustrates the history of Paris over the last 400 years. On the ground floor exhibits cover trades and guilds, Renaissance furniture and paintings, models and engravings of Paris, posters, an important series of documents, busts, furniture and portraits relating to the Revolutionary period, plus Empire and 19th-century exhibits. On the first floor, rooms show the 17th and 18th centuries, with two rooms devoted to Madame de Sévigné, her family and friends, and rooms 61, 62, and 63 contain a series of views of Paris in the mid 18th century by Nicolas Raguenet. A major part of the 18th-century furniture comes from the Bouvier collection, donated in 1965. The wealth of the collections, and lack of space, have led to reorganization of the museum and exhibits from the Revolution to the 20th century are being transferred to the annex in the Hôtel Le Pelletier Saint Fargeau next door at 29 Rue de Sévigné. The library, or **Bibliothéque de la Ville de Paris** open, except Sundays, 0900−1800, has been transferred to the Hôtel Lamoignon, 24 Rue Pavée. 7J5 *Saint-Paul.* **29, 69, 76, 96.**

Cernuschi 7 Ave Velasquez, Paris 8. Open daily, except Mondays and public holidays, 1000−1740. The major part of this important collection of oriental art was donated to Paris by the politician and economist, Henri Cernuschi, and is composed of items he brought back from his journey to the Far East, 1871−3. 2E3 *Villiers, Monceau.* **30, 94.**

Chasse et Nature (see Hôtel Guénégaud p.94).

Cinéma Palais de Chaillot, Place du Trocadéro Paris 16. Guided visits every day except Tuesday. Over 3000 exhibits allow the visitor to trace the history of the Seventh Art from its earliest days to modern times. At the end of the east wing of the Palais, the **film library** contains over 50,000 reels of film. Daily film shows are held in the theatre which also has an annex in the Centre Georges Pompidou. 5D4 *Trocadéro.* **32, 63, 72.**

Cluny 6 Place Paul-Painlevé, Paris 5. (Behind the Boulevard St Michel.) Open daily, except Tuesdays, 0945−1230 and 1400−1715. The present building was built between 1485 and 1500 on the site of the 13th-century residence of the Abbots of Cluny, which in turn had been built over ruins of 2nd-century Gallo-Roman baths, probably erected by the Nautes, or river merchants. Visitors can still admire the outstanding collection of medieval tapestries including the world-famous Dame à la Licorne exhibited in a rotunda in Room IX. Other rooms exhibit embroidery, Gothic carvings, paintings and sculptures, ivories, jewellery and precious religious ornaments. Steps lead down from the ground floor to the **Roman baths** which comprise a large vaulted room, which was the frigidarium, the tepidarium and the caldarium, or steam room. The courtyard has a pillar dedicated to Jupiter, dating from the reign of Tiberius (AD 14−37), which was discovered near Notre Dame. Finally, bulldozers, on a site in the centre of Paris in 1977, unearthed 21 of the 28 original heads of the Gallery of Kings of Judah dating from 1220, which originally adorned the west façade of the cathedral of Notre Dame. These heads are in the Roman Baths room. 6G5 *St Michel, Odeon, Luxembourg.* **21, 27, 38, 63, 81, 85, 86, 87, 96.**

Cognacq-Jay 25 Bd des Capucines, Paris 1. Open daily, except Mondays and public holidays 1000−1740. One of the most charming in Paris, this museum has a collection which belonged to Ernest Cognacq, founder of the department store La Samaritaine, and his wife Louise Jay. 3F4 *Opéra, Madeleine.* **20, 21, 22, 27, 29, 42, 52, 53, 66, 68, 81, 95.**

Découverte, Palais de la Avenue Franklin Roosevelt, Paris 8. (West wing of Grand Palais.) Open daily, except Mondays, 1000−1800. This is not merely a

Hôtel Carnavalet

museum but also a centre whose aim is to stimulate public interest in science. There are models, maps, temporary exhibitions,

public demonstrations of scientific experiment and a **planetarium**. Lectures and film shows are held regularly.   2E4
Champs-Elysées-Clemenceau,   Franklin Roosevelt. **28, 49, 80, 83**.

Galliéra 10 Avenue Pierre I de Serbie, Paris 16. Open daily, except Mondays, public holidays and in between exhibitions, 1000–1740. The Renaissance-style mansion, built for the Duchesse de Galliera in 1878, now houses the **museum of costume and fashion.**   2D4
Alma Marceau, Iéna. **32, 63**.

Georges Pompidou Centre National d'Art et de Culture (see p.90).

Grand Palais Avenue Winston Churchill, Paris 8. Open daily, except Tuesdays, 1000–2000; Wednesdays 1000–2200. Many of the great national exhibitions of French and foreign art are held in the Art Nouveau buildings. A library, containing catalogues of past exhibitions, posters and publications on art, is open.   2E4
Champs-Elysées-Clemenceau. **49, 72**.

Grévin 10 Bd Montmartre, Paris 9. Open daily 1400–1900; Sundays and public holidays 1300–2000. Situated on the Grands Boulevards, Paris' **waxworks museum** includes effigies of personalities from the past and present. There are also scenes of great events of French History   3G4
Rue de Montmartre. **48, 67, 74, 85**.

Grévin Forum des Halles, Grand Balcon. Open daily. A *Son et Lumière* show of life in Paris during the *Belle Epoque* period.
Châtelet-les-Halles.

Guimet 6 Place d'Iéna, Paris 16. Open daily, except Tuesdays, 0945–1200 and 1330–1715. A matchless collection of Asian and Oriental art.   2D4
Iéna. **32, 63**.

Histoire de France 60 Rue des Francs-Bourgeois, Paris 3. Open daily, except Tuesdays, 1400–1700. The main collection of French **national archives** is in the magnificent Hôtel de Soubise built, between 1706 and 1712, on the site of the mansion of the de Guise family. The woodwork and panelling of the apartments (which may be visited on prior written application) are decorated with paintings by Boucher, Natoire and Van Loo. Among the documents on display are papers dating from the 7th century, a letter from Joan of Arc, the Charters founding the Sainte Chapelle and the Sorbonne, the Edict of Nantes of 1598 and the Revocation of that Edict in 1685.7H4
Rambuteau, Hôtel de Ville. **29, 66, 67, 72, 75, 77, 96.**

Histoire Naturelle Muséum National d' (see Jardin des Plantes p.106).

Homme Palais de Chaillot (west wing), Place du Trocadéro, Paris 16. Open daily, except Tuesdays, 0945–1715. A result of the amalgamation of the Musée d'Ethnologie and the Galerie d'Anthropologie, the museum encompasses the human race and its evolution.   5D4
Trocadéro. **22, 30, 32, 63, 72, 82.**

Jacquemart-André 158 Bd Haussmann, Paris 8. Open daily, except Mondays and Tuesdays and August, 1330–1730. This rich collection was brought together by the painter Nellie Jacquemart and her husband Edouard André, who bequeathed it to the nation. The museum houses outstanding examples of Renaissance Italian and 18th-century European art.   2E3
St-Philippe-du-Roule. **22, 43, 52, 83.**

Louvre Palais du Louvre, Paris 1. Open daily except Tuesdays 0945–1715. The Louvre is one of the world's largest museums receiving more than 4 million visitors annually. In view of the importance, and diversity of the collections, their upkeep and the reorganization of the museum, not all the galleries are open every day. At the time of writing, panels at the main entrance (Porte Denon Cour Carrée) indicate those which are open. It should be noted, however, that following the decision to move the Ministry of Finance to new buildings at Bercy, this main entrance will be changed and moved to the Cour Napoleon opposite the Carrousel, where libraries and information centres are also being built. A vast glass pyramid, ordered by President Mitterand, and destined to stand in front of this new entrance is scheduled for completion in 1988. Guided tours in English and their times are indicated by the Bureau des Informations in the Salle des Manèges.

Greek and Roman Antiquities Occupying the Galeries Daru and Mollien, the Cour du Sphinx and surrounding rooms on the ground floor, the south-west end of the Cour Carrée, the Salle Henri IV and the Salle des Cazes, this department is in process of reorganization. The Venus de Milo situated in Room 9 in the south-west end of the Cour Carrée, and the Winged Victory of Samothrace on the Escalier Daru, are essential viewing but there are also many other masterpieces of classical sculpture such as the copper-encrusted Apollo of Piombino (R2), the Rampin Head (R1), part of the Parthenon Frieze (Rs4 & 5), the Borghese Gladiator (R10), the Venus of Arles and the Apollo Sauroctone (lizard slayer) in the Salle des Caryatides. Roman sculpture includes the statue of Augustus and the head of his wife Livia in black basalt in the Salle d'Auguste. Just as important are the rooms displaying bronzes, ceramics and pottery, Etruscan mirrors engraved with mythical subjects and, in the Salle des Bijoux, the jewellery, gold and silver ware, including the silver found at Boscoreale near Pompeii.

Egyptian Antiquities Access is either through the Passage des Arts, to the right of the Pavillon des Arts exhibiting Greek Antiquities, or through the Porte Champollion. There are many important exhibits and visitors should try not to miss the immense rose granite sphinx in the crypt, the Mastaba, a funeral chapel, (R2); the Serpent King's Stele (R2); the Seated Scribe (R5) found in the well of a Mastaba; the wooden statue of the Chancellor Nakhti; the group in black granite representing Amon protecting Tutankhamen, statues from the tombs of the Valley of the Kings and Ramses III's engraved granite sarcophagus, all of which are situated in the Galerie Henri IV. Pass through Gallery 130, with examples of Coptic Art, before going up the Percier Staircase to the first floor where sculptures, figurines, jewellery and gold and silver ware are exhibited.

Oriental Antiquities This collection is on the ground floor of the Cour Carrée, and best reached by the Porte St Germain l'Auxerrois (opposite the church of the same name) or the Crypte Sully by the Porte Henri. Important exhibits include the Stele of Mesha, King of Moab, recording Israel's defeat at the hands of Ahab, Ahaziah and Omri; the Vulture's Stele and the Stele of Naram-Sin, which are all in the Sully Crypt. R3 has the seated alabaster Mari official Ebih-il, and R4 has the black basalt Law Code of Hammurabi, King of Babylon. Rooms 5–12 show exhibits from Persia and civilizations east of Mesopotamia, and include bronzes and ceramics, a grey marble capital and an enamelled brick frieze of archers, taken from Darius I's palace. The Marengo crypt has Punic, Syrian and Phoenician exhibits along with a remarkable series of Assyrian bas-reliefs (R22–24).

Objets d'Art and Furniture In the east wing and part of the west and north wings of the Cour Carrée, Apollo and Colonnade Galleries.

Galerie d'Apollon: the ceiling with Apollo vanquishing the Serpent Python is by Delacroix. Among the exhibits are the **Crown Jewels**, with the 137-carat Regent diamond, the 105-carat Côte de Bretagne ruby and a reliquary crown of Saint Louis. Case 6 holds the 12th-century vase in the form of an eagle, given to the Basilica of Saint Denis by the Abbé Suger.

Salles de la Colonnade: decorated with fine wood panelling and coffered ceilings, the rooms include a 10th-century ivory Harbaville Triptych (R4), a 13th-century ivory virgin from the Sainte Chapelle and another of painted ivory depicting the Coronation of the Virgin (R5). R7 is hung with a remarkable series of tapestries, The Hunts of Maximilian, which were woven for the Emperor Charles V around 1530 and, in the central cases, there is a fine collection of Italian and Limoges enamels.

North Wing of Cour Carrée (Rs9–35): the rooms in this wing contain tapestry (R7) from the same workshop as that of the Dame à la Licorne in the Musée de Cluny, examples of furniture by Boulle (R13, 14) and by Cressent (R16), a collection of snuff, pill and sweet boxes, many set with precious stones (R23) and Marie Leczynska's room (R25) has Gobelins' tapestries, furniture by Boulle and her *nécessaire* (dressing-case) dating from 1729, a gift on the occasion of the birth of the Dauphin. R30 contains a superb desk by Benneman used by Napoleon, and Marie Antoinette's furniture, including pieces by Riesener is in R33–35.

Sculpture On the ground floor of the Galerie du Bord de l'Eau, between the Porte de la Trémoille and the Pavillon de Flore, exhibits are arranged in chronological order. The first three rooms are devoted to Romanesque and Gothic sculpture and include a wooden polychrome descent from the Cross, statues of Solomon and the Queen of Sheba and effigies of Saint Louis and Marguerite of Provence portrayed as Charles V and his wife Jeanne de Bourbon. The Salle P. Vitry (R5) has the 15th-century rood screen from the Bourges Cathedral and the Burgundian tomb of Philippe Pot. Renaissance rooms include bas-reliefs from the Fontaine des Innocents and the Three Graces and the Chancellor of Birague by Germain Pilon. Italian sculpture, which is in the Galerie Basse and on the ground floor includes Michelangelo's Slaves, Benvenuto Cellini's Nymph of Fontainebleu, Terracottas by Della Robbia and the St John the Baptist and La Belle Florentine attributed to Donatello. French 17th- and 18th-century are in Rs13–17, access by the Porte Jaujard Pavillon de Flore end of the gallery. Sculptures include the Pont au Change by Simon Guillain, the Seine and the Marne by Coysevox, and a series of busts by Houdon.

Paintings The Louvre's collection of paintings is probably the largest of any museum in the world. Begun by François I who created a Cabinet des Tableaux, it was considerably enriched by his successors, notably Louis XIV, and later by donations and purchases. The greatest number of paintings is, not unnaturally, French, with works dating from the *Por-*

trait of Jean le Bon (Salle Duchatel), the oldest known portrait north of Italy, painted around 1360, to the works of the 19th-century Romantics. Of particular interest

d'un ballet sur la scène, 1874 Degas

are Fouquet's *Charles VII* (Salle Duchatel) and the Piéta of Avignon, shown on the second floor of the Cour Carrée, together with works by artists of the Fontainebleau School (Salon Carrée), such as Clouet and Quesnel, and paintings influenced by the Italian schools, such as Poussin's *Les Bergers d'Arcadie*. In the Grande Galerie hang masterpieces by La Tour, the Le Nain brothers, Fragonard, Watteau, Poussin's *The Poet's Inspiration*, Bouchet's *Le Repos de Diane*. The Salle Mollien groups together works by David including his *Portrait of Madame Récamier*, the *Oath of the Horatii* and his monumental *Coronation of Napoleon*, as well as works by Ingres, Gérard and Prud'hon. After the French, the Italians receive the best coverage in the Louvre. Occupying various galleries in the second part of the Grande Galerie, the collection of Italian Primitives includes works by Cimabue, Giotto, Fra Angelico, Botticelli and Mantegna. The great Renaissance masters hang in the Salle des Etats, and the Vestibule, and they include Leonardo da Vinci's *Mona Lisa*, the *Virgin on the Rocks* and other works; Raphael's *Portrait of Balthazar Castiglione* and *La Belle Jardinière*; Titian's *St Jerome in the Desert* and *Lady at her Toilet*; and Veronese's *Marriage at Cana*.

Flemish, Dutch and German Paintings hang in the Salle Van Dyck, Galerie Médicis, the Salle des Sept Mètres and the Petits Cabinets, and include early works by artists such as Memling and Van Eyck, Holbein's *Portrait of Anne of Cleves* and Van Dyck's *Portrait of Charles I*. The Salle des Sept Mètres exhibits works by Franz Hals; the third wing of his room, on the left, has twenty works by Rembrandt, including three self-portraits, *Tobias and*

the Angel and the Pilgrims of Emmaus.

The collection of 18th- and 19th-century **English** paintings on the second floor of the west wing of the Cour Carrée is small, but nevertheless includes works by Gainsborough, Lawrence, Reynolds and Constable's *Weymouth Bay*, *Hampstead Heath* and a *View of Salisbury*. Finally, the **Spanish** collection, hanging at the far end of the Pavillon de Flore on the first floor, includes a *Christ on the Cross* by El Greco, the *Club Foot* by Ribera and several works by Goya, including the recently acquired *Marquise de Santa Cruz*.   6F4

Art Graphique (Pavillon de Flore) Examples of the Louvre's magnificent collection of drawings, engravings and watercolours are exhibited in the form of temporary exhibitions in the *Cabinet des Dessins*.
Palais Royal, Louvre. **21, 24, 27, 67, 69, 72, 81, 85.**

Marine Palais de Chaillot (west wing), Place du Trocadéro, Paris 16. Open daily, except Tuesdays and public holidays, 1000–1800. French maritime history throughout the ages is on display here, with models of ships of all types and sizes, and paintings.   5D4
Trocadéro. **22, 30, 32, 63, 72, 82.**

Marmottan 2 Rue Louis Boilly, Paris 16. Open daily, except Mondays, 1000–1800. Although this museum is known mainly for its collection of Impressionist paintings, especially those of Monet, it also exhibits Flemish and Italian Primitives, and some 16th- and 17th-century tapestries.   5B5
Chaussée de la Musette. **32, 63, PC.**

Monnaies 11 Quai Conti, Paris 6. Open daily, except Saturdays, Sundays and public holidays, 1100–1700. A fine double staircase leads to the museum on the second floor. Since this was **the Mint**, the collection includes stamping presses, punches, scales, coins, medals and historical documents.   6G5
Pont Neuf. **24, 27, 58, 70.**

Nissim de Camondo 63 Rue de Monceau, Paris 8. Open daily, except Mondays and Tuesdays, 1000–1200 and 1400–1700. This collection recreates the atmosphere of a residence of the 18th century. 2E3
Villiers. **84, 94.**

Opéra 1 Place Charles Garnier, Paris 9. Open daily, except Sundays, public holidays and two weeks after Easter, 1000–1700. Busts, portraits, relics, and souvenirs of great composers, dancers and lyric artists predominate, but there are also models of sets, programmes and posters plus an important library devoted to dance, music and the theatre.   3E4
Opéra, Havre Caumartin. **21, 22, 27, 42, 48, 66, 68, 81.**

L'Orangerie Place de la Concorde. Open every day except Tuesdays 0945–1715. Recently restored, the very fine Walter Guillaume collection of Impressionists and early 20th-century artists is on permanent exhibition here. Examples include works by Renoir, Cezanne, Sisley, Matisse, Modigliani, Picasso and Soutine. L'Orangerie is also now the permanent 'home' of Monet's group of 'Les Nymphéas' waterlily paintings.
Concorde. **14, 72, 84, 94.**

Orsay, Musée de 1 Rue de Bellechasse, Paris 7. Open every day except Mondays and Public Holidays 1030–1800, Thurs-

Venus de Milo

days till 2145, Sundays 9000–1800. Guided visits in English and other languages take place daily.

Inaugurated in December 1986, the Museum is installed in the Gare d'Orsay built in 1900, that year of the Universal Exhibition, and threatened with demolition in the 1960s. In 1973 the Direction of the Musées de France envisaged the plan of transforming the station into a museum of late 19th-century art.

Ground Floor − *Left Wing* Section B: This section contains works by Daumier, famous for his caricatures illustrating the social life of the mid-19th century, including engravings and an amusing series of terracotta busts of contemporary members of parliament.

The Chauchard Collection contains examples of works by the Barbizon group of artists including Theodore Rousseau and Millet *Les Glaneuses* and *L'Angelus*, landscapes by Corot and the historical painter Meissonnier. Visitors can also admire examples of the Realist School of painting led by Courbet.

Section D: The Moreau-Nelaton and Edouardo Mollard collections in this section are composed of early works by Impressionists and include Manet's *Déjeuner Sur l'Herbe, Olympia* and his portraits of Emile Zola and Madame Gaudibert; a group of works by Boudin, Pissarro and Sisley and some early Renoirs. Also in this section are several paintings by Fantin Latour including *Un Atelier aux Batignolles* depicting Manet in his studio surrounded by friends and fellow artists such as Renoir.

Ground Floor *Right Wing* Sections A & C: These sections are devoted to works by Ingres, Delacroix, Isabey, Chasseriau and Puvis de Chavannes many of whose works decorate the Hotel de Ville, Le Pantheon and La Sorbonne. Also hanging in this wing are oils by Gustave Moreau, who influenced the young Matisse and Georges Rouault, and a series of early works executed before 1870 by Degas. Finally, visitors can admire examples of mid-19th century furniture, gold, silver, glass and porcelain ware illustrating the richness and variety of material used by the craftsmen of the period. Visitors should not miss the Duchess of Parma's dressing table, which took 6 years to make. The table is a unique mixture of baroque, renaissance and Islamic styles.

An escalator leads directly to the 2nd level which is devoted to the Impressionists, the Neo-Impressionists, followed by the Pont Aven Group, Toulouse Lautrec, Gauguin and the Nabis school. The Jeu de Paume, has been moved here and to it have been added the Personnaz, Gachet and Kaganovitch collections.

In room 1 hang the following: *Le Moulin de la Galette, L'Etude Torse de Femme au Soleil, La Femme à la Voilette* and *Le Chemin Montant* by Renoir; *Le Déjeuner* by Monet and series of paintings by Pissarro including *Le Coteau d'Hermitage* and *Les Toits Rouges.* Room 2 contains, amongst others, *Les Dindons à Giverny, La Gare St Lazare* and *La Rue Montorgeuil* by Monet, Renoir's portraits of Mme Alfonse Daudet, Madame Paul Darras and Madame Charpentier, scenes of Louvéciennes and the Flood at Port Marly by Sisley and Caillebotte's *Les Raboteurs du Parquet*. In the 2nd half of this gallery visitors can admire Manet's portraits of Georges Clemenceau and the poet Mallarmé, *La Femme à l'Eventail* and *Sur La Plage painted at Berck sur Plage* in 1873. The main part of this room, however, is devoted to Degas and includes the well-known *l'Absinthe, Les Danseuses Bleues, La Classe de Danse* and the bronze. *Danseuse Habillée* complete with her tulle tutu,

Madame Récamier *David*

hair ribbon and ballerina shoes. Room 4 contains works by Renoir, Pissarro and Monet after 1880 including, by Renoir: the *Danse à la Campagne* and *Danse à la Ville, Les Jeunes Filles au Piano, Les Liseuses* and *Les Baigneuses*. By Pissarro: *La Bergère* and *La Jeune Fille à la Baguette*, and by Monet, the Cathedral at Rouen series, the two *Femmes à L'Ombrelle, London Parliament* and *Les Nymphéas Bleus* prefiguring the famous Nymphéas series in l'Orangerie.

Examples of works by Monet, Pissarro, Sisley and Guillaumin form the main part of the Personnas Collection which also includes Mary Cassat's *Femme Cousant*.

The Paul Gachet Collection is divided into two parts — Van Gogh and Cézanne. Works by Van Gogh include *l'Arlésienne*, his room at Arles, a portrait of Dr Paul Gachet, *L'Eglise d'Auvers-Sur-Oise*, and a self-portrait executed in 1889. The Cézanne room contains several still lifes, *Les Baigneurs, Les Joueurs de Cartes, La Femme à la Cafetière* and the caricature portrait of his friend Achille Emperaire.

Toulouse Lautrec's panels *La Danse Mauresque* and *La Danse au Moulin Rouge* with La Goulue and Valentin hang in the Café des Hauteurs on this level. Other works by the artist, including *Jane Avril* and *The Clowness Cha U Kao* hang in a

small room further on. Immediately after, two oils by Le Douanier Rousseau precede the rooms devoted to the Pont Aven group of artists, with works by Emile Bernard, Serusier and Gauguin, who formed part of the group. The room containing examples of Gauguin's later work includes *Les Femmes de Tahiti, Le Repas, Arearea or the Red Dog* and *Le Cheval Blanc*. Bonnard, Dennis, Valloton and Vuillard represent the Nabis Group of artists in two rooms immediately after Gauguin.

The 20 paintings forming the Max and Rosy Kaganovitch collection form the final part of exhibits on this level and include works by Monet, Pissarro, Renoir and Sisley, as well as Van Gogh's *L'Hopital de St Rémy* and *Les Paysannes Bretonnes* by Cézanne.

The *Passage de la Presse* Gallery relates the history and development of the Press in France during the 19th century and the *Passage des Dates* outlines the principal cultural, political and social events of France and the rest of the world with the aid of video screens and cassettes.

The final part of the visit illustrates the Art and Decoration during the period of the 3rd Republic. Rooms P and Q show examples of the sculpture of the period with works by Barrias, Gérome and Fremiet amongst others. However, the lion's share of the terrace is devoted to Rodin, beginning with the early *Age of Airan*, exhibited at the Salon des Artistes in 1877. Other examples include *St John the Baptist*, the Symbolist marble bust *La Pensée*, and a series of fellow artists and critics. At the top of the gallery stands the monumental *Porte d'Enfer*, with its two main themes inspired by Dante's Divine Comedy — Paulo and Fransesca on the right and Ugolin and his children on the left.

Paintings in Room R (Left Wing) include examples of the Naturalist School including the Swiss Eugène Burnand *St Peter and St Paul Hurrying to the Tomb*, the German Max Liebermann and the Russian Valentin Serov *Portrait of Madame Lwoff*. The Symbolist Movement is also represented in this room with works by Gustave Moreau, Odilon Redon, Wilmslow Holmer and Edward Burne-Jones whose *Wheel of Fortune* illustrates the Pre-Raphaelites.

Room S (Right Wing) contains paintings by French artists after 1900 — Bonnard, Rousseau *The Serpent Charmer*, the Austrian Gustave Klimt and Matisse *Luxe, Caime et Volupté* painted in 1904.

Rooms T, U, V and W are devoted to Art Nouveau, with examples of enamel ware, jewellery, stained glass and porcelain. Glass and porcelain by Gallé are exhibited in a small annexe to the left of Room T.

Furniture and interior design exhibits include the reconstruction of a dining room in the country home of a French banker with wood panelling and a stone fountain, a fine walnut and wrought iron bookcase by Carabin and Gallé's glass cabinet with its mahogany and oak base.

Finally, just before the exit, is a small section illustrating the birth and earliest stages of the cinema.

Temporary exhibitions are held frequently in rooms on all levels. In addition, Orsay possesses an important library and videothèque which can be consulted free of charge during opening hours.

Solferino, RER C. **24, 63, 64, 68, 83, 84, 94.**

Petit Palais Avenue Winston Churchill,

Opéra

Paris 8. Open daily, except Mondays, 1000—1740. Temporary exhibitions are held here, but visitors often ignore the fact that the Palais also contains a permanent collection made up from private donations. 2E4

Champs-Elysées-Clemenceau. **28, 49, 63, 72, 83.**

Picasso Musée Hotel de Sale, 5 Rue de Thorigny, Paris 3. Open daily except Tuesday 0945—1715 (2200 Wednesday).

This magnificent 17th-century mansion now houses the world's most important collection of works by Picasso acquired by the State against death duties payable by his inheritors. More than 200 paintings, 158 sculptures, including *Les Figures aux Bords de la Mer, La Femme au Jardin,* a series of busts and *Le Chèvre;* paper collages, ceramics and drawings illustrating Picasso's genius and the extraordinary range of techniques he used can be seen here.

The visit has been arranged to trace the whole evolution of Picasso's art from his earliest days to his death in 1973. Examples of the Bateau Lavoir period, the Cubist, Classical and Surrealist years, his political engagement during the Spanish Civil War and his private life with portraits of his family are included in the collection.

Amongst those works which the visitor

should not miss are the Auto-portrait Bleu in Room 1, Room 4 devoted to the Cubist period with, in particular, *La Nature Morte à la Chaise Cannée* and *Le Violon,* the portraits of Olga and his son Paul as Harlequin and *La Flute de Pan* (Rooms 6 and 6bis) the *Grande Nature Morte au Gueridon* (Room 10) the *Crucifixion* and the two *Corridas* hanging in Room 11, *Les Femmes à leur Toilette,* a collage originally destined as a cartoon for a tapestry executed by the Gobelins tapestry works 30 years later (Room 12), the portraits of Dora Maar, Marie-Thérèse and his daughter Maya and the Guernica studies in Room 13. Room 5 contains Picasso's personal collection with works by Cézanne, Renoir and Rousseau and friends — Braque, Matisse and Miró.

Temporary exhibitions are held on the 2nd floor and film projections on the 3rd floor. The gardens, with a view of the back of the Hotel de Salé, can also be visited.

St Paul, St Sebastien. **20, 65, 96.**

Rodin 77 Rue de Varenne, Paris 7. Open daily, except Tuesdays, 1000—1700. Auguste Rodin, the sculptor, lived and worked on the ground floor of this beautiful 18th-century mansion, which was also occupied at various times by Isadora Duncan, Matisse and Jean Cocteau. Rodin bequeathed this collection to the nation, and it includes many of his important works, such as *L'Age d'Airan, Le Baiser, St John the Baptist, Le Penseur* and several preparatory works for the Porte d'Enfer. Room 13 exhibits paintings by Renoir, Monet and Van Gogh. 6E5

Varenne. **69.**

Techniques 292 Rue St Martin, Paris 3. Open daily 1300—1730, Mondays to Saturdays; Sundays 1000—1715. Closed 6 and 7 April. This museum in the buildings of the Conservatoire National des Arts et Métiers shows all aspects of technical and mechanical science. 3H4

Arts et Métiers, Réaumar Sébastopol, Strasbourg St Denis. **38, 47.**

Victor Hugo (see p. 95).

The code references given in main entries refer to Central Paris maps between pages 41 and 57.

LA VOIE TRIOMPHALE

Known as La Voie Triomphale (Way of Triumph), this walk starts out from the Métro Palais Royal. Enter the Jardin du Carrousel through the archways on the **Rue de Rivoli** opposite the Place du Palais Royal. From the **Arc de Triomphe du Carrousel** the view stretches along the **Champs-Elysées** to the **Arc de Triomphe** of the **Etoile**, with the Obelisk rising in the centre of the **Place de la Concorde**. Walk up the central alleyway of the gardens. On either side are terraces which overlook the **Tuileries**. The Terrasse du Bord de l'Eau on the Seine side gives you a fine view of the Left Bank. Underneath the terrace is a passage leading from the cellars of the old palace which provided a fortunate escape route for Louis Philippe in 1848. The two sphinxes at the end of the Avenue du Général Lemonnier were

brought back from Sebastopol in 1855. Throughout the gardens and round the ponds stand statues dating from the 17th and 18th centuries by G. and N. Coustou, Coysevox, Van Clève and Le Pautre.

The bust on the north side of the large octagonal fountain is a copy of Coysevox's bust of Le Nôtre who landscaped the main part of the Tuileries gardens. At the west end of the gardens on the left, just in front of the terrace overlooking the Place de la Concorde, a tablet commemorates the balloon ascent of Robert and Charles in 1783. On the left of this terrace is the Musée de **l'Orangerie**, and on the right, the Musée du **Jeu de Paume** (closed). In the centre are Coysevox's Chevaux Ailés, of Fame and Mercury on winged horses. Steps lead down to the Place de la Concorde, on the far side of which,

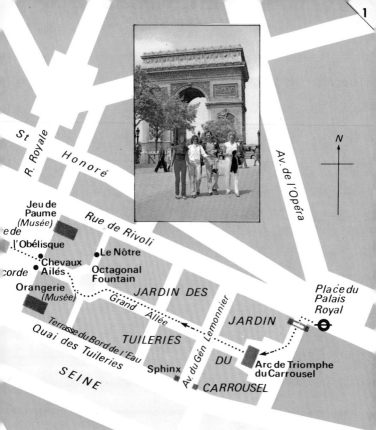

1

Jeu de
Paume
(Musée)

Rue de Rivoli

e de
l'Obélisque

Le Nôtre

corde

Chevaux
Ailés

Octagonal
Fountain

Orangerie
(Musée)

JARDIN DES

Place du
Palais
Royal

Grand Allée

Av. du Gén Lemonnier

JARDIN

Terrasse du Bord de l'Eau

Quai des Tuileries

TUILERIES

DU

Arc de Triomphe
du Carrousel

SEINE

Sphinx

CARROUSEL

In the walks which follow, a name picked out in **heavy type** *is featured as a main entry in Museums and Galleries or the Gazetteer. These entries are listed in the index.*

flanking the Champs-Elysées, are the Chevaux de Marly (Marly Horses) by Coustou, brought here, like the pair by Coysevox, from the Château de Marly, which was demolished during the Revolution.

Walking up the Champs-Elysées you come to, on the left, the Avenue Winston Churchill with the **Petit** and **Grand Palais**, and, on the right, the Avenue de Marigny where, by the theatre, an open-air stamp market is held on Thursdays and Sundays. Leading off left from the **Rond Point des Champs-Elysées**, are the Avenue Franklin D. Roosevelt and the Avenue Montaigne with the fashion house of Christian Dior at No. 30; to the right, the Avenue Matignon, with several well-known art galleries, leads to the Rue du Faubourg St Honoré.

Today, the Champs-Elysées has lost its 19th-century aristocratic appearance – when it was lined with mansions, fountains and elegant restaurants and cafés – and the stretch from the Rond Point to the Etoile is largely commercial with shops, offices, hotels and banks. Nevertheless its cafés remain the central meeting place in Paris, and it is the gathering place for Parisians intent on demonstrating national pride as, in 1940, when the people gathered to express their silent emotion at the events which had overtaken their city and, again, in 1944 when they gathered to celebrate at the Liberation procession. There was another march along this famous Avenue to reaffirm confidence in General de Gaulle after the student riots of May 1968 had threatened the stability of the state.
Mètro: Etoile

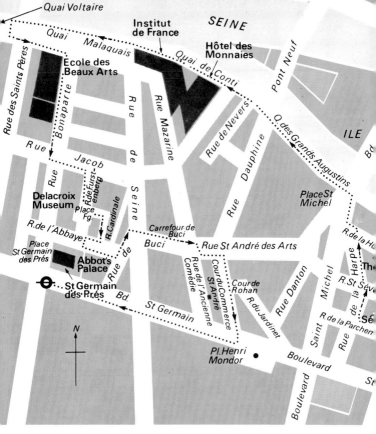

LES QUAIS- ST GERMAIN DES PRÉS

The walk, which begins on the Right Bank
at the Métro Sully Morland, takes in the
most picturesque of the quays by the
Seine and then explores the old streets
running up from the river to the Boulevard
St Germain and the Place St Germain des
Prés. Those interested in antiques and
paintings will enjoy this area, as many of
Paris' leading antique dealers and art
galleries are situated here. Cross over the
Seine and the eastern tip of the **Ile St
Louis** by the Pont de Sully to the Quai de la
Tournelle on the Left Bank. From here, as
you walk in a westerly direction, you will
have fine views of the Quai de Béthune and
the Quai d'Orléans on the Ile St Louis. At
15 Quai de la Tournelle is the famous old
restaurant La Tour d'Argent, situated at
the top of the building. Continue past the
Pont de l'Archevêché to the Quai

Montebello. Both the Quai de la Tournelle
and the Quai Montebello have several fine
17th-century houses, now being carefully
restored. The walls by the river sport open
bookstalls selling second-hand books and
posters. Known as the *bouquinistes* the
existence of the stalls was threatened a few
years ago when it was proposed to
transform the Left Bank of the Seine into
an expressway similar to the Voie
Pompidou running along the Right Bank.
Fortunately, after an outcry, the idea was
abandoned – at least for the present.
Opposite, on the **Ile de la Cité**, stands the
cathedral of **Notre Dame**.

Turn into the Square René Viviani. On
the right is the church of **St Julien-le-
Pauvre** and, almost next to it, via the Rue
Galande, the church of **St Séverin**. Turn
into the Rue de la Parcheminerie which
runs along the back of the church on the
south side, and then right into the ancient

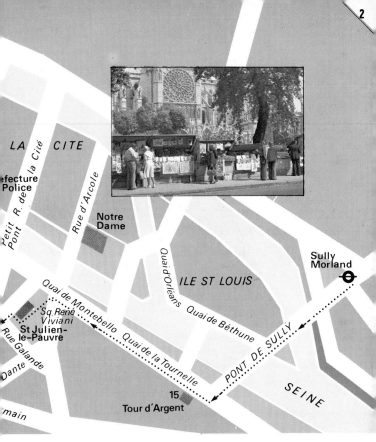

LA CITÉ

Préfecture
Police

Rue d'Arcole

Petit R. de la Cité

**Notre
Dame**

Quai d'Orléans

ILE ST LOUIS

**Sully
Morland**

Quai de Montebello

Sq. René
Viviani

**St Julien-
le-Pauvre**

Rue Galande

Dante

Quai de la Tournelle

Quai de Béthune

PONT DE SULLY

SEINE

15
Tour d'Argent

main

Rue de la Harpe which leads to the Rue de
la Huchette, where there are several small
night clubs and the Théâtre de la
Huchette, which is the smallest in Paris.
Retrace your steps along the narrow Rue
de la Huchette until you reach the Place St
Michel, from where you have a good view
of the Préfecture de Police – familiar to
readers of Georges Simenon's Maigret
novels – on the Ile de la Cité. Then to the
Quai des Grands Augustins whose houses
have vast high-ceilinged rooms with
windows which give the inhabitants a fine
view of the Ile de la Cité and the Right
Bank. On the corner of the Quai de Conti
and the Rue Dauphine is the curious Rue
de Nevers built under an arcade. The Quai
de Conti has two buildings well worth
stopping to examine: the 18th-century
Hôtel des Monnaies, the Mint, at No. 11
and, at No. 23, the 17th-century **Institut
de France**. The next two Quais –

Malaquais and Voltaire – have several
galleries and antique shops.

Retrace your steps to the Quai Malaquais and turn into the Rue Bonaparte,
past the Ecole des Beaux Arts and left into
the Rue Jacob. The Rue de Furstenberg
and the *place* of the same name run off to the
right. Delacroix's studio at No. 6 of the
place was also used for a time by Monet.
Turn right into the Rue Cardinal, which
has several ancient houses, and leads into
the Rue de Bourbon le Château. Turn right
into the Rue de l'Abbaye to examine the
buildings of the Abbot's Palace (Nos. 3–5)
built in 1586, then back, and across the Rue
de Seine which has several art galleries,
into the Rue de Buci, site of a colourful
daily market. Just after the Carrefour de
Buci is the entrance to the Cour du
Commerce St André on the Rue St André
des Arts. No. 4 was part of a tower on the
perimeter wall built by Philippe Auguste

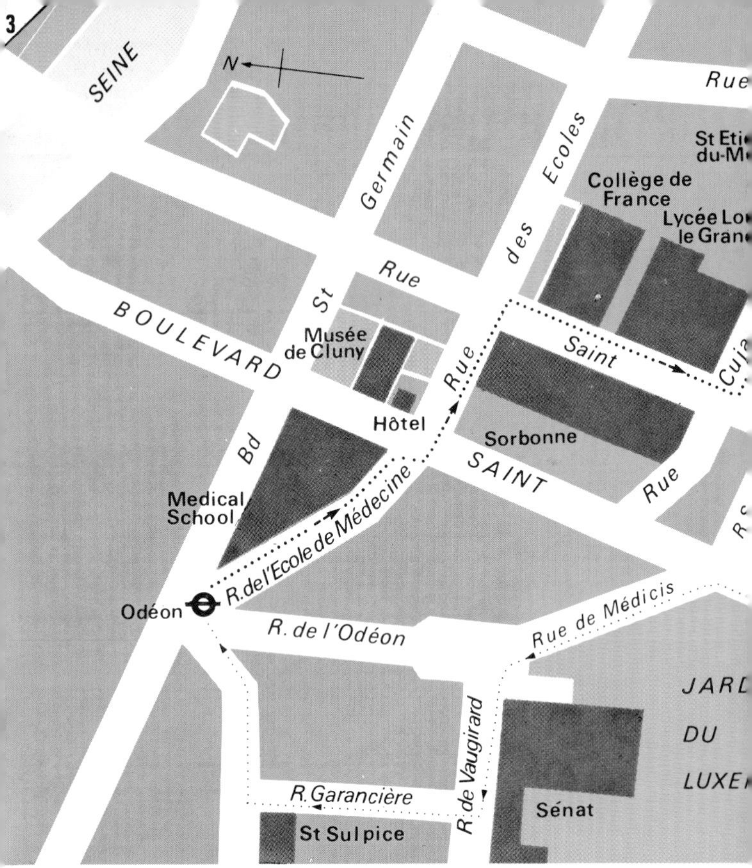

SEINE

N

Rue

Germain

St Eti
du-M

Collège de
France

Lycée Lo
le Gran

des Ecoles

Rue

BOULEVARD

St

Rue

Musée
de Cluny

Rue

Saint

Cuja

Hôtel

Sorbonne

SAINT

Bd

Rue

Medical
School

R. de l'Ecole de Médecine

R.

Odéon

R. de l'Odéon

Rue de Médicis

JARD

DU

LUXE

R. de Vaugirard

R. Garancière

St Sulpice

Sénat

at the turn of the 12th century. Immediately to the left is the Cour de Rohan, part of the residence of the Archbishops of Rouen. The 16th-century building in the second courtyard is all that remains of Diane de Poitier's home. Leave the Cour du Commerce St André at the exit on the Boulevard St Germain, opposite Danton's statue on the Place Henri Mondor, and turn right along the Boulevard. The first street leading off right is the Rue de l'Ancienne Comédie, named after the **Comédie Française** which was situated there from 1689 to 1770 at No. 14. No. 13 is the ancient literary café, **La Procope**. Continue west along the Boulevard past the Rue de Buci and the old Rue de l'Echaudé until you come to the Place St Germain des Prés. The 11th-century **church** was once part of the Benedictine Abbey founded in 558 by Childebert I. Métro: St Germain des Prés.

LE QUARTIER LATIN

The walk begins at the Métro Odéon and continues up the Rue de l'Ecole de Médicine, past the colonnaded medical school on the left, to the **Boulevard St Michel**. On the left lies the Hôtel and **Musée de Cluny**. Turn right into the Rue St Jacques, past the **Collège de France** and the Lycée Louis le Grand on your left and the **Sorbonne** on your right, and then left into the Rue Cujas for the Place du Panthéon. Skirt round the **Panthéon** to the Rue Clovis. The church of **St Etienne-du-Mont** is on your left and the Lycée Henri IV on your right. The Gothic tower in the Lycée is the remains of the church of the Abbaye de Ste Geneviève. The Saint was originally buried in the abbey crypt and her tombstone was removed to the church of St Etienne when the abbey was demolished in 1802. A little

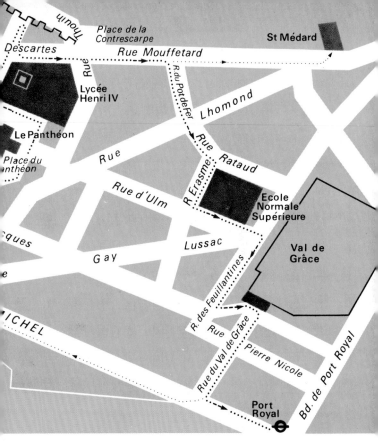

further along the Rue Clovis is part of the wall built round Paris at the turn of the 12th century by Philippe Auguste.

Retrace your steps and turn left into the Rue Descartes which, after crossing the Rue Thouin, leads to the **Placc de la Contrescarpe** and the **Rue Mouffetard** (the church of **St Médard** is at No. 41). Turn right into the Rue du Pot de Fer, cross Rue Lhomond, continue along the Rue Rataud until you reach the Rue Erasme on the right, and turn left down the Rue d'Ulm. The college on the left is the Ecole Normale Supérieure for the training of teachers and Lycée professors. Former students include Bergson the philosopher, Giraudoux the playwright, Romain Rolland, and Jules Romains the novelists, and Président Pompidou. At the bottom of Rue d'Ulm, turn into the Rue des Feuillantines, then left into the Rue St Jacques to visit the **Val de Grâce**.

The street of the same name leads back to the Boulevard St Michel where, to the left, is the Métro Port Royal on the line to Denfert-Rochereau from which there are connections to the Etoile. If you turn right down the Boulevard you come to the **Jardins du Luxembourg**, leading to the Senate, the church of **St Sulpice** and, ultimately, the Odéon and the métro.

Panthéon

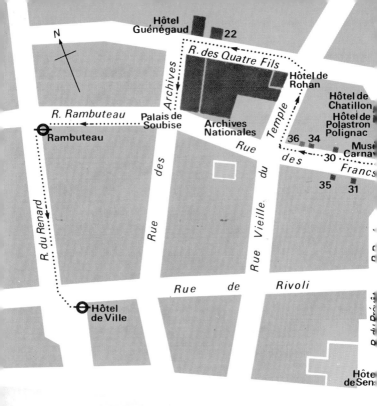

SEINE

LE MARAIS

The walk begins at the **Place de la Bastille** and, continuing in a more or less westerly direction, it takes in most of the main sites of interest in the Marais. From the *place*, take the Rue St Antoine and turn right along the Rue des Tournelles, then left into the Rue du Pas de la Mule, where a few steps will lead you into the **Place des Vosges**. Come back on to the Rue St Antoine by the Rue de Birague on the south side, and turn right as far as the **Hôtel de Béthune-Sully** at No. 62, which was built in 1624. Cross the street and take the little Rue de l'Hôtel St Paul, named after the palace built by Charles V, and turn left into the Rue Neuve St Pierre, then right into the Rue Beautreillis which (together with the Rue Charles V and the Rue des Lions running off it) has several period mansions worth looking at. At the bottom

turn left, then right into the Rue du Petit Musc, and right again on to the Quai des Célestins. Hôtel Fieubet at No. 4, built by Hardouin-Mansart, has been much restored. On the corner of the Rue du Figuier is the turreted **Hôtel de Sens** built between 1474 and 1507. A short walk along this street and the Rue du Prévôt leads you back to the Rue St Antoine.

Cross over to the Rue Pavée, past the **Hôtel Lamoignon** at No. 24 and turn right into the Rue des Francs Bourgeois, then left into the Rue de Sévigné, to the **Musée Carnavalet** at No. 23. No. 29 is an annex to the museum and once belonged to Le Pelletier St Fargeau who was responsible for turning the vote in favour of Louis XVI's death, in 1793. Turn left along the Rue du Parc Royal which has a row of fine 17th-century mansions and left again down the Rue Payenne. The Hôtel de Polastron Polignac at No. 11 and the Hôtel

de Chatillon at No. 13 date from the late 17th century. Turn right, back into the Rue des Francs Bourgeois. Nos. 34-36 and 35 were built in 1634; No. 30, the stone and brick Hôtel Alméras, built in 1598, possesses one of the finest doorways in the Marais, decorated with a ram's head. On the opposite side, at No. 31, is the Hôtel d'Albret which was the residence of Louis XIV's mistress, Madame de Montespan. A few paces to the right, along the Rue Vieille du Temple, bring you, at No. 87, to the Hôtel de Rohan, built in 1713 for Armand de Rohan. Also known as the Hôtel de Strasbourg, the name is a reminder that Armand de Rohan and his three successors – from the same family – were all Cardinals of Strasbourg. The building is now part of the **Archives Nationales.**

Turn left into the Rue des Quatre Fils where, at No. 22, Madame du Deffand held her famous literary and political salon in the 18th century. On the corner, entrance at 60 Rue des Archives, is the 17th-century **Hôtel Guénégaud** built by François Mansart, which is now the Musée de la Chasse. Turning left down the Rue des Archives brings you to the Palais de Soubise which houses the main part of the Archives Nationales (entrance 60 Rue des Francs Bourgeois). The palace is on the site of a mansion, built in the 14th century for the Constable of France, Olivier de Clisson. It later became the property of the Guise family and during the Religious Wars, it was their main headquarters where plans were laid for the St Bartholomew Massacre, which began in 1572. After 1700, when Anne de Soubise bought it, the mansion was demolished except for its turreted doorway which was retained and incorporated in the present building.

Métro: Rambuteau, Hôtel de Ville.

5

N

BOIS DE

BOULOGNE

Route de Suresnes

Université
Paris IX

Rte de la Muette à Neuilly

Boulevard Lannes

Chemin de Ceinture du Lac Inférieur

Lac
Inférieur

Ferry

Porte de
la Muette

Av. de St Cloud

Avenue Henri M.

Suchet

Musée
Marmottan

R.L.
Boilly

Raphael

Jardin
du

Route des Lacs à Passy

Bd.

Chaussée de la Muette

Lac
Supérieur

Av.

Ranelagh

PI.
du Ma
de Lat
Tassi

R. de la Fa

Av

LE BOIS

Paris has two extensive woods on its east and west borders, and there are several small parks within the town. This walk, beginning at the Trocadéro, passes through one of these parks before continuing to the **Bois de Boulogne**.

From the Place du Trocadéro, take the Rue Franklin which runs off the west side of the Palais de Chaillot; Benjamin Franklin's statue stands at the beginning and Clemenceau, who negotiated the Treaty of Versailles in 1919, lived at No. 8 which can be visited. At the Place de Costa Rica take the Rue de Passy which leads to the Chaussée de la Muette and the Jardin du Ranelagh, once part of the royal park surrounding the Château de la Muette, and laid out in the style of the London gardens of the same name. On the west side, at No. 2 Rue Louis Boilly, is the **Musée Marmot-** **tan**, containing an important collection of Impressionist paintings. The gardens end on their north-west side at the Porte de la Muette.

Cross over to enter the Bois de Boulogne by the Avenue de St Cloud which leads to the lakes. Boats can be rented on the Lac Inférieur and there is a ferry service to the islands in the middle. The Chemin de Ceinture du Lac Inférieur leads round the lake and, at the northern tip, the Route de Suresnes ends at the Place du Maréchal de Lattre de Tassigny (Porte Dauphine). The large white modern building on the right, at the corner of the Boulevard Lannes, is the University Paris IX. The **Avenue** **Foch** leads up to the **Etoile**. Running off to the right of the Avenue is the Rue de la Faisanderie with a small forgery museum at No. 16 – the Musée de la Contrefaçon. At

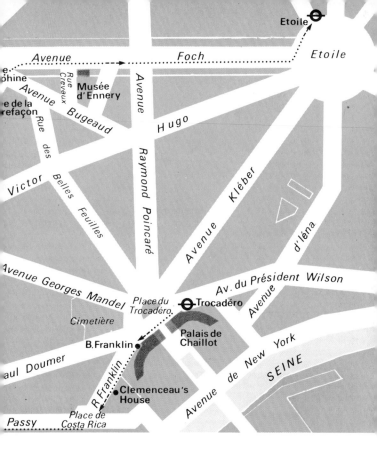

Etoile

Etoile

Avenue Foch

Rue Crevaux

Musée d'Ennery

Avenue Bugeaud

Avenue Hugo

Raymond Poincaré

Avenue Kléber

d'Iéna

Victor

Rue des Belles Feuilles

Avenue Georges Mandel

Av. du Président Wilson

Place du Trocadéro

Trocadéro

Avenue

Cimetière

Palais de Chaillot

Avenue de New York

SEINE

B. Franklin

aul Doumer

R. Franklin

Clemenceau's House

Avenue

Passy

Place de Costa Rica

59 Ave Foch there is the little Musée d'Ennery with a collection of Oriental and Armenian art.

Note: there are no métro stations on this avenue between those of the Porte Dauphine and the Etoile.

Bois de Boulogne

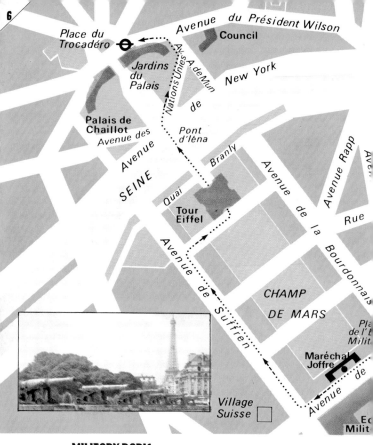

6

MILITARY PARIS

Setting off from the **Place de la Concorde**, cross over the Pont de la Concorde to the Left Bank. Facing you is the Greek-style façade of the **Palais Bourbon**, seat of the Assemblée Nationale. Turn right on to the **Quai d'Orsay** and continue past the Ministère des Affaires Etrangères at No. 37. Next to it is the **Esplanade des Invalides** on the other side of the Rue de Constantine. At No. 5 of this street is the Canadian Cultural Institute and, almost next door at No. 9 is the British Council. Walk a little way into the centre of the Esplanade and pause for a few minutes to admire the perspective of the Invalides buildings behind the balustrade with its cannons and artillery. The Esplanade is crossed successively by the Rue de l'Université, the Rue St Dominique and the Rue de Grenelle all of which,

as they continue east towards the Boulevard St Germain, form part of the quarter known as the Faubourg St Germain. Many of the 18th- and 19th-century mansions standing in these streets are now ministries, government offices or embassies.

Entry tickets to **Les Invalides** include visits to both the museum and Napoleon's Tomb and are valid for two consecutive days. Pass through the main entrance into the Cour d'Honneur. Ancient cannon, including one dating from the late 15th century, are ranged along the walls. The statue of Napoleon in the centre, known as Le Petit Caporal, once stood on the top of the column in the **Place Vendôme**. After visiting the **Church of St Louis** (entrance in the façade opposite the main entrance) turn left along the Corridor de Nimes to

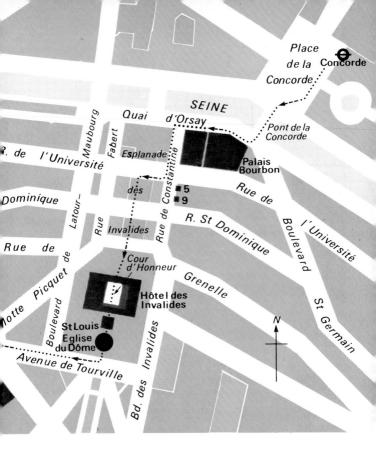

reach the **Dôme des Invalides**. It is well worth taking time here to admire to the full the harmony of design and proportion of both the outside and the interior of the church before going on to the gallery surrounding the crypt containing Napoleon's tomb.

On leaving the Dôme, turn right along the Avenue de Tourville to the **Ecole Militaire**. The Central Pavilion faces the Champ de Mars. In front of it is the statue of Maréchal Joffre. Just behind the junction of Avenue de la Motte Picquet and the Avenue de Suffren on the west side of the Champ de Mars is the **Village Suisse**, a group of antique shops. The **Champ de Mars** is laid out partly in the French style and partly in the English style of landscaping. At the foot is the **Tour Eiffel**. At the height of the tourist season

you will probably have to join the queue to take the elevator and admission prices vary according to the platform visited, the highest being the most expensive, but the view from the summit, especially on a clear day, is worth the outlay.

Cross over the Pont d'Iéna to the gardens and fountains of the Palais de Chaillot. Steps lead up to the terrace of the buildings, or, you can skirt round the gardens and reach the Place du Trocadéro via the Avenue des Nations Unies, to the right, and the Avenue Albert de Mun. The building on the corner of this avenue and the Avenue du Président Wilson, leading to the Trocadéro, is the headquarters of Conseil Economique et Social (Economic and Social Council).

The Métro from the Trocadéro is a direct line to the Etoile.

GAZETTEER

Champs-Elysées

RIGHT BANK

ÉTOILE-LA MADELEINE

It is best to approach this area from the Etoile (officially called Place Charles de Gaulle). Looking along the Avenue des Champs-Elysées, you can see the Obélisque at the far end, in the Place de la Concorde. This section takes in, clockwise, five of the twelve avenues radiating from the Etoile: on the extreme left, the Avenue de Wagram runs down to the Place des Ternes. Then come the Avenues Hoche, which leads to the Parc Monceau; Friedland, which leads to the Boulevard Haussmann and the Place St Augustin; the Champs-Elysées and finally Marceau on the right leading south west to the Place de l'Alma and the Seine. From there, the Cours Albert I and the Cours la Reine, bordering the river, lead back to the Place de la Concorde. Crossing the 8th *arrondissement* (district) diagonally from the Place des Ternes to the Rue Royal, is the fashionable shopping street, the Rue du Faubourg St Honoré which also houses the American and British Embassies.

Arc de Triomphe　　2D4

Place Charles de Gaulle Begun on the orders of Napoleon in 1806, in honour of the Imperial Army, the archway was not completed until 30 years later under Louis-Philippe. You can climb to the top (51m/164ft high) for a magnificent view of Paris with the twelve avenues radiating from the Etoile, while beneath the arch lies the **Tomb of the Unknown Soldier**, where the Eternal Flame is rekindled every evening at 1830.

Métro: Etoile. Buses 22, 30, 31, 52, 73, 92.

Champs-Elysées, Avenue des　　2E4

Perhaps the most beautiful avenue in the world, it is divided into two parts, separated by the Rond Point. The section between the Rond Point and the Etoile was a favourite spot for walks and promenades up until the Napoleonic era. It became residential in the 19th century and is now commercial, with airline offices, banks, car showrooms, cinemas and shops. On fine days and summer evenings the café terraces can be cheerful but crowded. The section leading from the Rond Point to the Concorde is flanked by gardens.

Métro: Etoile, George V, Franklin Roosevelt, Champs-Elysées-Clemenceau,

Concorde. Buses 22, 28, 32, 49, 52, 73.

Concorde, Place de la 2F4

Before the town of Paris decided to place an equestrian statue here in honour of Louis XV, the site was wasteland. Highly flattered, Louis granted letters patent to the municipality permitting the building of the square to enhance his statue. Admirably proportioned, the buildings on the north side were designed by Gabriel who was also the architect of the Ecole Militaire (p.100). During the Revolution the square was one of three principal execution sites and Louis XIV and Marie Antoinette, Danton and Robespierre were guillotined there. The centre is dominated by the **Obélisque,** given to Charles X in 1829 by Mehmet Ali, viceroy of Egypt. The monument (23m/75ft high) is over 33 centuries old and originally stood at Luxor.
Métro: Concorde. Buses 24, 42, 72, 84, 94.

Elysée, Palais de l' 2E4

35 Rue du Faubourg St Honoré. The official residence of the President of the Republic. Napoleon signed his abdication here, in 1815, and Wellington occupied the building during his stay in Paris. It is not open to the public.
Métro: Champs-Elysées-Clemenceau, Concorde. Buses 24, 42, 49, 52, 72.

Etoile (Place Charles de Gaulle) 2D4

Twelve avenues, one of which is the Champs-Elysées, radiate starwise from the Etoile. At the end of the 18th century only five existed, the other seven avenues were added by Baron Haussmann in 1854. The façades of the buildings facing the Arc de Triomphe were designed by Hittorff.
Métro: Etoile. Buses 22, 30, 52, 73, 92.

Gabriel, Avenue 2E4

Named after the architect of the Place de la Concorde, the avenue runs past the gardens of the American and British Embassies and the Palais de l'Elysée.
Métro: Concorde. Buses 24, 42, 72, 84.

Païva, Hôtel 2E4

25 Avenue des Champs-Elysées. Now the French branch of the Traveller's Club, this mansion was the residence of the Marquise de Païva, a famous hostess, and spy, in Louis Napoleon's reign.
Metro: Franklin Roosevelt. Buses 73, 32, 49, 80.

Pont Alexandre III 6E4

Spanning the Seine from the Avenue Winston Churchill to the Quai d'Orsay on the Left Bank, this heavily decorated steel bridge is considered by many Parisians to be the most beautiful in the city.
Métro: Champs-Elysées-Clemenceau. Buses 63, 72, 83.

Rond Point des Champs-Elysées 2E4

The Rond Point separates the commercial half of the Avenue des Champs-Elysées from the other, and is crossed by the Avenue Matignon. The building at No. 7 houses the offices of the magazine *Jours de France,* whilst opposite, at No. 14, are the recently restored offices of *Le Figaro.*
Métro: Franklin Roosevelt. Buses 28, 42, 32, 49, 80.

Royale, Rue 2F4

Situated between the Place de la Madeleine and the Place de la Concorde, this is a fashionable shopping street. Madame de Stael, renowned woman of letters, lived briefly at No. 6 and Maxim's, the famous restaurant, is at No. 3.
Métro: Concorde, La Madeleine. Buses 24, 42, 52.

St Marie Madeleine 2F4

Place de la Madeleine. Known only as 'La Madeleine', the present building, in the style of a Greek temple surrounded by 52 Corinthian columns, was completed in 1842. On the east side of the church there is a small flower market, whilst all round the *place* are the most luxurious food shops in Paris.
Métro: Madeleine. Buses 24, 42, 52, 84, 94.

St Philippe du Roule 2E4

154 Rue du Faubourg St Honoré. Built between 1774 and 1784 in the style of a Roman basilica, the semicircular chancel was added in the mid 19th century. The interior contains a fresco representing The Descent from the Cross, by Chassériau.
Métro: St Philippe du Roule. Buses 28, 32, 49, 80.

MONTMARTRE

The hill, La Butte de Montmartre, derives its name from the Latin *Mons Martyrum,* because it was here that St Denis, first bishop of Paris, is supposed to have been martyred by beheading. The Quartier des Abbesses, at the bottom of the hill, gained its name from a Benedictine Abbey founded in the 12th century. Montmartre began to attract the artists, writers and musicians who made it famous in the 19th century mainly because it was both cheap and picturesque. Baudelaire, Berlioz, Flaubert and Musset were among the first to frequent the area, and Toulouse-Lautrec contributed largely to its es-

Place du Tertre

Montmartre, near Sacré Coeur

Rue Norvins

Place du Tertre

tablishment as an artistic centre with his paintings of the Moulin Rouge and the artistes who performed there. Van Gogh lived at 54 Rue Lepic, where many of the houses have been restored, and, at the beginning of this century, Picasso and Modigliani had their studios in the Bateau Lavoir.

Métro: Abbesses, Lamarck-Caulaincourt, Anvers from where a funicular service runs up the hill to the terminus close by Sacré Coeur. Buses 30, 54, 80, 85. There is a minibus service from the Place Pigalle via the old streets of les Abbesses, the Moulin de la Galette, and the Place du Tertre to the Mairie of the 18th *arrondissement*.

Bercy   7J6

Le Palais Omnisports, 8 Bd de Bercy, Paris 12. Opened in 1984, this large modern pyramid entirely covered with green lawns growing up it at an angle of 45° is the new Paris sports stadium. With a seating capacity of 17,000, sports meetings of all disciplines ranging from athletics to motorcycle competitions are held here, as well as performances of large scale opera productions and concerts.

Métro: Bercy, Gare de Lyon. Buses 24, PC.

Blanche, Place   3G3

At 82 Boulevard de Clichy, which runs along the north side of the *place*, is the **Moulin Rouge**, the cabaret famous for the can-can girls in the 1880s and 1890s.

Métros: Blanche, Pigalle. Buses 54, 30.

Parc de la Villette   4K2

Cité des Sciences et de l'Industrie, Ave Corentin Cariou, Paris 19. Open Tues, Thurs, Fri 1000—1800, Wed 1200—2100, Weekends and Public Holidays 1200—2000. Situated on the old Villette Meat Market this modern complex offers a selection of activities for adults and children. *Explora*, the heart of the Cité des Sciences, is devoted to the following themes: a) The Earth and the Universe, with a Planetarium; b) Matter and the Human Brain, showing the latest robots and their use in modern Science; c) Language and Communication with examples of the latest audio-visual techniques; d) Agriculture, biotechnology and meteorology. Apart from *l'Explora*, visitors should note the *Mediathèque* a scientific, technological and industrial library, the *Inventorium* designed for children where they can command the weather at will, *l'Espace Entreprises* where exhibitions are held and *Science Actualités* where journalists lecture on the latest developments. Scientific and industrial films are shown in the *Salle Louis Lumière*. La *Géode*, the dome, is

Europe's largest hemispheric cinema, linked to Omnimax international circuit.

Métro: Porte de la Villette. Bus 251, 150, 152, PC.

Montmartre, Cimetière de   3F3

Entrance across the iron bridge on Rue Caulaincourt. Many artists, musicians and writers are buried here – Berlioz, Degas, Offenbach and Stendhal are just a few. The tomb of Alphonsine Plessis, who created the leading role in Alexandre Dumas' *La Dame aux Camélias*, can also be visited.

Moulin de la Galette

Avenue Junot/Rue Girardon In the 19th century two windmills, sole survivors of a number which once stood on the hill of Montmartre, were brought to this site and became known as the Moulin de la Galette, a very popular dance hall which inspired many artists including Van Gogh and Renoir whose painting of the mill now hangs in the museum of the Jeu de Paume.

Sacré Coeur   3G3

Rue du Chevalier-de-la-Barre The Sacré Coeur is modelled on the construction of the Basilique de St Front in Périgueux. French Catholics decided to build a church dedicated to the Sacred Heart as an expression of contrition and hope following the French disasters in the Franco-Prussian War of 1870-1. Financed mainly by public subscription from three million Frenchmen, the church was inaugurated in 1910. The Sacré Coeur is one of the landmarks of Paris and the terrace in front gives a superb view across the town.

St Pierre   3G3

2 Rue du Mont-Cenis Situated to the east of the Place du Tertre, this is one of the oldest churches in Paris, its construction dating from the 12th century. The interior contains the tomb of Queen Adelaide of Savoy, who founded the Benedictine Abbey of Montmartre in 1133. The vaults of the nave were rebuilt in the 15th century.

Tertre, Place du

Famous for its cafés and cabarets, two of the best known are La Mère Catherine and Le Clairon des Chasseurs. On summer evenings you can dine or sip a drink under the trees, or have your portrait sketched by one of the numerous artists who exhibit their paintings on the *place* and in the galleries of the surrounding streets.

Vignoble

Rue des Saules This is the only remaining vineyard in Paris, whose wines were renowned during the Middle Ages. It is the property of the municipality, and the grapes which are gathered early in October amid public festivities, yield a white wine which can be tasted in most of the cabarets and bars of Montmartre. Profits from the sales are given to charity.

LES GRANDS BOULEVARDS

The Grands Boulevards begin with the Boulevard de la Madeleine and, although the names change, the same road continues east, in a slight curve, finishing at the Place de la République. Extremely fashionable in the 19th century, artists, politicians and writers met in the cafés lining the street and mingled with dandies and their courtesans and also with shady members of the underworld, as described in Balzac's novels. On the Boulevard Haussmann, which joins the Boulevard des Italiens, stand two large department stores, Le Printemps and Les Galeries Lafayette where, according to the loudspeaker inside: 'Something is always going on'. To the north of the Carrefour (junction) Richelieu-Drouot is the Rue Drouot where the rebuilt auction house, the Hôtel Drouot, stands and, on the south side, is the Rue de Richelieu, which runs down to the Place André Malraux and the Comédie Française. At the junction of the Boulevards Montmartre and Poissonnière is the Rue Notre Dame des Victoires, which crosses the Sentier Quarter, the centre of the wholesale garment and haberdashery trade. The Rue Réaumur, also in this area, is the newspaper and printing centre of Paris. The Musée Grévin is on the left of the Boulevard Montmartre, on the right the Rue Vivienne leads to the Bourse (Stock Exchange). This area; its history, architecture, and activities, is linked to the Opéra and Palais Royal.

Bourse   3G4
Place de la Bourse. Visitors are admitted to the gallery of Paris' Stock Exchange between 1100 and 1430, except at the weekends, and a guided commentary is given every 40 minutes.
Métro: Bourse. Buses 20, 29, 39, 74.

Jean-sans-Peur, Tour   3G4
20 Rue Etienne Marcel Situated in a courtyard, the square tower was built by King John the Fearless, in 1408, to protect himself after the assassination of the Duke of Orléans. It was part of the Hôtel de Bourgogne.
Métro: Étienne-Marcel. Buses 29, 38, 47.

Notre Dame de Bonne Nouvelle   3H4
25 Rue de la Lune Situated just off the Boulevard de Bonne Nouvelle, this was originally a sanctuary, dating from the reign of Louis XIII (1610-43), although only the ancient belfry now remains. The

church was rebuilt during the Revolution. Notre Dame de Bonne Nouvelle is the patron saint of radio and television.
Métro: Bonne-Nouvelle. Buses 20, 39.

Notre Dame des Victoires   3G4
Place des Petits Pères Louis XIII laid the foundation stone of this church, built like a basilica, to celebrate the capture of La Rochelle from the Huguenots after a long siege (1627-8). The fine wood carvings in the choir are 17th century and the organ case dates from the 18th century.
Métro: Bourse. Buses 20, 29, 48.

Porte St Denis   3H4
At the junction of Boulevard St Denis and Rue du Faubourg St Denis. One of the city's great triumphal arches, erected in 1672, and financed by the city of Paris to commemorate Louis XIV's victories on the Rhine. The decorations, set in pyramid reliefs, are allegorical and represent scenes from campaigns in Holland and the Rhine.
Métro: Strasbourg-St-Denis. Buses 20, 38, 39, 47.

Porte St Martin   3H4
At the junction of Boulevard St Denis and Rue du Faubourg St Martin. This triumphal arch was also put up (in 1674) to celebrate Louis XIV's victories against William of Orange and his allies.
Métro: Strasbourg-St-Denis. Buses 20, 38, 39, 47.

Victoires, Place des   3G4
Designed by Hardouin-Mansart in 1685, much of the original decoration of this circular *place* has vanished, but the semicircular windows with their wrought-iron balconies give some idea of the former aspect. The statue of Louis XIV in the centre, by Bosio, was put there in 1822 to replace the former statue melted down for cannon during the Revolution.
Métro: Bourse. Buses 29, 48.

Place des Victoires, Louis XIV

LOUVRE-L'OPÉRA

Rich in history and monuments, this area, which comprises the 1st *arrondissement* and part of the 2nd, is best approached from the Place de la Concorde. Parallel to the Jardins des Tuileries, which stretch from La Concorde to the Louvre, runs the Rue de Rivoli. Leading off the Rue de Rivoli are the Rue de Castiglione and the Place Vendôme, the Place André Malraux (formerly known as the Place du Théâtre Français) and the Palais Royal and its gardens. Just behind the gardens stands the Bibliothèque Nationale and, along the Rue des Petits Champs, on the right, is the Banque de France. Both the Rue du Quatre Septembre and the Avenue de l'Opéra lead to the Place de l'Opéra.

Banque de France   3G4

1/5 Rue La Vrillière France's national bank was founded in 1800, at the instigation of Napoleon, by a group of bankers. Most of the present architecture dates from the mid and late 19th century. The gold and monetary reserves of France are kept in the vaults under the bank.
Métro: Pyramides. Buses 27, 29, 48, 85.

Bibliothèque Nationale see p.59

Carrousel, Arc de Triomphe du   6F4

Place du Carrousel Modelled on the arch of Septimus Severus in Rome, and built by Fontaine and Percier, in 1806, the arch commemorates Napoleon's victories in Italy in 1805. The marble columns flanking the middle and two side arches were taken from the Château at Meudon, and the bronze chariot group and figures on the top are by Bosio. Standing in front of the main entrance to the former Palais des Tuileries, it is the only surviving remnant of the palace, which was destroyed by fire in 1871.
Métro: Louvre, Palais-Royal. Buses 27, 39, 48, 68, 69, 95.

Carrousel, Place du   6F4

Now part of the Louvre, it owes its name to the brilliant tournament and parade given there by the Sun King, Louis XIV, in 1662 to celebrate the birth of his first child. The king, on horseback and dressed as a Roman Emperor, paraded round the square followed by the Princes of the blood royal and high-ranking members of his Court, costumed as Armenians, Turks and Indians. Up until the 19th century when Napoleon III cleared it, the *place* was small and bore a number of dilapidated houses.
Métro: Louvre, Palais-Royal. Buses 27, 39, 48, 68, 69, 95.

Comédie Française   3G4

Place André Malraux Noted for the performance of classic French dramatists, particularly Molière, the Théâtre de la Comédie Française was built in 1786. Louis XIV founded the Comédie Française troupe in 1680, decreeing that Molière's company should amalgamate with the actors of the Hôtel de Bourgogne, a rival group. The statutes governing the company's affairs were drawn up, in 1812, on the orders of Napoleon, who also granted a handsome state subsidy. Members of the Comédie Française are known as 'Sociétaires', and have official status; the Administrator is nominated by the Government. Houdon's **statue of Voltaire** can be admired in the foyer of the Salle Richelieu.
Métro: Palais-Royal. Buses 21, 27, 39, 48, 67, 72.

Gaillon, Place   3G4

On the east side of the square is the Restaurant Drouant where every autumn, the members of the literary Académie Goncourt award a prize, the *Prix Goncourt*, for the best novel of the year. On the north side, the fountain, was decorated by architect Visconti.
Métro: Quatre-Septembre. Buses 20, 21, 27, 29.

Louvre, Palais du   3FG4

Historically speaking, the Louvre cannot be considered separately from Les Tuileries, since up to the riots of the Commune of 1871, both of these palaces existed on the site now occupied by the museum and the Place du Carrousel. The Palais des Tuileries, burnt down in 1871, was not rebuilt. The origins of the Louvre date from the last years of the 12th century when Philippe Auguste decided to build a fortress which would defend the Right Bank of Paris, whose economy was rapidly expanding, and also house his Arsenal, Archives and Treasure. The fortress was transformed in the 13th century into a sumptuously furnished royal residence by Charles V who placed the royal library of 973 manuscripts (an enormous amount for the time) in the north tower, the Tour de la Fauconnerie. Little used as a residence – the French Kings preferred to live in the Hôtels de la Tournelle and de St Pol in the Marais – it was not until 1548 that François I, responsible for the construction of Renaissance masterpieces such as the Châteaux of Blois, Chambord and Fontainebleau, entrusted Pierre Lescot with the task of drawing up plans for a palace more in accord with his (the king's) taste. Demolition work began on the fortress almost immediately, but François died the

François I *Clouet*

Gilles *Watteau*

Louvre, Pavillon de l'Horloge

Coronation of the Virgin *Fra Angelico*

following year, before the actual construction work had begun. The Renaissance façade, however, on the south west, decorated by Jean Goujon, and the west and south wings were completed under his son Henri II and his grandchildren.

In 1564 Catherine de Médicis, Henri II's widow, asked the architect Philibert Delorme to draw up plans for a separate palace for her personal use, to be built a short distance away on the former site of a tile works known as La Sablonnière or Les Tuileries. Under Henri IV construction work on both palaces continued. In addition, Henri took up Catherine's original plan, known as the Grand Design, for providing a link between the two palaces in the form of a covered gallery running alongside the Seine – the Galerie du Bord de l'Eau. Three-quarters of the vast Cour Carrée, which was part of Lescot's original design, dates from the reigns of Louis XIII and Louis XIV. Louis XIII demolished the Tour de la Fauconnerie, replacing it with the Pavillon de l'Horloge and, on the north side of the courtyard, added an exact replica of the Henri II wing opposite. Louis XIV's architects Le Vau, Le Brun and Perrault added the Apollo wing on the south side and the colonnades on the east side.

With the removal of the Court to Versailles, in 1682, the Louvre and Tuileries palaces fell into disrepair and neglect. Let out to members of the Académie and to artists, the interiors were modified in haphazard fashion and smaller buildings sprouted like mushrooms in the Cour Carrée, in the other courtyards and all round the buildings. Despite the serious efforts of Louis XV's Director for Royal Buildings, Marigny, who saved the palaces from demolition and carried out some repairs, the ravages continued under the auspices of the Revolution, although credit should be given to the members of the Convention, who had established themselves in the Louvre, for the decision to transform it into a museum.

Napoleon's decision to build along the Rue de Rivoli between the Place du Palais Royal and the Concorde, marked a new phase in the construction of the palaces. Taking up Catherine's Grand Design again, his architects built the north gallery, joining it to the Tuileries with the Pavillon de Marsan. Finally, Napoleon III completed more than three centuries of building, by adding the Pavillons Denon and Richelieu on the north and south sides of the Place du Carrousel. He also entirely redecorated the interior of the Tuileries in the style of the mid 19th century, fitting it out as apartments for himself and the Empress Eugénie.

The Palais des Tuileries was destroyed during the Commune in 1871, in the fire which also burnt down the Palais Royal. Although the interior was completely ruined, the Renaissance façades, overlooking the gardens, suffered less and could have been restored. Instead the decision was taken to raze them and to restore only the Pavillons du Flore and de Marsan.

Viewed from the exterior, the most notable parts of the Louvre are: **The Cour Carrée**. Entering through the Pavillon Marengo from the Rue de Rivoli, Lescot's west and south wings, admirable in design and proportion, are in the far right-hand corner. Jean Goujon's carvings with their reliefs, statues and garlanded friezes display Renaissance architectural decoration at its zenith. On the Pavillon Henri II, note the crowned H surmounting a cipher of an H with two crescents which can be read either as two C's in honour of Henri's wife, Catherine de Médicis, or two D's in homage to Diane de Poitiers, his mistress. The ciphers on the other wings allow us to retrace the different stages in the construction of the Louvre. The ciphers of Henri III (H), Charles IX (K, signifying Karolus), and Henri IV (HDB) appear on the south wing whilst, to the right of the Pavillon de l'Horloge, the interlaced L and A and LMT denote the buildings completed during the reigns of Louis XIII and Anne of Austria, and Louis XIV and Marie-Thérèse. The outlines of the old Louvre are still visible from the tracings on the paving on the south west of the Cour Carrée. **Colonnade** Facing the Place du Louvre, these columns were designed by Claude Perrault, brother of Charles, the author of the famous *Contes de Perrault*. Claude was a man of many talents, since he was also a well-known doctor, and a precursor of modern building techniques, with his columns reinforced with iron. Louis XIV's monogram appears at the top, and his bust which replaced Napoleon's, removed during the Restoration, is in the centre. **Galerie du Bord de l'Eau** From here there is a fine view of the Left Bank across the Pont des Arts. (For a description of the museum, see p. 62.)

Métro: Louvre, Palais-Royal. Buses 21, 24, 27, 67, 69, 72, 81, 85.

Molière, Fontaine   3G4

At the corner of Rue Molière and Rue de Richelieu. Erected by Visconti, in 1844, at the suggestion of a member of the Comédie Française and financed by public subscription, the fountain is decorated with statues by Pradier. Molière's house (place of his death) is situated nearby at 40 Rue de Richelieu.

Métro: Pyramides. Buses 39, 48.

Opéra de Paris   3F4

Place de l'Opéra Also known as the Palais Garnier, after the architect, the façade is decorated with sculptures. Carpaux's La Danse, on the façade facing the *place*, is a copy. The original has been removed to the Louvre. The ceiling of the Opéra was decorated by Chagall.
Metro: Opera, RER Auber. Buses 20, 21, 22, 27, 29, 42, 52, 53, 66, 68, 81, 95.

Palais Royal   5G4

Place du Palais Royal The original palace was built by Cardinal de Richelieu in 1629. On his death there, in 1642, the palace was bequeathed to Louis XIII. It remained the property of the Orléans branch of the royal family, with brief interruptions under the Révolution and Napoleon, when it became a centre of gambling. Louis Philippe set off from this palace for the Hôtel de Ville, in 1830, to be crowned king. Destroyed by fire during the Commune in 1871, it was rebuilt and is now the offices of the *Conseil d'Etat*. The striped columns in the courtyard are by Buren (1986).
Métro: Palais-Royal. Buses 21, 27, 39, 48, 67, 69, 72, 81.

Palais Royal, Jardins du   6G4

The galleries on the north, east and west sides, in the gardens of the Palais Royal, were built in 1781 by Philippe-Egalité and, because he was constantly in debt, they were rented out as apartments and shops. The little cannon standing on an ivy pedestal in the gardens used to detonate at midday when the sun hit the magnifying glass and ignited the charge. The shops under the arcades sell antiques, stamps and curios, and among those who had apartments overlooking the gardens were Jean Cocteau and Colette, the novelist.
Métro: Palais-Royal. Buses 21, 27, 39, 48, 67, 69, 72, 81.

Pyramides, Place des   3G4

Rue de Rivoli The gilded equestrian statue, by Frémiet, in the centre of this arcaded square portrays Joan of Arc.
Métro: Tuileries. Buses 69, 72.

Rivoli, Rue de   6F4

The arcaded stretch of this street, between the Places de la Concorde and du Châtelet, was built to celebrate Napoleon's Italian victories. Several large hotels are situated here, including the Hôtel Meurice at No. 228, where General Von Choltitz, Commander of Paris in the last years before the Liberation, had his military headquarters.
Métro: Concorde, Tuileries, Palais-Royal. Buses 67, 69, 72.

Place Vendôme

Joan of Arc, Place des Pyramides

St Germain l'Auxerrois 6G4

2 Place du Louvre With its 12th-century belfry, 13th-century choir, Flamboyant Gothic porch and nave and Renaissance doorway, St Germain l'Auxerrois represents five centuries of religious architecture. One of the most striking features of the exterior is the carved balustrade above the porch, which continues round the church and the flying buttresses supporting the central bays. Above the porch is a fine rose window. The interior, which has double aisles round the nave and the choir, has suffered greatly from 18th century alterations and poor restoration work in the 19th century. The 18th century transformed the piers into fluted columns and altered the choir arches, whilst in the 19th century the magnificent rood screen, fragments of which are in the Louvre, was destroyed along with much of the stained glass, and the only remains now are the rose and transept windows. In front of the 18th-century wrought-iron choir railings are statues of St Vincent and St Germain and a fine 14th-century Virgin. On the left side of the nave, behind the wooden canopied churchwarden's pew, there is a 15th-century carved wooden triptych and, in the Lady Chapel opposite, a 15th-century Flemish carved altarpiece.

The church served as parish church to the Valois royal family and, in the early hours of the morning of 25 August, 1572, the three silver bells in the belfry rang out to signal the St Bartholomew Massacre of the Huguenots.

Métro: Louvre, Pont Neuf. Buses 21, 67, 69, 72, 74, 76, 81, 85.

St Roch 3F4

Rue St Roch Founded in 1653 by Louis XIV, this Baroque church was completed in 1736, partly financed by John Law, the Scots financier. The medallion to the left of the entrance shows the dramatist, Pierre Corneille, who is buried here.

Métro: Tuileries. Buses 69, 72.

Vendôme, Place 3F4

One of the finest examples of Louis XIV urban architecture, the buildings, uniform in style, were designed by Hardouin-Mansart. In the centre of the arcaded square stands the **Vendôme Column**. In the style of Trajan's Column in Rome, it replaced, in 1806, an equestrian statue of Louis XIV. The Place Vendôme houses the most prestigious jewellers in Paris and, at No. 15, the Ritz Hotel, where the dress designer Chanel spent the last years of her life.

Métro: Tuileries. Buses 69, 72.

Sunday on Rue de Rivoli

BASTILLE-RÉPUBLIQUE

The Bastille and the République are linked by one long boulevard which has three changes of name: Boulevard du Temple, Boulevard des Filles du Calvaire and Boulevard Beaumarchais – once collectively known as the Boulevard du Crime, due to the bloodcurdling dramas that took place there and to the undesirable characters frequenting the area. Travelling south from the Place de la République to the Place de la Bastille, the Marais district lies to the west. The Rue du Faubourg du Temple, the Avenue de la République and the Boulevard Voltaire, all radiating from the Place de la République, lead respectively to the park of the Buttes Chaumont, the cemetery of Père Lachaise and the Place de la Nation. Running between the Places de la Bastille and la Nation is the Rue du Faubourg St Antoine which, together with the place de la Bastille, shares close historical links with Le Marais. The Cours de Vincennes on the east side of the Place de la Nation leads to the Château and Bois de Vincennes.

Aligre, Place d'   7K5
Situated near the Rue du Faubourg St Antoine, this is a well-known and very lively food and flea market open every day of the week.
Métro: Ledru Rollin. Buses 76, 86.

Bastille, Place de la   7J5
The Bastille which stood here was built as a fort, on the orders of Charles V, in the 14th century. Its fall to the hands of the mob on 14 July, 1789 marked the beginning of the French Revolution. Throughout the summer and autumn of that year the Bastille was demolished, only the paving stones tracing its outline remain on the ground. Underneath the *place* is an ancient Sephardic (Jews of Spanish, Portuguese or North African descent) cemetery, resting place of many of those who lived in and around the Marais. The **Colonne de Juillet** (July Column) which with the figure of Liberty at its summit is 52m/169ft high, stands in the centre and is dedicated to those who fell during the fighting in the July 1830 Revolution. A new opera house is being built on the east side of the Place.
Métro: Bastille. Buses 20, 29, 65, 69, 76, 86, 87, 91.

Buttes Chaumont, Parc des
see p.112.

Faubourg St Antoine, Rue du   7K5
This long street running between the Places de la Bastille and de la Nation used to be a notable centre of agitation, and its inhabitants played a leading role during the civil war of the *Fronde* (named after a catapult/sling used by street urchins), and during the Revolutions of 1789, 1830 and 1848. Still a popular street, it is one of the few remaining refuges for craftsmen in Paris, and is noted for its furniture and cabinet-making workshops. Many of the houses with their 18th-century façades hide a maze of little alleyways and courtyards where the furniture is made and the wood stocked. The Ecole Boulle, named after the celebrated cabinet-maker, is nearby in the Rue Pierre Bourdan, off the Boulevard Diderot.
Métro: Bastille,   Ledru-Rollin, Faidherbe-Chaligny, Nation. Buses 46, 76, 86.

Lyon, Gare de   7J6
Boulevard Diderot The rail terminus for journeys to the south and south east of France. The well-known restaurant on the first floor, Le Train Bleu, is decorated with frescoes depicting scenes from the route between Paris and Monte Carlo.
Métro: Gare de Lyon and RER. Buses 20, 57, 61, 63, 65, 91.

Ménilmontant, Rue and Place   4K4
Affectionately known as 'Ménilmuche', this area, with its narrow winding streets, stairways, little cottages and gardens, remains one of the last authentic popular quarters although, unfortunately much of the area is being redeveloped. Maurice Chevalier began his career here and Edith Piaf began hers on the pavements of neighbouring Boulevard de Belleville.
Métro: Ménilmontant, St Fargeau. Buses 26, 96.

Nation, Place de la   7L5
Up until the Revolution of 1789, this was called the Place du Trône because of the throne placed there for Louis XIV and his queen Marie-Thérèse on their triumphal entry into Paris in 1660. The revolutionaries changed the name to the Place du Trône Renversé to signify the overthrow of the monarchy. During the Terror, in 1793, over 1000 people were guillotined on the *place*. The bronze group in the centre, the Triumph of the Republic, is by Dalou.
Métro: Nation, RER. Buses 56, 86.

Père Lachaise, Cimetière du   7K4
Boulevard de Ménilmontant The largest and most fashionable cemetery in Paris took its name from Louis XIV's confessor. Crowds gather here every year to place chrysanthemums in pots on tombs on All

Honoré de Balzac

Edith Piaf

Frédéric Chopin

Saints' Day (1 November). The names of celebrities from all walks of life buried here are too numerous to list, but they include Balzac, Chopin, Modigliani, Edith Piaf and Oscar Wilde. It was in this cemetery that the last rebels of the Commune of 1871 were lined up against the north-east wall and shot. The wall is now named Le Mur des Fédérés.
Métro: Père Lachaise. Buses 61, 69, 76.

Picpus, Cimetière de   7L6
35 Rue de Picpus Burial ground of many of the victims of the Revolution and their descendants. The writer and diplomat Chateaubriand, and La Fayette, soldier and statesman, are buried here.
Métro: Picpus. Buses 29, 62, 56.

Quinze-Vingts, Hôpital des   7K5
28 Rue de Charenton An asylum for the blind founded in the 12th century by St Louis, this is now an important eye hospital. The buildings were used in the 18th century as a barracks to house the famous company of Black Musketeers whose name derived from the colour of their horses.
Métro: Bastille, Ledru-Rollin. Buses 29, 61, 76

République, Place de la   4J4
This was once called the Place du Château d'Eau because of a water tower, made up of three separate reservoirs superimposed on each other and surmounted by a fountain,

which stood there until 1867 when the square was enlarged by Baron Haussmann. It is now a very busy thoroughfare for traffic east and west. The Statue to the Republic on the square is by Morice and stands on a base with bas-reliefs depicting events in the history of the Third Republic from 1871 to 1880.
Métro: République. Buses 20, 54, 56, 65, 75.

St Louis, Hôpital de   4J4
Rue Bichat Founded in 1606 by Henri IV after the great plague of that year, the buildings of pink brick and stone are very similar in style to those on the Place des Vosges (p. 95).
Métro: Goncourt, Jacques Bonsergent. Buses 46, 54, 75.

St Marguerite   7K5
Rue St Bernard An early 17th-century church with 18th-century additions. Behind the high altar there is a fine Pietà by Girardon. According to some historians, Louis XVII may have been buried here after his imprisonment with his father in the Donjon du Temple in the Marais.
Métro: Faideherbe-Chaligny. Buses 76, 86.

Trogneux, Fontaine   7J5
61 Rue du Faubourg St Antoine Standing at the junction with the Rue de Charonne, this charming little fountain was erected in 1710.
Métro: Faideherbe-Chaligny. Buses 61, 86.

BEAUBOURG-HÔTEL DE VILLE

Between the Louvre and the Marais, and bordered by the Seine, this area – part of which was the site of the old central market, Les Halles – offers a striking contrast between ancient and contemporary Paris. Many of the old streets and picturesque alleyways, such as Rue de la Ferronnerie where Henri IV was assassinated in 1610, and the Rue des Lombards, named after the Italian bankers and moneylenders who lived there in the Middle Ages, evoke the city's historic past, whilst the modern national arts and cultural centre, with its steel construction and brightly-coloured exterior pipes, and the glass Forum on the actual site of the old market, both illustrate Paris' determination to remain in the forefront of modern urban development.

Beaubourg, Plateau   6H5

Collective name for the area comprising the old site of Les Halles on one side of the Boulevard de Sébastopol, and the modern Centre Georges Pompidou on the other, plus many surrounding streets which are now pedestrian precincts. Beaubourg was a village outside Paris until Philippe Auguste included it within his ramparts which defined the limits of Paris at the turn of the 13th century. In the centre of the site where Les Halles stood, is the glass Forum, modelled on a Roman forum and surrounded by gardens. Four storeys high, its 16 glass-enclosed 'streets' contain banks, cinemas, restaurants, shops and two theatres. Gardens are planned for the front.

Métro: Halles, Rambuteau. Buses 29, 47, 38.

Billettes, Temple des   6H5

22 Rue des Archives The name 'Billettes' came from the heraldic device sewn on to the habits of the order of the Brothers of Charity who built a monastery on the site in the 14th century. The Carmelites, who succeeded the Brothers of Charity, rebuilt the monastery which was secularized during the Revolution. It finally became a Lutheran Temple in 1812. The medieval cloister, which survived demolition by the Carmelites, in 1756, is the only remaining example of its kind in Paris.

Métro: Hôtel de Ville. Buses 67, 76, 96.

Centre National d'Art et de Culture *or* Centre Georges Pompidou   6H4

Rue Saint Martin This immense modern edifice, admired by some, deplored by others, was built at the instigation of President Georges Pompidou. Inaugurated in 1977, the centre comes under the responsibility of the Ministry of Culture whose Secretary of State nominates the Director every three years. Its objectives are not only to serve as a permanent exhibition centre for modern art, but also to encourage the public to consider art as an everyday factor of modern life, and to exist as a forum for all areas of artistic and technical creativity. The museum includes the following: **The CCI** (Centre for Industrial Creativity) situated on the first floor, with information and exhibitions of modern industrial research and techniques. Reference library on the ground floor, exhibitions on the mezzanine floor. **The BPI** (Public Information Library) a vast general public library situated on the first, second and third floors, (access on the second). The contents of the library are catalogued under author, subject matter and according to general areas of interest. In addition, microfilm of texts which are rare, out of print or not normally on the shelves, and cassettes in more than 40 languages are at the disposal of the public. **IRCAM** (Institute for Research and Coordination Acoustics Music). Situated underground in vast soundproofed specially-built auditoriums and equipped with the latest electronic and recording devices, the IRCAM, headed by Pierre Boulez, is one of the world's most important music research centres. **Musée National d'Art Moderne** Situated on the third and fourth floors of the building, the museum brings together the major works of art of the 20th century. Exhibits come from part of the collection which used to be housed in the Avenue du Président Wilson and from the collection of the National Contemporary Art Centre. In addition, the museum has benefited from several important private donations, including some from the families of Kandinsky, Matisse and the Fondation Maeght. The exhibits start with the Fauvist Movement, which marked a strong departure from the Impressionists, and from there on, the visitor can follow, more or less in chronological order, the evolution of modern art to the present day. The number and diversity of paintings, mobiles and sculptures on display make it impossible to cite more than a few on each floor. **Third Floor** The visit starts with the Cabinet d'Arts Graphiques — drawings, engravings and photographs. Next is the Salon Kandinsky, a reconstruction of the artist's music room (1922). The first rooms of the permanent collection include many examples from the Fauvist and Cubist Movements, important exhibits include Braque's *Le Guéridon et l'Homme à la Guitare;* Picasso's *Nu Couché, Nu Assis* and his *Femme Assisedans un Fauteuil* and *Joueur de Guitare.* In addition, there are works by the German

Expressionist Group, Russian Primitives and Italian Futurists. The Salles (Rooms) Kandinsky contain a number of works by the artist and others, including Chagall. **Fourth Floor** Exhibits include a collection of bronzes and still-lifes by Matisse, and canvases by Dufy, Soutine and Utrillo. The rooms grouped together under the heading 'Les Naïfs' contain works by Picasso, including several of his female portraits, abstracts by Paul Klee and a series of works by Chagall, including the important canvases dedicated to his wife, to Russia and his Clair de Lune. The Surrealist rooms contain works by Max Ernst, Miro, Magritte and Tanguy, and American abstract and pop art is represented in works by Samuel Francis, Jackson Pollock, notably his *The Deep*, Jasper Johns and Andy Warhol **Fifth Floor**. Current exhibitions are held in galleries on this floor.

Métro: Châtelet, Hôtel de Ville, Les Halles, Rambuteau. Buses 29, 38, 47, 48, 67, 69, 72, 75.

Châtelet, Place du   6H5

Named after the gateway and fortress which used to stand there, commanding the Pont au Change, the *place* is now a very busy thoroughfare for traffic and an important junction for the métro and RER lines. The **Théâtre du Châtelet** on the west side has now become the Théâtre Musical de Paris where concerts and light operas are performed.

Métro: Châtelet. Buses 58, 67, 69, 70, 72, 74, 75, 76.

Commerce, Bourse du   6G4

40 Rue du Louvre The centre of the corn, sugar and alcohol trade, this 18th-century circular building is all that remains of the 12 pavilions of the old central market, now established in the southern suburb of Rungis. The Doric column on the south side is all that survives of the Hôtel de la Reine, built here for Marie de Médicis; it was probably part of her astrologer's observatory.

Métro: Louvre. Buses 67, 74, 85.

Hôtel de Ville   6H5

Place de l'Hôtel de Ville It was Etienne Marcel, the powerful Provost of the Merchants, who was responsible for the transfer of the municipal assembly, or 'Parloir des Bourgeois' as it was then called, from the neighbouring Place du Châtelet to the present site, in 1357, when he bought the Maison des Piliers from the town. By the 16th century, the premises had become too small for the Assembly which had grown in numbers and in power and, with the assent of François I, a new

magnificent Town Hall was built. The Hôtel de Ville has played an influential role throughout France's history. Its members supplied the mob with the powder and arms used to storm the Bastille on 14 July, 1789, and it was here that, three days later, Louis XVI was forced to kiss the Tricolore. In 1830, Charles X's reign came to an end after fierce fighting in the *place* and on the Pont d'Arcole. Finally, in 1848, the Provisional Government was established in the buildings and, a few weeks later, the Second Republic was proclaimed. On 24 May, 1871, The Renaissance buildings were burnt down during the Commune. Almost immediately it was decided to reconstruct the Hôtel, as far as possible in the same style, and the buildings, by Ballu and Deperthes, were completed in 1883. Centuries of conflict between the municipality of Paris and the French Government, meant that it was 1977 before the first Mayor of Paris, Jacques Chirac, was elected.

Métro: Hôtel de Ville. Buses 58, 69, 70, 72, 74, 96.

Hôtel de Ville, Place de l'   6H5

Known as the Place du Grève until 1806, one of the squares main functions was as a place of execution, and amongst those who met their death here were Ravaillac, Henri IV's assassin, and the poisoner Madame de Brinvilliers. During the Revolution it was one of the principal execution sites of Paris.

Métro: Hôtel de Ville. Buses 58, 69, 70, 72, 74, 96.

Innocents, Fontaine des   6H4

Square des Innocents Originally, the fountain was set into the wall of the church of the Innocents which stood here. The graveyard was Paris' largest cemetery until 1785 when the graves were dug up and the skeletons removed to the Catacombs (p.105). The fountain, erected by Pierre Lescot, in 1548, and decorated with bas-reliefs by Jean Goujon, now stands on the south side of the square.

Métro: Rambuteau, Châtelet. Buses 38, 47.

Quincampoix, Rue   6H4

Running between the Boulevard de Sébastopol and the Rue Saint Martin, this is one of the oldest streets in Paris, despite the fact that the rococo façades and wrought-iron balconies of the houses date only from the mid 17th century. John Law, the Scots financier, set up his bank here at No. 43, in 1719.

Métro: Halles, Rambuteau. Buses 21, 29, 38, 47, 67, 69.

Centre National d'Art et de Culture (Beaubourg)

Tour St Jacques

Fontaine des Innocents

Hôtel de Ville

Place des Vosges, Le Marais

St Eustache   6G4

2 Rue du Jour Standing on the corner of the Rue Montmartre and the Rue Montorgueil, this is one of the loveliest churches in Paris. It is also one of the largest, stretching 100m/328ft in length, 44m/144ft in breadth, and rising 34m/112ft high. Begun in 1532 it was not consecrated until the mid 17th century. The church is Gothic in concept – the main west door was a classical addition of the 18th century. Above the rose window on the west side is a stag's head with a crucifix between its antlers, recalling the stag seen by Eustace, a Roman general, when out hunting one day. The stag prompted him to change his way of life and he was converted to Christianity.

Inside the plan is based on Notre Dame, with double aisles continuing round the choir. Above the pillars in the aisles are arches and a Renaissance gallery. Several of the chapels are decorated with frescoes and paintings, notably Chapel No. 6, which has an early Rubens, *The Pilgrims of Emmaus*, and Chapel No. 4, which contains Santi di Tito's *Tobias and the Angel*. Above the west door is the 17th-century artist Vouet's *Martyrdom of St Eustace*. In the chancel, the stained glass windows were based on sketches by Philippe de Champaigne. The church has seen the baptisms of many notable Frenchmen, including Molière and Cardinal de Richelieu, and the First Communion of Louis XIV, whose minister Colbert is buried in a tomb, designed by Lebrun, in the first chapel on the north aisle.

St Eustache is also a church with a strong musical tradition: the composer Rameau's tomb is in the second chapel of the south aisle and Berlioz and Liszt created several of their works here. Concerts are given on the magnificent organ and, on Christmas Eve, the choir at Midnight Mass attracts many people.
Métro: Halles, Etienne Marcel. Buses 29, 67, 74.

St Gervais-St Protais   6H5

2 Rue François Miron Standing just behind the Hôtel de Ville, the parish of St Gervais is the oldest on the Right Bank, with a church founded in the 6th century. The present building was begun towards the end of the 15th century and completed in the mid 17th century. The façade by Salomon de Brosse the first example of its kind in Paris, is remarkable for its superimposed Corinthian, Ionic and Doric pillars. Inside, the vaulted nave is Flamboyant, and the high stained glass windows are by Pinaigrier and Chaumet. The stained glass of the fifth and sixth chapels in the south aisle is 15th century

and the seven painted panels depicting the Life of Christ in the third chapel are 17th century. On the left of the transept is a 16th-century Flemish wood painting of the Passion and a Gothic figure of the Virgin and Child. The organ dates from 1601 and was played by François Couperin and other members of his family who succeeded him as organist.
Métro: Hôtel de Ville. Buses 67, 69, 72, 76, 96.

St Jacques, Tour   6H5

Square St Jacques Standing on the square just north of the Place du Châtelet, the tower is the last surviving remnant of the church of St Jacques-La-Boucherie which was one of the departure points for pilgrims going to the shrine of St James of Compostella in Spain. During the Revolution the church was demolished and the tower used as a shot-tower. In the square of the same name, there is a statue of Pascal, writer and scientist, who verified his barometric experiments, begun in the Auvergne, from the top of the tower.
Métro: Châtelet. Buses 58, 67, 69, 70, 72.

St Merri   6H5

78 Rue Saint-Martin Named after St Médéric who died, in the 7th century, in an oratory on the site, the present church, which was the parish church of the Lombards, is a little gem set in between craftsmen's houses in the picturesque quarter of St Merri. Access to the church is through the 18th-century presbytery doorway at 74 Rue de la Verrerie. Much of the Flamboyant Gothic interior was altered in the 18th century when the rood screen was demolished, the arches rounded and the pillars encased with marble or stuccoed. However, the transept has retained its fine ribbed vaults, some of the original stained glass and the 16th- and 17th- century paintings in the chapels. The bell, dating from 1331, is probably the oldest in Paris.
Métro: Châtelet, Rambuteau. Buses 38, 47, 67, 75.

LE MARAIS

Lying to the east of the Plateau Beaubourg and stretching to the boulevards linking the Place de la Bastille and the République, the Marais is bordered on its south side by the Seine and the Quais de l'Hôtel de Ville, des Célestins and Henri IV. Le Marais means 'marsh' and this low-lying ground often used to be flooded by the Seine. The St Paul Quarter, between the Seine and the Rue St Antoine, was the site of the royal residence built in the 14th century by Charles V and inhabited by French kings until the 16th century. With the creation of the Place Royale in the early 17th century, the Marais became a highly fashionable residential area for the aristocracy and the wealthy, many of whose houses still stand (now being carefully restored). This is an area to visit at leisure. Rich in history, it is well worth taking the time to walk down the narrow streets, stopping to examine the carvings above the window here, or to peer through an open doorway revealing a fine courtyard there.

Amélot de Bisseuil, Hôtel   6H5

47 Rue Vieille du Temple Built in 1655, its door with decorations of masks and allegories, is one of the finest in the Marais. Beaumarchais, the dramatist, lived here while writing the *Marriage of Figaro*, in 1784, supporting himself by means of the traffic of arms to American Independence fighters and, after that had ruined him, an institute for nursing mothers.
Métro: Hôtel de Ville. Buses 29, 75.

Archives Nationales

see Histoire de France p 61.

Arsenal, Bibliothèque de l'

see p.58

Beauvais, Hôtel de   6H5

68 Rue François Miron It was from the balcony of this building, which has a fine interior courtyard and a circular vestibule with Doric columns supporting a cupola, that Anne of Austria and Cardinal Mazarin watched the entry of Louis XIV and his young bride, Marie-Thérèse, into Paris in 1660. And in 1763, Mozart, aged seven, was the guest of the Bavarian Ambassador during his French tour.
Métro: St Paul. Buses 69, 76.

Béthune–Sully, Hôtel de   7J5

62 Rue St Antoine The courtyard and pavilions of this early 17th-century mansion, which was the residence of Sully, Henri IV's minister, are particularly fine examples of the architecture of the period. Part of the building is occupied by the **Caisse Nationale des Monuments Historiques** and exhibitions devoted to Paris and its history are held there.
Métro: Bastille, St Paul. Buses 69, 76.

Brinvilliers, Hôtel de   7J5

12 Rue Charles V A family drama took place in this restored mansion, built in 1620 for Balthazar Gobelins. It was here that his daughter, the Marquise de Brinvilliers, with the assistance of her lover and the compliance of her husband, successively poisoned off her father and

two brothers in order to pay her gambling debts. A highly organized lady, she took care first to try out the doses on the patients of the neighbouring hospital, l'Hôtel Dieu. The case was the subject of consuming interest and crowds, including the famous letter writer, Madame de Sévigné, flocked to witness her execution. The house is now the property of a religious order.
Métro: Sully Morland. Buses, 67, 86, 87.

Carnavalet, Musée see p.59

Guénégaud, Hôtel   7J4

60 Rue des Archives Built by the architect François Mansart between 1648 and 1656, the left wing of the building houses the **Musée de la Chasse et de la Nature**, comprising an important collection of ancient hunting weapons and fire-arms, spears, daggers, knives and animal trophies brought back from hunts in Africa, America and Asia. Open daily 1000–1700 except Tuesdays and public holidays.
Métro: Rambuteau. Buses 29, 75.

Juif, Quartier   7J5

Rues des Rosiers, d'Ecouffes, Ferdinand Duval A Jewish community is known to have existed on the Right Bank of Paris under the Merovingian dynasty, since a document dating from Chilperic's reign, in the 6th century, forbade them to circulate in the streets during Easter. As elsewhere in Europe, the Jews were subject to periodic persecution and it was St Louis who imposed on them the wearing of a discriminatory badge in the form of a wheel, in the 13th century. By the 18th century, however, the community was completely accepted and many of its members served in the Royal Guard and, under Napoleon, in the Imperial Army. The quarter is mainly concentrated around these three streets, and the Rue Ferdinand Duval was known only for a long time as 'Rue des Juiffes'. Many orthodox Jews still inhabit the area and the shops, especially in the Rue des Rosiers, are still signposted in Hebrew and specialize in kosher products.
Métro: Hôtel de Ville. Buses 67, 96.

Lamoignon, Hôtel   7J5

14 Rue Pavée Facing the Musée Carnavalet, this mansion was built for Diane, legitimized daughter of Henri II and Mlle Philippe-Duc. Boileau, the poet and critic, and Madame de Sévigné often visited Monsieur de Lamoignon, President of Parliament, who lived there during the reign of Louis XIV. The building is now the **Bibliothèque Historique de la**

Ville de Paris and contains a particularly rich collection of documents on the Revolution, as well as ancient maps, posters and other manuscripts. The beamed ceiling of the reading room is decorated with paintings reflecting Diane's passion for hunting.
Métro: St Paul. Buses 29, 75, 96.

Notre Dame des Blancs Manteaux   6H5
Rue des Blancs Manteaux Situated near the Rue Vieille du Temple, the interior of this church is notable for its fine wood carvings and, in particular, for the ivory and pewter inlaid Flemish pulpit.
Métro: Hôtel de Ville. Buses 29, 75.

St Louis-St Paul   7J5
99 Rue St Antoine Built for the Jesuits in 1627 by Louis XIII who laid the foundation stone, the interior contains Delacroix's *Christ in the Garden of Olives.* The Mater Dolorosa in the chapel to the left of the high altar is by Pilon (16th century), and the holy water stoups at the entrance were donated to the church by Victor Hugo, in 1842. Extremely fashionable during the reign of Louis XIV, the church was the recipient of gifts in the form of works of art and relics amongst which, one of the most precious was the heart of Louis XIII enclosed in a golden envelope. During the Revolution the treasures were dispersed and Louis XIII's heart, together with those of later members of the royal family, were sold to two painters who ground them up as lubricant for their paints.
Métro: St Paul. Buses 69, 76, 96

Salé, Hôtel de
5 Rue de Thorigny This 17th-century mansion now completely restored, is the home of the Picasso Museum opened in 1985. The house got its name from a French pun on 'salt' (*salé* means salty), because the original owner was also the collector of the salt tax.
Métro: St Sebastian. Buses 20, 65, 96.

Sens, Hôtel de   7H5
Quai des Célestins/Rue de Figuier One of the three largest private medieval residences of Paris, it was, in the 16th century, a notable centre of intrigue under Cardinal Guise during the religious wars. In 1605 it became the residence of Queen Marguerite de Valois. **The Bibliothèque Forney**, entrance in the Rue de Figuier, is an important reference library devoted to the fine arts and industrial techniques.
Métro: Pont Marie, Sully Morland. Buses 67, 86, 87.

Temple, Quartier du   7J5
Rues de Béranger, de Bretagne, de Picardie and du Temple The area enclosed by these four streets was the site of the buildings occupied by the military and religious order of the Templars established in Paris in 1140. Documents relating to the Temple show it to have been more military than religious, since it possessed a fortified keep and was surrounded by ramparts. Extremely wealthy and powerful, the Templars formed a mini-state within the kingdom, until, in 1307, Philippe le Bel brought a trumped-up charge against them which resulted, in 1314, in the burning at the stake of the Grand Master, Jacques de Molay, and the division of the property between the Crown and the Order of Malta. In 1790 the keep became a state prison, replacing the Bastille, amongst whose illustrious prisoners were Louis XIV and his son the Dauphin. Louis was decapitated in 1793 but mystery shrouds the final destiny of the Dauphin – although his death was announced there two years later, many historians believe he was either allowed to escape or died in prison six months after his father and an idiot child was substituted for him.
Métro: Temple, République. Buses 20, 65, 75, 96.

Vosges, Place des   7J5
This remarkable square, built of rose brick and stone, with arcaded buildings whose doors open on to interior courtyards and gardens, has had a long and varied history. Place des Vosges was formerly the site of the Hôtel de Tournelles, where the Duke of Orléans was assassinated in 1407, and Henri II lost his life by being pierced through the eye during a tournament. The present square was built to order of Henri IV according to a plan whereby he was to live on the southern, sunny, side and his Queen opposite. Although he was assassinated two years before the construction was completed in 1612, the 'Place Royale' as it was then called, became the fashionable centre of Paris almost immediately, a position which it held for over 100 years. A number of famous people have lived there, including the churchman Bossuet, Cardinal de Richelieu and Madame de Sévigné, woman of letters, who was born at No. 1 bis. The best-known 19th-century inhabitant is without doubt **Victor Hugo**, whose house at No. 6 is now a museum containing relics and souvenirs; open daily 1000–1740 except Mondays and public holidays. It was while living in the Place des Vosges, in 1930, that Georges Simenon began writing his famous series of novels featuring Maigret.
Métro: St Paul. Buses 69, 76.

Notre Dame

Ile de la Cité

Conciergerie, Clock Tower

Ste Chapelle & gate of Palais de Justice

Pont Royal and Louvre

ÎLE DE LA CITÉ

Joined to the Right and Left Banks on either side by a series of bridges, this island is the 'birthplace' of Paris. The earliest Gallo-Roman settlements were established here around 200 BC and the government headquarters of the Romans and the Merovingian kings were also situated here. Until Charles V fled the island after the revolts of 1358, all the monarchs of France lived and governed the kingdom from the Palais de Justice. A good general view of the Conciergerie, part of the royal palace, can be had from the Quais de la Mégisserie and de Gèsvres on the Right Bank, whilst the Quai de Montebello on the other side of the Seine is a good spot to admire the perspective of the flying buttresses and Notre Dame's central spire. Métro: La Cité. Buses 21, 38, 47, 85, 86, 86, 96.

Conciergerie, La   6G5

1 Quai de l'Horloge One of the most famous prisons of France, the buildings form part of the old royal palace. Of the three pepperpot towers facing the Right Bank, the crenellated west Tour Bonbec is the oldest, the other two having been built during the reign of Philippe le Bel, around 1311. The rectangular Tour de l'Horloge (Clock Tower) on the corner dates from the 14th century, although the dial was restored in the 19th century. Inside, the three Gothic Rooms date from the 14th century: the Salle des Gardes by the entrance, the magnificently vaulted four aisled Salle des Gens d'Armes and the Kitchen with a vast fireplace at each corner. The Conciergerie was the seat of the Tribunal during the Revolution. Poorer prisoners slept on the ground in the bay above the Salle des Gens d'Armes, others were housed in small cells elsewhere according to their means. Before leaving for execution all of them had to pass through the gallery leading to the Salle des Toilettes, where their hair was cut, their collars ripped open and their hands tied behind their backs. **Marie Antoinette's cell**, situated to the right of the Galerie des Prisonniers, also included a chapel which now contains souvenirs, documents and a guillotine blade. Next to her cell is the one where Danton and Robespierre were imprisoned.

Justice, Palais de   6G5

Boulevard du Palais The entrance to the Palais, which is the Law Court of Paris, is through the wrought-iron gates of the Cour de Mai and up the steps leading to the Galerie Marchande and the Salle des Pas Perdus. This hall, formerly the Great Hall of the Palace, was rebuilt in the 17th century and restored after damage by fire during the Commune, in 1871. It is here that barristers, robed in black with white jabots, meet their clients and discuss the last details before their cases are heard in the adjoining court rooms.

Notre Dame de Paris, Cathédrale de   6H5

Place du Parvis de Notre Dame The site of Notre Dame has been the centre of religious worship for 2000 years. A Roman temple dedicated to Jupiter stood on the spot and, in the Middle Ages, there were two cathedrals, St Stephen and Notre Dame, on the island. The decision to give Paris a great cathedral worthy of the capital was taken by the Bishop of Paris, Maurice de Sully, and the foundation stone was laid in 1163. The predecessor of other Gothic masterpieces, such as Beauvais and Chartres, the purity of Notre Dame's architecture has suffered greatly from 17th- and 18th-century modifications and from the ravages of the Revolution when many of the original statues were destroyed and the treasures inside stolen or dispersed. The 19th-century architect, Viollet le Duc, was responsible for carrying out much of the restoration work decided upon after the Concordat between Napoleon and the Pope in 1801. Intimately linked with France's history, it was in this cathedral that Henry IV of England was crowned King of France, in 1438, and that the marriages of Mary Stuart to François II, Henry of Navarre to Marguerite de Valois and (by proxy) Charles I of England to Henrietta Maria took place. Napoleon and Josephine were crowned here in 1801 and, in 1944, the Te Deum celebrating the Liberation of Paris was performed in the presence of Charles de Gaulle.

Exterior Crossing the Place du Parvis de Notre Dame, the three-tiered western façade, with its two great towers, presents an aspect of total harmony. At the base are the three great doors, the Portals of St Anne, The Last Judgement and The Virgin Mary. The Portal of St Anne, on the right, depicts scenes from her life. To the right of the tympanum the kneeling figure is Louis VII and the prelate, Maurice de Sully. The Portal of the Virgin Mary on the left, is devoted to scenes from the Resurrection and Coronation of the Virgin. Both these doors, constructed in the 12th century retain their original hinges. The central door was restored by Viollet le Duc in the 19th century, after 18th-century modifications. On the gallery above the doors, the statues represent the 28 kings of Judah. Above this, the Great Rose window, which is one of the finest examples of its kind, is flanked by arched windows. Finally, the delicately arcaded Great Gallery forms the base for the towers. The great bell of Notre Dame hangs in the South Tower, suspended from oak scaffolding. The Cloister door on the northern side of the Cathedral depicts scenes from the Miracle of Theophilus and has a fine late 13th-century statue of the Virgin Mary on the pier. A little further along on this side is the Porte Rouge, with carvings from the life of St Marcel. The apse, the elegant flying buttresses and the spire of Notre Dame can best be admired from the garden surrounding the east and south sides. The 13th-century South Porch is dedicated to St Stephen.

Interior The best general view is obtained by standing below the great organ at the west end of the nave. Pure Gothic, the arcades of the nave are flanked by double aisles continuing round the choir. The surmounting vaults are supported by cylindrical pillars. Of the three great rose windows the northern one is the best preserved. A 14th-century statue of Notre Dame stands against the south-east pillar of the transept and against the south-west pillar is a 17th-century statue of St Denis, first bishop of Paris. A tablet on this pillar commemorates the dead of the British Empire in the 1914-18 War. The high altar is a 19th-century addition but in front of it Geoffrey Plantagenet was buried in 1196. Behind the altar are statues of Louis XIII and Louis XIV and a Piéta by Nicholas Costou. Most of the chapels in the ambulatory contain 19th-century statues and paintings, but the 15th-century statues of Jean Jouvenal des Ursins and his wife and Pigalle's mausoleum for Count Claude Henri d'Harcourt (1771) can be seen in the arcaded chapel of St Guillaume.

Sainte Chapelle, La   6G5

Within the precincts of the Palais de Justice, to the left of the Cour de Mai, stands this chapel built on the orders of St Louis to house the relics of Christ's Passion given to him by the Emperor of Constantinople in return for paying his debts. It was consecrated in 1248. The low chapel, unfortunately disfigured by re-decoration in the 19th century, was intended for the servants and courtiers, the upper one being reserved for the shrine which was placed in the centre of the apse within a gallery protected by a wooden canopy, and for the king and his family. The red and blue stained glass windows surrounding this upper chapel are the oldest existing in Paris, and show scenes from the Old and New Testaments. Remarkable for their colour and for the vividness with which the scenes are depicted, they also convey an ex-

traordinary impression of light. The rose window, greenish-yellow in tone, portrays scenes from the Apocalypse and is a late 15th-century addition.

ÎLE ST LOUIS

The little Pont St Louis connects this island with Ile de La Cité. Originally, two islands existed here, both the property of the Canons of the Cathedral who rented them out to weavers and laundrywomen. During the reign of Louis XIII, the engineer Marie and his two assistants obtained permission to join up both islands and build on them. One of the conditions was that the island should be linked to the Right Bank by a bridge, named after Marie, placed exactly opposite the Pont de la Tournelle on the other side. Benefiting from its proximity to the Marais, the Ile Saint Louis is remarkable for the number of well-preserved 17th-century houses lining the riverside Quais and in the streets behind.

Métro: Cité, Pont Marie, Sully Morland. Buses 24, 67.

Adam Mikiewitz, Musée   6H5

6 Quai d'Orléans The museum contains souvenirs of the poet Mikiewitz and Chopin (including his death mask), and also houses an important Polish library.

Lambert, Hôtel   7H5

Quai d'Anjou (entrance 2 Rue St-Louis-en-l'Ile) Designed by Le Vau, Voltaire lived here for a short while and Chopin was entertained in the house by the Czartoryski family, whose descendants still own the building. (Not open to the public.)

Lauzun, Hôtel de   7H5

17 Quai d'Anjou Magnificently decorated inside with gilt panelling, painted ceilings and fine tapestries, this was the centre of Baudelaire's and Theophile Gautier's Hashish Eaters' Club. (Permission to visit obtained from the Syndic du Conseil de Paris, Hôtel de Ville.)

Richelieu, Hôtel du Duc de   6H5

16 Quai de Béthune This privately-owned house was once the property of the Duc de Richelieu, great-nephew of the Cardinal, and, according to legend, great lover despite his small toad-like appearance.

St Louis-en-l'Ile   6H5

19 Rue St Louis-en-L'Ile Notable for its curious iron clock and open-work spire, this 17th-century church, Jesuit in style, is richly decorated inside with marble and gilt work.

AUTEUIL & PASSY

The 16th *arrondissement*, which includes the old villages of Auteuil and Passy, stretches crescent-wise from the Etoile, via the Avenue de la Grande Armée, along the Bois de Boulogne to the Porte de Saint Cloud. From there, it is bordered on its south side by the Seine to the Place de l'Alma, where the Avenue Marceau, running up to the Etoile, forms its eastern limit. This is one of the smartest residential areas, and from the visitor's point of view the main attractions are the museums on or near the Place du Trocadéro and the impressive view of the Eiffel Tower and the Champ de Mars obtained from the terrace and gardens of the Palais de Chaillot.

Auteuil   5B5

The charm of Auteuil lies in the small groups of cottages and gardens, known as 'Villas' or 'Hameau', often hidden from the streets by wrought-iron gates which one comes across unexpectedly. Two of the best known are the Villa Montmorency, behind the Boulevard Montmorency, where the literary Goncourt Brothers lived at 52 Avenue des Sycomores, and the Villa and Hameau Boileau between the Boulevard Exelmans and the Rue d'Auteuil. Others less well known include the Villa de la Réunion, off the Rue Chardon Lagache, and a group of three tucked away between the Rue Claude Lorraine and the Rue Parent de Rosan – the Villas Cheysson, Dietz-Morin and Emile Meyer. Auteuil was once a spa and during the Revolution many members of the nobility were hidden here disguised as patients or staff. Several illustrious inhabitants lived here, amongst whom were the poet and critic, Boileau, who lived at No. 26 of the street bearing his name, and Molière, who rented a house at 2 Rue d'Auteuil.
Métro: Porte d'Auteuil, Chardon Lagache, Eglise d'Auteuil. Buses 72, 52, PC, 62.

Auteuil, Cimetière de   5B6

Situated at the west end of the Rue Claude Lorraine and lying behind the Rue Michel Ange, this private cemetery includes the graves of the composer Gounod and the philosopher Helvetius.
Métro: Exelmans. Bus 62.

Chaillot, Palais de see Cinéma

p. 60, Homme p. 61, Marine p. 64, Monuments Français p. 64.

Congrès, Palais des   2C3

Place de la Porte Maillot Officially, Centre International de Paris (CIP), this is Paris' largest conference centre, with an audi-torium equipped for simultaneous translation in six languages. The building holds the offices of the Orchestre de Paris and, at ground level and in the basement, restaurants, shops and the Air France Terminal for departures to the Charles de Gaulle airport at Roissy. From the top of the 42-storey hotel above the Palais there is a panoramic view of Paris.
Métro: Porte Maillot. Buses 73, 82, PC.

Foch, Avenue   2C4

This wide tree-lined avenue, laid out by Baron Haussmann in the 19th century, used to be called the Avenue du Bois, because it was the fashionable route for carriages driving out to the Bois de Boulogne. No. 59 is a small museum devoted to Armenian works of art and jewellery.
Métro: Etoile, Porte Dauphine. Buses 82, PC.

Galliéra, Musée see p.61

Guimet, Musée see p.61

Passy   5C5

The best way to explore this area, which has retained its village-like atmosphere, is to take the Avenue Paul Doumer which starts at the Place du Trocadéro and runs up to the busy commercial Rue de Passy. On the left of the Avenue is the Rue Franklin where, at No. 8, the apartment of the statesman Clemenceau is now a museum containing souvenirs of his life. South of the Rue de Passy, at 2 Rue Singer, which runs between the Rue Raynouard and the Rue des Vignes, Benjamin Franklin put up the first lightning conductor in France on the house in which he lived for a short period.
Métro: Trocadéro, Muette, Passy. Buses 22, 32, 52.

Radio, Maison de la (ORTF)   5C5

116 Avenue du Président Kennedy Standing at the foot of the Rue de Boulainvilliers, facing the Seine, this circular building housed both France's Radio and Television centres until reorganization in 1974. Concerts are given on the ground floor.
Métro: Muette, Passy. Buses 70, 72.

Raynouard, Rue   5C5

The most famous inhabitant of this street was Balzac whose house at No. 47, where he lived from 1840-7, is now a museum containing relics, drawings and souvenirs.
Métro: Passy. Buses 70, 72.

Tokyo, Musée du Palais de

see Museums and Galleries.

LEFT BANK

INVALIDES-TOUR EIFFEL

In view of its traditions, this area could well be called Military Paris. Monuments and museums here mainly reflect this aspect, and several of the surrounding streets are named after distinguished soldiers and military architects. It is best approached from the Right Bank, either from the Pont Alexandre III leading to Les Invalides, or from the Pont d'Iéna at the bottom of the gardens and steps of the Palais de Chaillot opposite the Eiffel Tower and the Champ de Mars. The area also takes in the Faubourg St Germain – an extremely fashionable residential quarter inhabited by the aristocracy in the 18th and 19th centuries – lying to the north and the south of the Boulevard St Germain. On the Rue de Grenelle and the Rue de Varenne, many embassies now occupy these former aristocratic homes and the Prime Minister's offical residence is at 57 Rue de Varenne.

Bourbon, Palais   6E4

128 Rue de l'Université The seat of the Assemblée Nationale or French Parliament. It was originally the property of the Duchesse de Bourbon, daughter of Louis XIV and Madame de Montespan, who built it in 1727 as a residence with gardens leading down to the Seine. In 1807 Napoleon ordered that the façade facing the river be rebuilt in Greek style to harmonize with La Madeleine on the other side of the Place de la Concorde. The Legislative Assembly established itself in the buildings in 1827 (they are not open to the public without prior written request being made to the Questor's office at 126 Rue de l'Université). Inside, the President of the Assembly faces the deputies from his 'perch' opposite the benches arranged in a semicircle. Many of the decorations in the building are pompous and of little interest, but the library is decorated by Delacroix and also contains Houdon's busts of Voltaire and Diderot.
Métro: Chambre des Députés, Concorde. Buses 24, 63, 73, 83, 84, 94.

Champ de Mars   5D5

Originally a series of market gardens, they were made into a parade ground by Gabriel, architect of the Ecole Militaire, In 1790, in preparation for the Fête de la Fédération commemorating the first anniversary of the Fall of the Bastille, patriotic Parisians turned out spontaneously to help the 12,000 workmen building stands. In 1791 and 1793, when the country was threatened with war, crowds gathered here to enlist in the Revolutionary Armies. Also in 1793, the first hydrogen-filled balloon was launched from the spot. Now one of Paris' best loved open spaces, the Champ de Mars was the site of the first French industrial exhibition in 1798, inaugurated with great pomp by Napoleon, and this became a tradition with the Universal Exhibitions held there between 1867 and 1937.
Métro: Ecole Militaire, Trocadéro. Buses 42, 69, 80, 82.

Dôme, Eglise du   6E5

Avenue de Tourville Although this can be reached via the Corridor de Nimes, after visiting the Church of St Louis in the Invalides, the main entrance faces the Place Vauban, named after the military engineer. Designed by Hardouin-Mansart in 1675 to complete the Invalides, and finished by Robert de Cotte in 1735, the Dôme ranks, along with St Paul's Cathedral in London and St Peter's of Rome, as one of the three most remarkable in Europe. The base of the cupola, which has arched windows, is decorated with consoles. The gilded roof is lead and decorated with trophies, garlands and helmets, each of which conceals a window illuminating the interior. A lantern and a spire complete the construction.

Inside, the cupola is painted with scenes depicting the victorious St Louis presenting the sword with which he conquered the Arabs to Christ. Below are medallions of the Kings of France and the 12 Apostles and, at the base, the four Evangelists, Matthew, Mark, Luke and John. **Napoleon's body**, placed in six coffins, each inside the other, lies in a tomb of red porphyry on a green pedestal, standing in an open crypt surrounded by a circular gallery. Below, and just in front of a statue of Napoleon is the tomb of L'Aiglon, Napoleon's only son, King of Rome who died of consumption at the age of 21. In 1940 his remains were transferred by the Germans from the Habsburg crypt in Vienna and placed in the church exactly one century after his father had been laid to rest here. The tombs of Jerome and Joseph Bonaparte, Vauban and the Marshals Foch and Lyautey are in surrounding chapels.
Métro: Invalides, Latour-Maubourg. Buses 49, 69, 82, 92.

Ecole Militaire   5D5

Avenue de la Motte Picquet The school was built at the instigation of Madame de Pompadour, Louis XV's mistress, in order to provide a military education for poorer members of the nobility. Architecturally, the Central Pavilion with its eight Corinthian columns, carved pediment and quadrangular dome is the most interesting. The main courtyard and the rear façade of the Central Pavilion is best viewed from the Place Fontenoy and across the Champ de Mars. Amongst the students here was Napoleon aged 15, who was also confirmed in the chapel which is open to the public on Sundays. The school is now a Staff College and the Higher School of National Defence and Army Ordnance.

Métro: Ecole Militaire, La Motte Picquet. Buses 28, 49, 80, 82.

Eiffel, Tour 5D5

Champ de Mars Without doubt the best known of all France's monuments, the tower has been reproduced in countless souvenirs and publications and has inspired numerous artists including Pissarro, Dufy and Seurat. Its construction was the subject of public outcry and a petition against it was signed by such celebrities as the composer Gounod and the writers François Coppée and Guy de Maupassant. Built between 1887 and 1889, it was only intended to stand for some 20 years but was spared demolition because of its use in radio telegraphy. Since 1918 it has been used as a transmitter, first for radio and, since 1957, for television. Originally 300m/984ft high, the television transmitters added to its summit in recent years have brought the height to a total of 320m/1051ft above ground level. The tower, which is built on the same mechanical principles as Eiffel's other masterpiece, the Viaduct at Garabit in the Auvergne, is composed of 12,000 pieces of metal joined together by 2½ million rivets. The four feet at the base are supported by sunken piers, and the whole weighs 7000 tons. The views from the three platforms, which can be reached either by elevator or by climbing 1652 steps, are remarkable, especially about an hour before sunset, and on a clear day can extend to over 64km/40mi. The third platform, however, is closed from mid-November to mid-March and is not recommended on a windy day.

Métro: Trocadéro, Bir-Hakeim, Ecole Militaire. Buses 42, 69, 80, 82, 87.

Invalides, Esplanade des 6E5

Facing the Pont Alexandre III, the Esplanade was laid out early in the 18th century by Robert de Cotte. From the north side, by the Quai d'Orsay and the Air France Terminal, it affords an impressive vista of the perspective of the façade of the main buildings of Les Invalides with the church of the Dôme behind. Beside the Place des Invalides there is a garden with a dry moat and ramparts lined with bronze cannons and pieces of captured artillery.

Métro: Invalides. Buses 28, 49, 63, 83.

Invalides, Hôtel des 6E5

In 1674 Louis XIV signed a 'perpetual and irrevocable' edict decreeing that a refuge and hospital should be built for disabled soldiers. The idea was not new, since Louis XIII and Henri IV before him had set aside the Château de Bicêtre for this purpose, but Louis XIV must be given the credit for endowing soldiers with an establishment worthy of their past service – it also perpetuated his own name.

Begun in 1671, according to the design of Liberal-Bruant, the buildings were finished five years later. The façade, facing the Esplanade, can only be described as majestic, both in harmony of design and proportion. It is 210m/230yd long, and the magnificent doorway in the centre is surmounted by an equestrian statue of Louis XIV with the figures of Justice and Prudence on either side, and bas-reliefs.

Inside, the buildings facing the cobbled Cour d'Honneur are arcaded and the slate roofs are surmounted at each corner by horses trampling on the attributes of war. Some of the buildings are still inhabited by disabled servicemen but the main East and West Pavilions of the Cour d'Honneur house three museums. Opposite the main entrance to the courtyard is the Chapel, now the **Church of St Louis des Invalides**, also designed by Liberal-Bruant. The cold, austere interior is decorated with captured flags from enemy armies. The adjoining Napoleon Chapel contains the funeral relics of the Emperor including the pall covering his coffin and the gun carriage which bore his body from his house, Longwood, to St Helena.

Métro: Invalides, Latour-Maubourg, Varenne. Buses 28, 49, 63, 82, 87, 92.

Invalides: Musée de l'Armée 6E5

Open daily 1000–1800 from 1 April–30 Sept, closed at 1700 from 1 Oct–31 March. Housed in the East and West Pavilions on either side of the Cour d'Honneur, the museum was formed from the fusion, in 1905, of the Musée de l'Armée with the Musée de l'Artillerie, and since then it has received a number of important donations. The result is without doubt one of the world's largest and richest military museums. The rooms are divided into two main themes, the first follows the evolution and development of military history from prehistoric times to the end of the Second World War, and the second theme is based on souvenirs of French military history.

Invalides, Eglise du Dôme

Palais Bourbon (National Assembly)

Maine-Montparnasse complex

Tour Eiffel

Jardins du Luxembourg

West Pavilion Among the most interesting exhibits is a series of beautifully chased rapiers and swords, often with embossed pommels, displayed in the Salle (Room) Henri IV. You can see there a sword whose pommel bears the arms of Eleanor of Aquitaine, another belonging to the Connétable de France, a high-ranking dignitary, embossed with a fleur-de-lys and a sword belonging to François I, inlaid with gold and enamel, more a work of art than weapon. In showcase 40 is Henri II's armour bearing the monogram H entwined with a C (Catherine de Médicis) wife, and a D (Diane de Poitiers) mistress. Salle Pauilhac contains an interesting collection of offensive and defensive arms dating from the 13th to the 17th centuries, including firearms belonging to Louis XIII and the Emperor Charles V, also included here is the first known arquebus which belonged to Philippe V of Spain. Salle Louis XIII includes a battle-axe belonging to Edward III of England and several coats of armour belonging to Louis XIII. The Salle Louvois has on display a series of ceremonial arms and arms which were given as reward for distinguished service under the Directory, the Consulate and Napoleonic eras. Exhibits from China, Japan and Asia are displayed in the Salle Orientale. Documents, models, maps and uniforms from the two World Wars are exhibited on the second floor.

East Pavilion Flags and ensigns, including some captured from the enemy, dating from the Revolution to present times are displayed on the ground floor in the Vestibule and the Salle Turenne. On the same floor, the Salle Vauban exhibits the history of the French cavalry from 1800 to 1940. The second floor is mainly devoted to souvenirs, paintings and engravings which evoke the glorious periods of French history. In the Salle Louis XIV is the cannon ball which killed Marshal Turenne, in 1694, and a small gilded cannon given to Louis XIV when the Franche Compté (a region of E. France) became part of France in 1678. The Salle Lafayette and the Salle Rochambeau contain souvenirs and relics of those two Generals. Two rooms, the Salle de Boulogne and the Corridor de Tarascon contain momentoes of Napoleon, and include his famous grey overcoat, his tent and furniture, and the flag which flew at Fontainebleau in 1814 on his abdication. His last years on St Helena are represented in relics in the Grande Galerie de la Restauration.

Invalides: Musée de l'Ordre de la Libération   6E5
Open Mon–Sat 1400–1700; closed August and public holidays. *51 bis Boulevard de Latour-Maubourg* Occupying the Pavilion of Les Invalides built by Robert de Cotte in 1747 for army officers, the museum – originally created at Brazzaville in the Congo by General de Gaulle in honour of those whose contribution to the Liberation of France had been of outstanding importance – has since expanded and exhibits cover French Resistance inside and outside France, the German Occupation and the deportation of French Jews and Resistance Fighters.
Métro: Latour-Maubourg, Les Invalides. Buses 28, 49, 63, 69, 82, 83, 92.

Invalides: Musée des Plans-Reliefs   6E5
Open 1000–1215 and 1400–1800 from 1 Apr–30 Sept (1645, 1 Oct–31 Mar); closed Sunday mornings, Tuesdays, and public holidays. Situated on the first floor of the East Pavilion, the museum contains exhibits of considerable historical and topographical interest. Maps, models and plans of French fortifications and military strongholds are on display and include the models of Strasbourg and Neuf-Brisach (by Vauban), Briançon, Marseille, Mont St Michel and Toul.
Métro: Les Invalides. Buses 28, 49, 63, 82, 92.

Matignon, Hôtel   6F5
57 Rue de Varenne Built in 1721, and at one time the property of the statesman Talleyrand, this is the official residence of the Prime Minister of France. Not open.
Métro: Invalides, Varenne. Buses 63, 69.

Quai d'Orsay   6E4
This quay, which runs from the Pont de l'Alma to the Pont de la Concorde, has given its name to the Ministry of Foreign Affairs, situated at No. 37.
Métro: Invalides, Concorde, Chambre des Députés. Buses 24, 63, 73.

Quatre Saisons, Fontaine des   6F5
Rue de Grenelle, near Boulevard Raspail This fountain was erected in 1745 to supply water to the local inhabitants whose only reserves up until that date had been what could be drawn directly from the Seine. It is decorated with statues representing the City of Paris (seated) contemplating the Seine and Marne rivers, and the Four Seasons.
Métro: Rue du Bac. Buses 63, 83, 84, 94.

UNESCO   5E5
Place de Fontenoy (United Nations Educational, Scientific and Cultural Organization) Inaugurated in 1958, these

modern buildings in the form of a Y are decorated inside with works by Calder, Miro, Henry Moore and Picasso.
Métro: Ségur. Buses 49, 87.

Village Suisse 5D5

A group of antique and curio shops clustered together in the streets behind the junction of Avenue de la Motte Picquet and Avenue de Suffren. They are open from Thursdays to Mondays.
Métro: Ecole Militaire, La Motte Picquet. Buses 80, 82.

MONTPARNASSE-JARDIN DES PLANTES

It could be said that Montparnasse lives on its past, for, while possessing few monuments of note, its position as an artistic and literary centre in the early 20th century still makes it an area of interest for visitors. Chagall, Gauguin, Modigliani and Whistler lived and worked in and around Montparnasse, and writers, poets and musicians, such as Jean Cocteau, Ernest Hemingway, Henry Miller and Stravinsky frequented the Dome, Coupole, Rotonde and Select cafés on the Boulevard du Montparnasse in the 1920s and 1930s. At the east end of the Boulevard the Observatoire de Paris lies to the right, and the ancient abbey of Val de Grâce stands on the Rue St Jacques just by the Boulevard du Port Royal named after the 17th-century Abbaye du Port Royal, associated with the philosopher Pascal and the Jansenist Movement. At the junction of this Boulevard with the Boulevard Arago, the Avenue des Gobelins leads south to the busy Place d'Italie. At 42 Avenue des Gobelins, the famous tapestry works can be visited during the week. Finally, walking in the direction of the Seine, along the Rue Censier and the Rue Buffon, you come to the Jardin des Plantes and the Quai St Bernard where the Pont de Sully leads across the eastern tip of the Ile St Louis to the Marais on the Right Bank.

Arènes de Lutèce 6H6

Rue des Arènes Situated off the Rue Linné and discovered as late as 1870, the exact date of this Gallo-Roman arena, built for games and gladiatorial contests, is unknown. Together with the Thermes de Cluny in the Latin Quarter, it is the last vestige of Roman civilization left in Paris.
Métro: Cardinal Lemoine, Jussieu. Buses 67, 89.

Catacombes, Les 6F6

Place Denfert-Rochereau Formed in 1785 out of a series of disused quarries dating from Roman times, the Catacombs stretch underground from Montparnasse to the suburbs of Monstouris and Montrouge. Several million skeletons dug up from cemeteries all over Paris, including the graveyard of the Innocents, were transported here. During the Reign of Terror (1793-4), the bodies of many of those guillotined were added to the macabre collection, and during the German Occupation of the Second World War, the Catacombs were used as a centre by the Resistance. Visits Tuesday to Friday 1400 —1600 hours, Saturdays and Sundays 0900—1100 hours and 1400—1600 hours. Take a torch.
Métro: Denfert-Rochereau. Buses 38, 68.

Contrescarpe, Place de la 6H6

The student tradition of this little *place*, situated at the north end of the Rue Mouffetard, near the Rue Thouin, is still prevalent today. During the Middle Ages, impecunious students lived and studied in the colleges in neighbouring streets. The tablet at No. 1 commemorates the Cabaret de la Pomme de Pin, rendered famous by Rabelais in the 16th century.
Métro: Monge. Bus 47.

Gobelins, Manufacture des 6H6

42 Avenue des Gobelins The name Gobelins came from the 15th-century scarlet-dyer Jean Gobelins, who set up his workshops on the banks of the River Bièvre, now flowing under the present buildings. However, it was Louis XIV's minister Colbert, who created the Royal Factory of Tapestry and Carpet Weavers by grouping together the various tapestry and carpet weavers established throughout Paris and the suburbs. In the early 19th century the Savonnerie carpet weavers were transferred to the Avenue des Gobelins and, after the Second World War, the Beauvais workshops were also brought here. Some of the original buildings still exist, although the main building of the factory is modern. All the weaving is done on looms according to the methods used in the 17th century, and several of the looms date from that period. Working on the reverse side of the tapestry, the weaver copies the design behind him which is reflected in a mirror. The work is long and intricate and output varies between .85 sq m/1 sq yd and 6.7 sq m/8 sq yd per year. In the former Chapel hang two specially woven tapestries inspired by sketches of Raphael. Visits of the exhibition rooms, 1400—1600; guided visits of the workshops Tuesdays, Wednesdays and Thursdays 1400—1600. (Last visit begins 1530.)
Métro: Gobelins. Buses 27, 47, 83.

Maine-Montparnasse   6F6

This modern complex, situated at the junction of the Boulevard Montparnasse and the Avenue du Maine, opposite the Rue de Rennes, comprises the 58-storey office block, now one of the landmarks of Paris, as well as a commercial centre, restaurants and a sports centre with a swimming pool and squash court. Behind, separated by a paved precinct, is the rebuilt Gare de Montparnasse from which trains depart to Brittany and Western France.
Métro: Montparnasse-Bienvenue. Buses 89, 91, 92, 94, 95, 96.

Mosquée, La   6H6

Place du Puits-de-l'Ermite Next to the Jardin des Plantes, on the south-west side, stands the Mosque of the Franco-Muslim Institute, tiled in green and complete with minaret. The interior is richly decorated with bronzes, cedar wood and Persian carpets. The patio was inspired by the Alhambra in Granada, Spain.
Métro: Monge. Buses 67, 89.

Mouffetard, Rue   6H6

A populous, narrow winding street with a lively market which is open every day. Many old houses are being restored and converted into expensive apartments.
Métro: Monge, Censier-Daubenton. Bus 47.

l'Observatoire   6F6

61 Avenue de l'Observatoire Founded by Colbert in the reign of Lous XIV, each side of the Observatory faces a cardinal point of the compass. It is the headquarters of the Bureau International de l'Heure (International Time Bureau), and there is a talking clock (tel: 3699) installed in the deep cellars. The Observatory also contains an interesting collection of astronomical and telescopic instruments.
Métro: Port Royal; RER Port Royal line B2/B4 (Châtelet direction Denfert Rochereau). Buses 38, 83, 91.

Plantes, Jardin des   7H6

Place Valhubert Originally a royal garden of medicinal herbs founded by Louis XIII's physician, Guy de la Brosse, in 1626, the Jardin was opened to the public 24 years later. Expansion to their present size and the importance and variety of the collections of alpine, herbaceous and wild plants were largely due to the naturalist Buffon who was superintendent of the gardens for 49 years, from 1739 until his death in 1788. It was he who created the maze, the museum galleries and the amphitheatre, encouraged and developed the botanical collection, and still found the time to write his monumental Encyclopedia of Natural History and correspond with scientists and naturalists throughout France and abroad. During the Revolution, under the supervision of Bernardin de Saint Pierre, the collection of wild animals established at Versailles was transferred to Paris, enabling the people to see exotic animals for the first time. Unfortunately, during the Siege of Paris in the Franco-Prussian War a century later, many of their descendants found their way into the kitchens of the starving Parisians.

Entering from the Place Valhubert on the south-east side, galleries devoted to palaeontology, botany, palaeobotany, mineralogy and zoology are on the left. Continue past the galleries and you come to the maze and the hillock which bears the famous cedar of Lebanon planted by the botanist Jussieu, in 1734. According to legend, he brought it back all the way from Syria, kept in his hat and moistened from his water ration, but in reality, he was given it by the authorities at Kew Gardens and it only crossed the Channel. In the centre of the gardens are the Jardin d'Hiver (Winter Garden) containing a collection of tropical plants, and the Alpine Garden with rock and alpine plants. The Botanical Garden which is the largest, situated between the Allée Buffon and the Allées Alfred Lacroix and Centrale, has a magnificent collection of wild and herbaceous plants. The aquarium, aviary, menagerie and vivarium are grouped together on the west side. In addition there are separate enclosures for lions and tigers, elephants and monkeys.

The Muséum National d'Histoire Naturelle, which comprises the galleries on the east side of the gardens, is the work of Buffon and his assistant Daubenton, whose tomb is in the maze. Their work in expanding the scientific and research activities of the Jardin des Plantes was acknowledged by the Convention in 1793 when the national natural history museum was established and 12 chairs created to continue Buffon's teaching. Many scientists of international repute have either studied or taught at the museum which is still acclaimed today. The library contains a particularly fine collection of ancient botanical and zoological manuscripts.
Métro: Gare d'Orleans Austerlitz, Jussieu, Monge. Buses 61, 65, 89.

St Médard   6H6

Rue Daubenton This pretty little church, begun in the 15th century, was the object of persecution, first by the Huguenots and then by Louis XV. He closed its cemetery due to the hysterical excesses of the Jansenists who believed that the tomb of the Abbé Paris, buried there in 1727, had the property of curing diseases miracul-

ously. Behind the pulpit is a fine 16th-century triptych and, to the right of the choir in the second chapel, the Christ is attributed to Philippe de Champaigne. The weather on St Médard's day (8 June) is said to set the pattern for the whole summer, as with St Swithin's Day in England.
Métro: Censier-Daubenton. Buses 47, 67, 89.

Salpêtrière, La 7J6
47 Boulevard de l'Hôpital Founded by Louis XIV as a home for the poor and aged, the buildings are comparable in style with those of Les Invalides and date from the same period. **The Church of St Louis** in the centre was designed by Liberal-Bruant, in 1670. Today, La Salpêtrière forms part of an important hospital group with La Pitié, which is next to it.
Métro: St Marcel. Buses 57, 91.

Schola Cantorum 8G6
269 Rue St Jacques The buildings of this singing school originally belonged to the English Benedictine Order of St Edmund, which founded a monastery on the site in 1640. James II of England, his son the Duke of Berwick and daughter Louisa Maria-Theresa were buried here and, during the Revolution, their bodies are thought to have been hidden by the monks in neighbouring catacombs. The school, which was founded in 1894 by pupils of the composer César Franck, can be visited on request.
Métro: Port Royal; RER Port Royal line B2/B4 (Châtelet direction Denfert Rochereau). Buses 83, 91.

Sciences de Paris, Faculté des 6H6
7 and 9 Quai St Bernard Formerly situated in the Sorbonne, the Scientific Universities VI and VII were installed in specially constructed modern buildings as the result of the 1968 University Reform. The site was once occupied by the ancient Abbaye de St Victor, disbanded in 1790, whose residents included Peter Abélard and Thomas Becket. It was also the site of wine warehouses, known as Halle Aux Vins, before the university stood there.
Métro: Jussieu. Buses 24, 63, 67, 86, 89.

Val de Grâce 8G6
277 Rue St Jacques During the 17th century the Quartier de Val de Grâce, situated in the south west of the 5th *arrondissement*, was a thriving centre of female religious orders. Many were founded by Anne of Austria, and the Benedictine Order which she founded on the present site was only one of many. Although they were disbanded during the Revolution, witness to their existence

remains in the names of streets such as the Rue des Feuillantines and Rue des Urselines. The Church of Val de Grâce was built by Anne in thanksgiving for the birth of Louis XIV after 23 years of childless marriage.

The design of the church was entrusted to François Mansart, who was succeeded as architect by Lemercier and finally by Le Muet and Le Duc who completed the construction in 1667. The façade, which is two-tiered with triangular pediments, is Jesuit in style. Above is the Dome, built by Le Duc. Inside, the cupola is decorated with paintings by Mignard. The high altar, with its twisted marble columns, and the ornate vaulted nave clearly denote the baroque inspiration of the period. The sculptures are by the Anguier brothers and Pierre Sarazin and, in the Chapel of the Sacrament, hangs a painting attributed to Philippe de Champaigne. Through the porch on the right is the double-arcaded cloister of the abbey.

The abbey buildings which were enlarged after the birth of Louis XIV, fortunately remained intact during the Revolution which merely left them unoccupied until 1793, when they were turned into a military hospital at the instigation of Napoleon. In 1852 The Val de Grâce became a medical school conferring degrees on military doctors and pharmacists. In the church courtyard is a statue by David d'Angers of Larrey, Napoleon's military surgeon.
Métro: Port Royal; RER, Port Royal line B2/B4 (Châtelet direction Denfert Rochereau). Buses 21, 27, 83, 91.

QUARTIER LATIN 1 & 2

Despite the reforms of 1968 which divided the University of Paris into 13 autonomous universities, the Latin Quarter still remains the student centre of Paris and many of the higher educational institutions, including several universities and the Grandes Ecoles (independent highly-specialized colleges) are situated in the area. The Latin Quarter is large and contains much to see, and a visit is best divided into two. The first section, stretching from the Place St Sulpice to the Seine, takes in the northern end of the Jardins du Luxembourg and the Palais, the Odéon and, after crossing the Boulevard St Germain, St Germain des Prés and the maze of streets leading to the Quais de Conti and Grands Augustins. The second section takes in the Boulevard St Michel, the Quartiers St Séverin and Maubert, the Sorbonne and the north side of the Luxembourg Gardens.

St Séverin

St Germain des Prés

Panthéon

St Julien-le-Pauvre

1 ST GERMAIN DES PRÉS

Brasserie Lipp   6G5

151 Boulevard St Germain Almost opposite the Café des Deux Magots, this café and restaurant, a favourite place for lunch with artists, journalists, politicians and writers, was a major centre of Resistance during the German Occupation.
Métro: St Germain des Prés. Buses 39, 48, 63, 86, 87.

France, Institut de   6G5

23 Quai de Conti Composed of five academies of elected members, the literary **Académie Française** is the oldest and best known. Founded in 1635 by Cardinal Richelieu and restricted to 40 members known as 'The Immortals', its task is to edit and continually update the official dictionary of the French language. Former members include Victor Hugo and André Maurois, but the list of those whose candidature was refused is far more impressive, since it includes Balzac, Descartes, Molière, Proust and Zola. An election to the Académie Française is always a notable event, beginning with the candidate's campaign and ending with his reception under the Dome in the Chamber. Here, the new member delivers his maiden speech, by tradition devoted to the merits of the deceased member whose armchair he now occupies. Up to 1980, only males were elected, but in March of that year, the writer Marguerite Yourcenar became the first woman member.
Métro: Pont Neuf (Right Bank), St Germain des Prés. Buses 24, 27, 58, 70.

Furstenberg, Place   6F5

Tucked away between the Rue de l'Abbaye, behind the Church of St Germain des Prés, and the Rue Jacob, this charming little square is associated with **Eugène Delacroix**, whose studio at No. 6 is now a museum. Open 0945–1715 except Tuesdays.
Métro: St Germain des Prés. Buses 86, 87, 63.

Luxembourg, Jardins du   6F5

Lying between the Palais du Luxembourg, the Rue Auguste-Comte and the Boulevard St Michel, these gardens are a great favourite with young people, students and children, especially on Wednesday and Sunday afternoons when Punch and Judy shows are given in the Théâtre des Marionettes on the west side. To the right of the palace is the Fontaine de Médicis, attributed to Salomon de Brosse.

The theme of the central niche depicts the jealous cyclops Polyphemus, waiting to crush Acis and Galatea with a rock.
Métro: Luxembourg. Buses 58, 82, 84, 89.

Luxembourg, Palais du   6F5

15 Boulevard de Vaugirard Occupying the whole of the north side of the Jardins du Luxembourg, the Palais was built for Marie de Médicis and financed by the gold she took from the Bastille where it was stored to pay for future wars. Many of the better paintings have been removed to the Louvre, but the library still contains some fine murals by Delacroix. It is now the Senate, the Upper Chamber of Parliament and can be visited by groups on written request to Secrétariat Général de la Questure du Sénat, 15 Rue de Vaugirard, 75291 Paris Cedex 06.
Métro: Luxembourg, Odéon. Buses 58, 84, 89.

Odéon, Place de l'   6G5

Built on the site of the Hôtel de Condé, the late 18th-century houses of this semicircular *place* are all uniform in style. The Café Voltaire at No. 1, now the **Institute of Benjamin Franklin Studies**, was a famous literary and artistic haunt, popular with the Encyclopedists.
Métro: Odéon. Buses 63, 84, 86, 87.

Odéon, Théâtre de l'   6G5

Opposite the Place de l'Odéon. The ceiling of this theatre, whose official name is Le Théâtre de France, was decorated by André Masson.
Métro: Odéon. Buses 63, 84, 86, 87.

La Procope, Café   6G5

13 Rue de l'Ancienne Comédie. Between Rue Mazarine and Boulevard St Germain. A famous literary café where Voltaire and the Encyclopedists used to meet in the 18th century. Its popularity continued during the Revolution with Bonaparte, Talleyrand and Robespierre among the clientèle. In the 19th century George Sand, Musset and, later on, Verlaine frequented it.
Métro: St Germain des Prés. Buses 24, 27, 58, 70, 96.

St Germain des Prés   6F5

3 Place St Germain des Prés A chapel dating from the 6th century stood here before the present building. The church, which is the oldest in Paris, survives from the powerful Abbey of St Germain des Prés. Built in the 11th century, the church was much restored in the 19th century. The Romanesque steeple, one of the oldest in France, dates from 1014; the spire was

rebuilt last century. Of three original towers, only the one above the façade remains. The flying buttresses and the chancel date from the same period as Notre Dame. Opposite, on the corner of the *place* and the Boulevard St Germain, is the famous **Café des Deux Magots**, where Jean-Paul Sartre and members of the Existentialist school of philosophy used to meet after the Second World War. (*Magot* means grotesque Chinese figure.)
Métro: St Germain des Prés. Buses 39, 48, 63, 86, 87, 95.

St Sulpice   6F5

Place St Sulpice Originally a parish church belonging to the Abbey of St Germain des Prés, the construction of St Sulpice, the work of six different architects, was the subject of great controversy. While the English historian Gibbon, judged it 'one of the noblest structures in Paris', Victor Hugo compared the two towers, unequal in height, to a pair of clarinets and the poet Raoul Ponchon in a celebrated outburst wrote: 'I hate the towers of St Sulpice'. Inside, the great organ, designed by Chalgrin, with its five keyboards, 20 pedals and 6500 pipes is one of the largest in Europe. The first chapel to the right of the nave facing the choir is decorated with frescoes by Delacroix and the holy water stoups on each side of the entrance, in the form of shells, are Venetian, given to François I by the Doge of Venice. Louis XV presented them to the church in 1745.
Métro: St Sulpice. Buses 63, 84, 86, 87, 96.

2 BOUL' MICH

Cluny, Musée de see p.60

Collège de France   6G5

Place Marcelin-Berthelot Next door to the Sorbonne and overlooking the Rue des Ecoles, the College, founded in 1530 by François I in order to combat the bigotry of the Sorbonne, still retains its independence and tradition of providing free higher education for the public, who can attend all lectures. The list of past and present professors is prestigious and includes Claude Bernard, Joliot-Curie and Lévi-Strauss, the anthropologist.
Métro: Maubert-Mutualité. Buses 86, 87.

Maubert, Place   6H5

Nicknamed 'La Maube', this is a traditional meeting place for students and a rallying point for demonstrations. On the corner with Rue Lagrange stands the Palais de la Mutualité where meetings, often political, are held.
Métro: Maubert-Mutualité. Buses 86, 87.

Panthéon, Le   6G6

Place du Panthéon Lying gravely ill at Metz, in 1744, Louis XV vowed that if he were cured he would rebuild the Abbey of Ste Geneviève. On his recovery this work was given to Marigny, brother of Madame de Pompadour. The monument alternated between its original purpose as a church and a last resting place for distinguished Frenchmen no less than five times before finally becoming a non-religious temple in 1885 when Victor Hugo's ashes were placed there. On the triangular pediment above the peristyle of Corinthian columns is a famous inscription 'Aux Grands Hommes, La Patrie Reconnaissante' (to great men, their grateful country). Inside, the dome has three cupolas, the second of which is decorated with a fresco representing Ste Geneviève, by Gros, and the walls of the choir are decorated with murals by Puvis de Chavannes. To the right of the choir is Jean Jacques Rousseau's tomb and in the crypt, the tombs, amongst many others, of Louis Braille, the inventor of the system of writing for the blind, Victor Hugo, Voltaire, Emile Zola and Jean Moulin, the French Resistance hero.
Métro: Luxembourg; RER Luxembourg B2/B4. Buses 84, 89.

St Etienne-du-Mont   6H6

1 Place Ste Geneviève Standing to the east of the Panthéon, the church is an interesting example of the transition from Gothic to Renaissance architecture. Inside, note the ribbed vaulting of the transept and the magnificent rood screen, the only one in existence dating from the 16th century. The decoration of the screen is pure Renaissance. Two spiral staircases lead to the rood loft. The Lady Chapel contains the tombs of Pascal and Racine. In the arcaded gallery of the cloister, called the Charnel House because of two small burial grounds discovered there, the 12 superb stained glass windows are early 17th century.
Métro: Luxembourg; RER Luxembourg B2/B4, Métro Cardinal Lemoine, Maubert Mutualité. Buses 84, 89.

St Julien-le-Pauvre   6H5

Rue Galande Situated almost next to the Church of St Séverin, St Julien, which is now a Melchite (Greek Catholic) church, was built between 1165 and 1220. Between the 13th and 16th centuries university assemblies and elections of the Chancellor were held in the church.
Métro: St Michel. Buses 24, 47, 63, 86, 87.

St Michel, Boulevard   6G6

Popularly known as the 'Boul'Mich', this lively street, with its libraries, second-hand bookshops and cafés full of students, is the very heart of the Latin Quarter. The Place St Michel, at the lower end of the Boulevard by the Seine was the scene of fierce fighting in 1944 between students and German troops and a plaque on the fountain commemorates the dead.

Métro: St Michel. Buses 21, 27, 38, 84, 85, 96.

St Séverin, Quartier de 6G5

The area lying east of the Place St Michel is made up of a number of ancient streets, collectively known as the Quartier St Séverin. The Rue de la Harpe, which was an old Roman road, leads via the Rue St Séverin to the **church** which stands in the Rue des Prêtres St Séverin. Gothic in architecture, part of the west front and the tower on the left date from the 13th century, while the upper storeys, balustrades and the rose window are 15th century. The interior which is notable for its breadth and for the absence of a transept, has a remarkable double ambulatory round the choir, with ribbed vaults rising from slender columns. The ribbing

continues in the form of spirals down the central pillar. The stained glass in the upper windows is 14th and 15th century.

Métro: St Michel. Buses 21, 24, 27, 38, 47, 85, 96.

Sorbonne, La 6G5

17 Rue de la Sorbonne Founded in 1253 by Robert de Sorbon, St Louis' chaplain, as a theological college for 16 poor students, the Sorbonne rapidly overshadowed all the other colleges of the University of Paris both in prestige and by the quality of its education. It played a leading role in many of the political and religious disputes during France's history, supporting Henry V of England in the Hundred Years War, and condemning the Protestants during the French Religious Wars and the Philosophes (free-thinking philosophers) in the 18th century. In May 1968, together with the college of Nanterre in the suburbs of Paris, the Sorbonne was the centre of student agitation which led to university reform throughout France. It is now the Universities of Paris III and Paris IV.

Métro: Luxembourg, Odéon; RER Luxembourg B2/B4. Buses 21, 27, 38, 63, 84, 85.

Café Deux Magots

PARKS & WOODLAND

Acclimatation, Jardin d'   1B3

This garden is in the north east corner of the Bois de Boulogne, near the Porte Maillot, and is a playground and amusement centre for children. It has a puppet theatre, a miniature railway and small zoo.

Métro: Port Maillot, Les Sablons. Buses PC, 43, 73.

Boulogne, Bois de   1B4

Known only as 'Le Bois', the woods stretch over 800 hectares/2000 acres to the west of Paris. The northern and southern limits are bounded respectively by the suburbs of Neuilly and Boulogne-Billancourt, its eastern limits border the 16th *arrondissement*, and the Seine flows along its western side. In former days, the Bois was strictly reserved for the royal hunt and it was not until the end of the 17th century that it was open to the public. Offered to the City in the mid 19th century by Napoleon III, Baron Haussmann, the Prefect of Paris at the time, demolished the surrounding walls and landscaped the area taking London's Hyde Park as his guide. The four **main entrances** to the Bois from Paris are the Porte Maillot in the north, the Porte Dauphine at the west end of the Avenue Foch, the Porte de la Muette which separates the Boulevard Lannes from the Boulevard Suchet, and the Porte d'Auteuil at the south end of the Boulevard Suchet. The entrances from the suburbs of St Cloud and Suresnes, on the opposite side of the Seine, are via the exit off the flyover of the A13 Motorway and from the Pont de Suresnes which leads directly to the Bois via the Route de Suresnes.

Several roads, with a speed limit of 40km/25mi per hour, run through the woods: the Allée de Longchamp crosses in a diagonal line from the Porte Maillot to the Carrefour de Longchamp; it is bisected by the Allée de la Reine Marguerite running from the Porte de Madrid in Neuilly to the Porte de Boulogne in the south, and the Route de l'Hippodrome which runs from the Porte de Passy (between the Portes de la Muette and Auteuil) to the Route de Suresnes and the bridge over the Seine.

Within the Bois de Boulogne there are several ornamental lakes, the two largest being the Lac Supérieur and the Lac Inférieur which are separated by the Route de l'Hippodrome. In addition there are several restaurants, two important race-courses – Auteuil and Longchamp, the Musée Nationale des Arts et Traditions Populaires (p. 59) near the Porte Maillot, and the little château of **Bagatelle** set within its own gardens on the north-west side of the Bois. In the 19th century it became one of the residences of Sir Richard Wallace, the English art collector. The gardens are famous for their displays of irises, rhododendrons, and magnificent roses in June. A windmill stands on the north side of the Longchamp racecourse, the relic of a former abbey which was demolished in 1789, and, near Carrefour de Longchamp, there is an artifical water-fall, La Grande Cascade. Continuing along the Route de la Grande Cascade you come to the restaurant, **Pré Catelan**. The gardens, contain a huge copper beech tree and a Shakespeare Garden with plants mentioned in his plays.

Métro: Porte Maillot, Porte Dauphine, Porte d'Auteuil. Buses PC, 32, 33, 43, 52, 63, 73, 82.

Buttes Chaumont, Parc des   4K3

Situated in the working-class 19th *arrondissement* on the east side of Paris, this is one of the least visited of Paris' parks. The original quarry site, known as Les Monts Chauves – the Bare Hills – was used as a rubbish dump until Baron Haussmann commissioned the engineer Alphand to transform it into an open space for the local inhabitants. Trees were planted, a small artificial lake hollowed out and the quarries turned into rock gardens. In 1871 the Buttes Chaumont was one of the last strongholds of the Communards.

Métro: Botzaris, Buttes-Chaumont. Buses 26, 60, 75.

Champ de Mars see p.100

Luxembourg, Jardin du see p.109

Monceau, Parc   2E3

The first park here was laid out in 1778 by Louis Carmontelle, designer and dramatist to Philippe-Egalité, Duc d'Orléans. Allowing his imagination to run riot, he produced a garden of fantasy, filled with follies, pagodas, a pyramid, a Roman temple, several windmills and a small farm. Although some of these disappeared during the Revolution and later, in 1852, when part of the park was sold off to make way for luxurious houses for the upper middle class, attracted by the surrounding area, quite a few still remain. The four entrances to the Parc Monceau have fine wrought-iron gilded gates. The rotunda which is the keeper's lodge, at the main entrance on the Boulevard de Courcelles, was taken from an 18th-century tollhouse which stood on the city wall. Skirting the

The Keep, Château de Vincennes

Tuileries

Palais du Luxembourg (Senate)

Tuileries, octagonal pond

north-east end of the artificial lake is a colonnade originally intended for the unfinished mausoleum of Henri II and Catherine de Médicis at St Denis and, nearby, a Renaissance arcade taken from the Hôtel de Ville.
Métro: Courcelles, Monceau, Villiers. Buses 30, 84, 94.

Montsouris, Parc   8G7
Laid out in the early years of the Third Republic on wasteland honeycombed by underground quarries, this 16 hectare/40 acre park is dominated at the centre by the **Meteorological Observatory**, where the temperature of the atmosphere is measured twice daily. The building is a replica of the Bey's palace at Tunis and was specially built, financed by the Bey, for the 1867 Universal Exhibition. On the day of the inauguration of the park, in 1878, the artificial lake unexpectedly and most inconveniently dried up, thus causing the suicide of the engineer responsible. In the streets surrounding the park is a number of small cottages and artists studios. Amongst those who lived and painted in the area were Georges Braque, Henri Rousseau and Seurat. Opposite the south side of the park is the Cité Universitaire de Paris, whose Brazilian and Swiss Halls were designed by Le Corbusier.
Métro: Cité Universitaire (Ligne de Sceaux). Buses PC, 21, 67.

Tuileries, Jardin des   6F4
Stretching from the Place de la Concorde to the Place du Carrousel, the gardens were originally laid out in two different styles. The earlier gardens were the private park of the Palais des Tuileries and designed in the Italian style. The formal French landscaping of the gardens stretching due west from the Avenue du Général Lemonnier to the terrace overlooking the Place de la Concorde, was the work of Le Nôtre who created the fine vista down the central alley, the artificial pools and the terraces bordering the gardens on each side. The Jardins des Tuileries have always been favoured by Parisians, first by the aristocracy before the Revolution, and later on by people from all walks of life, who came to admire the view of the Arc de Triomphe du Carrousel from the Place de la Concorde end, and the magnificent statues standing in the gardens.
Métro: Concorde, Tuileries, Louvre. Buses 68, 69, 72.

Vincennes, Bois de   7L6
Although Parisians shorten the name of the Bois de Boulogne, these woods are always known in full. Lying on the south-east edge of Paris on the Right Bank, they were a royal hunting reserve created by Philippe-Auguste early in the 12th century, closed to the public until 1731 during the reign of Louis XV. Within their confines a great number of attractions await the visitor. On the north side stands the fortified **Château de Vincennes** built by the Valois Kings. Continuing in a south-easterly direction you come to the **Parc Floral de Paris** whose superb displays of azaleas, roses and herbaceous plants in the summer attract thousands of visitors. Further east, encircled by a little ring road, is the Lac des Minimes, named after a monastery which once stood on the site, and next to the lake a tropical garden with a memorial to the Indo-Chinese who fought in the 1914-18 War. At the south-eastern corner of the woods is the **Breuil Horticultural School** whose gardens can be visited on written application to the director, and next to the gardens, Vincennes racecourse where trotting events are held. Evening meetings are floodlit. On the west side are a cycle track and the Lac Daumesnil with two islands in the centre. Finally, just north of the lake is the **Parc Zoologique**, stretching for 17 hectares/42 acres; it is France's largest zoo.
Métro: Porte Dorée, Château de Vincennes. Buses PC, 46, 56, 86.

IN GREATER PARIS & SUBURBS

Unlike most other large cities, the suburbs of Paris encompass a fairly small area and many, with woods and fields, have remained surprisingly rural, even up to the present day. Around Paris places of interest and châteaux abound and many of them can be reached easily by car or by the extensions of the métro.

Charenton
Musée du Pain 25 bis Rue Victor Hugo (tel: 368 43 60). Guided visits Tuesdays and Thursdays 1400–1700, closed 14 July–31 Aug. A unique collection devoted to the history of bread and pastry, with exhibits dating back to several centuries BC. The oldest piece of bread is probably the fragment found in an Egyptian tomb around 2400 BC. Cake moulds, waffle irons, Louis XIV's housekeeping accounts and figurines in brightly coloured bread dough are also among the exhibits on display.
Métro: Charenton-Ecoles.

Défense, La
Lying to the west of Paris, across the Pont de Neuilly, the towers of this modern suburb are visible on clear days from the summit of the Arc de Triomphe. Divided into several zones and forming part of the three communes of Courbevoie, Puteaux and Nanterre, the original objective of this

urban development was to provide Paris with a new business centre. *La Defense* has now also become a residential quarter with a large shopping centre *Les 4 Temps*, galleries, leisure and sports complexes.
Métro: RER La Défense, Pont de Neuilly.
Buses 73, 175.

Défense, Palais de la

On the north-west side of La Défense close by the RER station, this large concrete edifice, whose curiously inverted roof is supported at three points only, was inaugurated in 1959. Officially called the Centre National des Industries et des Techniques (CNIT), it is one of Paris' largest exhibition centres. In March, the Salon des Arts Ménagers (Ideal Homes Exhibition), previously held at the Porte de Versailles, is held here.
Métro: RER La Défense, SNCF Gare St Lazare.

Enghien-les-Bains

13km/8mi north of Paris, in the Val d'Oise département, Enghien is Paris' nearest spa, whose sulphurous waters are used in the treatment of throat and skin ailments and for rheumatism. In addition, Enghien possesses an important casino where galas are also held, and a racecourse.
SNCF Gare du Nord. Road: N14 Porte de Clignancourt, N192 La Défense.

Gros-Bois, Château de

Built at the end of the 16th century, this château was bought in 1805 by the Maréchal Berthier, Napoleon's Chief of Staff. He was mainly responsible for the magnificent decor and furniture from the late 18th century and the Empire.
Road: N19 SE of Paris. (8km/5mi from Brie-Comte-Robert.) RER Boissey-St Leger.

Louveciennes

24km/15mi west of Paris, on the road to St Germain-en-Laye, lies the little village of Louveciennes set on the edge of the Forêt de Marly. In the 18th century, Louveciennes was a popular country retreat for members of the aristocracy and several of the châteaux built at that time still remain – the most notable is the Pavillon de Musique which belonged to Madame Dubarry. It was built by Ledoux at the request of Louis XV. The Church of St Martin in the village was built in the 12th and 13th centuries, and beside the choir is a painting by Madame Vigée-Lebrun, who died in Louveciennes in 1842. Later, the area attracted many Impressionists.
SNCF Gare St Lazare. Road A13 Motorway.

Meudon

Situated just south of Sèvres, surrounded by forest, Meudon possesses two interesting museums, both of which can be visited in one afternoon at the weekend. The **Musée de Meudon** 11 Rue des Pierres, in the house of Molière's widow, is devoted to the history of the town and its châteaux.
The Musée Rodin Villa des Brillants, 19 Avenue Auguste Rodin, was the home of the sculptor and is an annex of the larger Musée Rodin (p.65) in Paris. The famous figure of Le Penseur marks Rodin's tomb in the garden. The inhabitants of Meudon have included Rabelais, and, for a brief period, Richard Wagner. Meudon is also the site of the **Observatoire d'Astronomie Physique** (astronomical observatory).
SNCF Gare Montparnasse. Bus 136 from Porte de St Cloud.

Puces, Marché Aux   3G2

Porte de Clignancourt This is Paris' largest flea market and, although it is now no longer possible to pick up inexpensive antiques, since many of the dealers also have premises in Paris, a visit here on a fine weekend is always entertaining. The market is divided into five sections, the Marchés Biron, Cambo, Jules-Vallès, Paul Bert and Vernaison, which specialize in china, curios, furniture and paintings. The Marché Malik, nearest to the métro, deals in records and second-hand clothes. Bargains in the form of 19th- and early 20th-century clothes can sometimes be found.
Open Saturdays, Sundays, Mondays.
Métro: Porte de Clignancourt. Buses PC, 85.

Reuil Malmaison

This suburb is associated with memories of Josephine, wife of Napoleon, who bought the Château de Malmaison in 1799 and spent the happiest years of her marriage here with the Emperor. Although many of the paintings from her private collection, including several magnificent works by Rubens and Rembrandt, were sold after her death to the Tsar Alexander I of Russia (and they now hang in the Hermitage Museum in Leningrad), the Château is open to the public.
On the ground floor are the Billiard Room which has a magnificent Savonnerie carpet, the Music Room with Josephine's harp and the Dining Room decorated with murals of dancers. The silver gilt centrepiece on the table is part of the service given to Napoleon by the City of Paris to mark the occasion of his coronation. Some of the furniture and contents of the Library, also on the ground floor, were originally in the Palais des Tuileries. The rooms on the first floor were

the private apartments of the Imperial couple and contain many personal souvenirs and relics, including Napoleon's canopied bed, Josephine's jewellery, her dressing case and table, and various portraits.

The second floor was occupied by La Reine Hortense, Josephine's daughter and mother of Louis Napoleon. The rooms contain many of her personal souvenirs and, in the Salle de Ste Hélène, which holds exhibits of Napoleon's internment on the island of St Helena, is the camp-bed on which he died, and his death mask. The gardens of the château include a very fine rose garden with examples of varieties planted by the Empress. On the Avenue de l'Impératrice, near the Château de Malmaison, lies the **Château de Bois-Préau**, once part of the domain. Bought by the American Edward Tuck, who bequeathed it to the state in 1926, it also contains souvenirs of Napoleon, including his grey rain coat and a black cocked hat. Métro: RER and then bus 158A from La Défense. Road N 13.

St Cloud, Parc de

The château of St Cloud, which was built by Louis XIV's brother (husband of Henrietta, Charles II of England's sister), was burnt down during the Franco-Prussian War of 1870. The Park, stretching for over 405 hectares/1000 acres, survives as a favourite spot with Parisians, particularly for walks at the weekends. The terrace of the Rond Point de la Balustrade overlooks the Seine and commands a fine view of Paris, the Bois de Boulogne and Meudon to the west. On the left is the Grand Cascade, a fountain decorated with allegorical figures, erected in the 17th century; the jet rises 42m/138 ft. The Jardin du Trocadéro, on the extreme south east, is laid out like an English garden. SNCF Gare St Lazare. Bus 72 Pont de St Cloud.

St Denis, La Basilique

Unfortunately disfigured by Debret, who undertook the restoration in 1813 after the damage caused by the Revolution, this Cathedral is nonetheless one of the most important examples of early Gothic architecture in France. Formerly an abbey, built in the 5th century, the present church was begun by the Abbé Suger in 1136 and construction continued until 1267. The chapels on the north side of the nave were added in the 14th century. The main façade has pointed Gothic and round Romanesque arches, a gallery with statues and the first rose window to feature in religious architecture.

In addition to its design, St Denis is notable for the fact that it is the burial ground for the Kings and Queens of France and their children. Among those whose tombs can be visited are François I and his wife Claude in the south transept, and, in the north transept, the 14th-century kings Philippe V, Charles IV, Philippe VI and Jean le Bon who died a prisoner in London. To the left of the ambulatory is the tomb of King Dagobert who was transported here at his own request, in order to die in the abbey in 638. Excavations in the crypt have brought to light the ruins of the former sanctuary and a royal Merovingian burial ground containing the tomb of Princess Aregonde, wife of the 6th-century king Clotaire I. Métro: Basilique St Denis. Road: A1 Motorway from Porte de la Chapelle.

Sceaux, Château

Lying to the south of Paris, the original château of Sceaux was built on a magnificent scale by Colbert between 1670 and 1677, but was destroyed during the Revolution. It was rebuilt in the style of a Louis XIII château by the Duc de Trévise in 1836, and is now the site of the **Musée Régional de l'Ile de France** which is devoted to the history and everyday life of the six *départements* making up the region. Exhibits include ceramic and porcelain from St Cloud and Sceaux, documents relating to De Dion Bouton's automobile factory and drawings and paintings depicting the surrounding areas of Paris and their architecture. The **Park**, laid out by Le Nôtre, is remarkable for its waterfalls leading to the small octagonal pond and then to the elongated artificial lake. The **Orangerie**, on the left of the château, was built by Hardouin-Mansart in 1685, and is now an exhibition and concert hall. Métro: Ligne de Sceaux. Buses 128, 194 from the Porte d'Orléans. Road: N20.

Porcelain clock in Sèvres museum

Sèvres

Musée National de Céramique Place de la Manufacture Nationale. Founded in 1805, the exhibits of this museum trace the development of ceramic and porcelain techniques from their earliest days to the 19th century. Although mainly devoted to France, examples of Arab, Dutch and Chinese ware are also included in the collection. Guided tours of the workshops, take place in the afternoons of the first and third Thursdays of the month.

Métro: Pont de Sèvres. Buses 169, 171, 179.

Versailles, Château de

Jealous of his finance ministers' château at Vaux-le-Vicomte and intent on creating an even more splendid monument which would perpetuate his name for ever, Louis XIV conceived the idea of rebuilding and enlarging his father's hunting lodge at Versailles, 22km/14mi to the west of Paris. Le Vau, first entrusted with the architecture, transformed the lodge into an Italianate building, but by 1678, it was too small to accommodate all the members of the Court (about 20,000 in all). From then on, for more than 50 years, the extension of Versailles continued. The cost of the conversion was enormous, amounting to over 60 million livres (a livre was equal to one pound of silver) and more than 30,000 workmen and 6000 horses were employed on the construction. After Louis XIV's death in 1715, the Regency left Versailles together with the Court, but Louis XV returned in 1722 and Louis XVI and Marie Antoinette lived there until forced to return to Paris in 1789. Abandoned during the Revolution, its furniture dispersed and the royal collections transferred to the Louvre, Versailles was turned into a museum by Louis Philippe in the 1830s. The famous Hall of Mirrors was used on two important occasions for France: on 18 January, 1871, after the French defeat in the war against his country, William of Prussia became First Emperor of Germany, and in 1919, the Treaty of Versailles between the Allies and Germany was signed there.

A complete tour of the château and its gardens in one day is almost impossible. Some rooms can only be visited in guided groups of 30. Check for visiting times. However you should try to see some of the following: **The Chapel**, decorated in white and gold, has superb carved gilt doors; sculptures are by Van Clève and Coustou. **The Salon d'Hercule** was a guardroom used to prevent unwelcome visitors from gaining entry to the State Apartments. Hercules is depicted on the ceiling of the room which also contains two fine paintings by Veronese. **Le Grand Appartement** is a series of six rooms where Louis XIV held court three times a week between 6 p.m. and 10 p.m. They were built by Le Vau and decorated under the supervision of Le Brun. The ceiling of each room is decorated with mythical figures. The rooms include: The Salon d'Abondance; the Salon de Vénus, which has ceilings decorated by Houasse, fine marble decorations and carved doors; the Salon de Diane, formerly the billiard room, which contains Bernini's bust of Louis XIV; the Salon de Mars, which was a concert room, and is decorated with early Gobelins' tapestries depicting scenes from Louis' life. The Salon de Mercure, formerly a gaming room, has a very fine Savonnerie carpet and an astronomical clock; finally, the Salon d'Apollon was the throne room. Louis XIV is depicted on the ceiling as Apollo in a chariot drawn by the seasons.

Next in order come the Salon de Paix and the Salon de Guerre, containing busts of Roman emperors and a huge oval medallion, by Coysevox, of Louis XIV on a horse trampling his enemies and being crowned by Minerva, Goddess of War. The **Galerie des Glaces**, Hall of Mirrors, is a truly sumptuous hall, whose 17 mirrors reflect the light from the 17 windows opposite. The deep red marble pilasters are decorated with bronze cock's heads, fleurs-de-lys and suns, and crowns are set along the cornice. Louis XIV appears in a stucco relief above the mantelpiece and in the magnificent painting on the ceiling by Le Brun, where he is represented in all his glory, surrounded by vanquished enemy countries. **Les Appartements du Roi** were Louis XIV's State Apartments. His bedroom and the bed on which he died in 1715, watched by a throng of courtiers, are preserved intact. Louis XV was responsible for the decoration of the adjoining **Council Chamber**. The decision to aid the Americans in the War of Independence was taken here. **Les Appartements de la Reine** include the bedchamber of Louis XIV's Queen, Maria-Theresa, and the Salon des Nobles de la Reine where visitors were presented to her. **Les Appartements prives du Roi** can only be visited if accompanied by a guide. Louis XV made these apartments into less formal suites which include Louis XV's bedchamber, where he died in 1774, his Inner Cabinet, the Library, where Louis XIV used to keep his most treasured works of art, and Louis XVI's Gaming Room, where Louis XIV also kept rare works of art. The decoration in the Queen's Apartments was redone for Marie Antoinette whose books are still

Marie Antoinette's retreat

Orangerie

Fontaine de Latone

Hall of Mirrors

housed in the library. **Madame de Maintenon**, Louis XIV's morganatic wife, lived in four rooms which comprise her bedchamber, containing several fine 17th-century works of art, two antechambers and her Grand Cabinet where she received and entertained members of the royal family. **Madame de Pompadour's Suite** is richly decorated with silk hangings and carved panelling and contains some very beautiful 18th-century furniture. In addition to all these rooms, there are the **16th, 17th, 18th and 19th century Galleries** containing portraits of those living at or associated with Versailles as well as decoration and furnishings appropriate to each period. Some are being restored and may not be open.

Les Jardins de Versailles Laid out by Le Nôtre, the gardens rank (with those at Vaux-Le-Vicomte) as one of the best-preserved examples of French classic landscape gardening, with their well-planned vistas, tree-lined alleys and lakes. Try not to miss the display of fountains at 1530–1700, three Sundays of the month, May to September, and the night fêtes held at the Bassin de Neptune (dates should be checked with the Office du Tourisme, 7 Rue des Réservoirs, behind the château).

Les Trianons Standing in the gardens, Le Grand Trianon, was designed by Hardouin-Mansart and Robert le Cotte. Built for Louis XIV and Madame de Maintenon, it was refurnished by Napoleon after his marriage to Marie-Louise of Austria. Much of its original marble decoration has, however, been retained. Le Petit Trianon, built during the reign of Louis XV, was a favourite retreat of Marie Antoinette who came here to escape the stifling etiquette of the Court
SNCF from the Gares Invalides, Montparnasse and St Lazare. A13 Motorway; bus 171 from the Pont de Sèvres.

Ville d'Avray

Situated to the south west of the Parc de St Cloud, this pretty little village with its two lakes is an agreeable halt on the old road to Versailles. The Church of St Nicholas, built in the 18th century contains frescoes and paintings by Corot.
SNCF Gare Montparnasse. Road N10 and then N185 (Rue de Versailles).

OUT-OF-PARIS TRIPS

Castles, monuments and other places of interest abound within a radius of 100km/62½ mi from Paris and the trips chosen represent only a small selection from the whole variety available. In addition to many private companies, the following also organize a wide choice of day and half-day excursions:

Caisse Nationale des Monuments Historiques et Sites, Bureau des Visites, 62 Rue St Antoine, 75004 Paris (tel: 887 24 14/15).
Comité Régional du Tourisme et des Loisirs d'Ile de France, 101 Rue de Vaugirard, Paris 6 (tel: 222 74 43)
Tourist Services of the RATP (Paris' public transport service), Place de la Madeleine (by the flower market), 75008 Paris (tel: 265 31 18) or 53 Quai des Grands Augustins, 75006 Paris (tel: 346 42 03). For further information on how to reach the various destinations telephone the **SNCF**: 260 51 51 or **France Information Loisirs**: 296 63 63 (for information in English: 720 88 98).

The figures in brackets at the head of the entries which follow are indications of the approximate distance from Paris.

Anet

Eure et Loire (80km/50mi) Situated 17km/10½mi north of Dreux, this Renaissance château was built by the architect Philibert Delorme for **Diane de Poitiers**, Mistress of Henri II. It was decorated by Jean Goujon, Germain Pilon and Benvenuto Cellini. Although the main part of the château was demolished just after the

Revolution, the main entrance, left wing and chapel still survive. Inside, the vestibule and staircase are later additions. The rooms contain tapestries, portraits and souvenirs of Diane. Her funeral chapel which contains her tomb, is on the Place du Château
SNCF Gare Montparnasse. Road N12 to Houdan, then D955.

Barbizon
Seine et Marne (56km/35mi) Set on the edge of the forest of Fontaine this charming village was the centre of the Barbizon school of painting. The landscape painter, Corot, lived here, 1830–5.
SNCF Gare de Lyon, then bus from Fontainebleau.

Beauvais
Oise (76km/47½mi) Although much of the town suffered from bombing during the Second World War, the magnificent Gothic Cathedral of **St Pierre** was virtually unscathed. Inside, the vaulting of the choir is supported by flying buttresses, and above the choir and the ambulatory chapels are windows and an open triforium. The stained glass dates from the 13th, 14th and 16th centuries. Specially woven tapestries dating from the 15th, 16th and 17th centuries, which used to hang in the cathedral, are now in a building by the remains of the Roman wall.
SNCF Gare du Nord. Road N1.

Châalis, Abbaye de
Oise (50km/31mi) Founded in 1136, only the ruins of this once powerful Cistercian abbey and its 13th-century chapel survive. The adjoining museum contains a collection of oriental and Roman antiquities and medieval and Renaissance furniture, sculpture and other works of art. Nearby the lakes and the large expanse of white sand, known as the Mer de Sable (sea of sand), provide a strange contrast to the surrounding forest of Ermenonville.
SNCF Gare du Nord to Ermenonville, then bus.

Chantilly
Oise (42km/26mi) Standing on a lake, two châteaux adjoin each other – Le Petit Château d'Enghien, now inhabited by the curator, and Le Grand Château, rebuilt in Renaissance style between 1875 and 1881 by the Duc d'Aumale. The museum in the Grand Château contains an outstanding collection of works of art amongst which are drawings by Clouet, paintings by Flemish and Italian masters, including Raphael, furniture and tapestries. The Cabinet des Livres in the Petit Château contains the original (15th-century) manuscript of the Très Riches Heures du Duc de Berry.
SNCF Gare du Nord. Road N16.

Chartres
Eure et Loire (87km/54mi) The spires of the Gothic Cathedral, one of the glories of French religious architecture, can be seen from a considerable distance, rising up from the plain of the Beauce. Among the most notable features of the cathedral are the magnificently carved portals, the nave and the choir and the stained glass dating from the 12th and 13th centuries, which is unique in France. In addition to the cathedral, Chartres is well worth a visit for its old quarter, and for its other churches and monuments.
SNCF Gare Montparnasse. Road N10 or Autoroute A11.

Chevreuse
Yvelines (36km/22mi) This pretty little village and its surrounding valley is a favourite area for Sunday drives from Paris. The 17th-century **Château de Breteuil** nearby (open Mon–Sat 1430–1800, Sundays and public holidays 1100–1800) contains a notable pearl-encrusted pedestal table and a fine collection of ancient copper and pewter kitchen utensils. The **Château de Dampierre** (4km/2½mi from the village) was built by Hardouin-Mansart in 1675–83, and the gardens were laid out by Le Nôtre.
RER St-Rémy-Les-Chevreuse then taxi.

Colombey-les-Deux-Eglises
Haute-Marne (240km/150mi)   La Boisserie was the home of **Charles de Gaulle**. He spent his periods out of office here, his weekends when he was President, and he retired here after the 1969 Referendum. The house is open to the public and you can visit the library where he wrote many of his speeches and memoirs. Just outside the village stands the huge rose granite Cross of Lorraine erected to his memory.
SNCF Gare de l'Est to Chaumont, then bus.

Compiègne
Oise (82km/51mi) The vast 18th-century palace, restored by Napoleon, is especially notable for its furniture and tapestries, and for mementoes of Marie Antoinette, Napoleon and his second wife, the Empress Marie-Louise. The building also houses a **transport museum**, with a collection of 18th-century coaches, early bicycles and automobiles. The palace park, modified by Napoleon, adjoins the forest.
SNCF Gare du Nord. Road Autoroute A11.

Ecouen

Val d'Oise (21km/13mi) Situated to the south east of the forest of Montmorency, this magnificent château houses the **Musée Nationale de la Renaissance** which groups together many of the exhibits formerly displayed at the Musée de Cluny in Paris. Notable are the Flemish tapestries David and Bathsheba, the furniture, ceramic ware and enamels.
SNCF Gare du Nord, then bus; or Métro St Denis, then bus 268C. Road N 16.

Ermenonville

Oise (47km/30mi) The forest at Ermenonville was a favourite haunt of the philosopher and writer, Jean Jacques Rousseau who lived in the château. The park is a fine example of 18th-century French landscaping. Nearby, is the abbey at Châalis (see above) and the zoo.
SNCF Gare du Nord.

Fontainebleau

Seine et Marne (65km/41mi) Built largely by François I in the 16th century, the **château** was much favoured by French monarchs. It was added to in the 17th and 18th centuries. The richly decorated interior contains fine examples of period furniture and tapestries and there are souvenirs of many royal inhabitants. The **forest** of Fontainebleau, stretching for over 17,000 hectares/42,000 acres, is one of the most interesting in France, with its light-coloured sand, strange rock formations and gorges. Oak trees predominate but there are also Scots pine, beech and birch between the glades. Several main roads traverse the forest and bus tours across it and to the most interesting sites, such as the Gorges du Franchard, run from the town. (Information from the Office de Tourisme, 31 Place Napoleon Bonaparte, tel: 6422 2568.)
SNCF Gare de Lyon.
Road Autoroute A6.

Giverny

Vernon (82km/51mi) Open daily 1 Apr–31 Oct, 1000–1200 and 1400–1800. The painter Claude Monet lived here from 1883 until his death in 1926. Hung with reproductions of his paintings, and his collection of Japanese prints, rooms visited include his bedroom, library, studio and tiled kitchen. The gardens, laid out by the artist, include bamboos, rhododendrons and a fine weeping willow by the Japanese bridge crossing the water lily pool which inspired his famous *Nympheas* series.
Gare St Lazare to Vernon, then taxi. Road Autoroute A13 to Mantes, then N13, then D5.

Maisons-Laffitte

Yvelines (20km/12mi) An important horse-racing and training centre, the town also possesses a 17th-century château built by François Mansart. Jean Cocteau was born here in 1889.
SNCF Gare St Lazare.

Milly-la-Forêt

Essonne (58km/36mi) Lying on the west side of the forest of Fontainebleau, Milly is a centre for the cultivation of medicinal herbs. A 15th-century market hall, constructed entirely of oak and chestnut, stands in the central square. At the exit of the village, on the road to Nemours, is the chapel of **St Blaise de Simples** decorated by Jean Cocteau, who is buried there.
SNCF Gare de Lyon to Fontainebleau, then bus. Road Autoroute A6 exit Fontainebleau.

Montmorency

Val d'Oise (20km/12mi) The philosopher and writer Jean Jacques Rousseau lived here from 1756 to 1762. His house, at 5 Rue JJ Rousseau, is a museum containing his documents, souvenirs and mementoes.
SNCF Gare du Nord.

Moret-sur-Loing

Seine et Marne (72km/45mi) Standing on the River Loing, Moret, once an ancient fortress and royal residence, still retains its 14th-century gateways. There is a good view from the bridge of the ancient church, the castle keep and the ramparts. Son et Lumière shows take place in the summer. (Information from Office de Tourisme, Place Samois, tel: 6070 4166 15 April–30 Sept.)
SNCF Gare de Lyon, then bus. Road A6 to Fontainebleau, then N6.

Orléans

Loiret (107km/67mi) Although it sustained considerable damage during the Second World War, this important town has been well restored. Rich in history, Orléans is particularly associated with **Joan of Arc** who delivered the town from the English in 1428. Her statue, erected in 1855, stands in the Place du Martroi in the centre, not far from the **Cathédrale Ste Croix**, originally founded in the 13th century but rebuilt by Henri IV and added to in the 18th and 19th centuries. Other places of interest in the town are Joan of Arc's house, containing documents and models of battles she fought, the **Musée des Beaux Arts** in the former town hall, the **Eglise de St Paul** contains a 16th-century Black Virgin, and the 11th-century crypt of the **Eglise St Aignan**.
SNCF Gare d'Austerlitz.

Pierrefonds

Oise (87km/55mi) The castle of Pierre-
fonds lies south west of the forest of
Compiègne. Built in the 14th century by
Louis d'Orléans, brother of Charles VI, it
was demolished two centuries later and lay
neglected until 1813 when Napoleon I
bought the ruins. But it was Napoleon III
who had the castle rebuilt, in the style of the
original, under the supervision of Viollet le
Duc. The quadrangular building has
impressive defence towers at each corner
and in the centre of each façade.
SNCF Gare du Nord. Road N2 to Villers-
Cotterets then D 973 to Compiègne.

Provins

Seine et Marne (85km/52½mi) Comprising
two distinct parts, La Ville Haute and La
Ville Basse – upper and lower towns –
Provins was an important commercial
centre in the Middle Ages. At the end of the
13th century, Edward of Lancaster,
through marriage to the Countess of
Champagne, became Lord of the town and
incorporated the red roses, which grew
there, into his coat of arms. Within the
ramparts, still partly surrounding the
upper town, stand the 13th-century
Grange aux Dimes (tithe barn) and the
12th-century keep and church of **St
Quiriace**. The lower town contains
several 13th-century buildings, the church
of **Ste Croix** (13th-16th century) and the
church of **St Ayoul.**
SNCF Gare de l'Est. Road N19.

Rambouillet

Yvelines (54km/36mi) Begun in the 14th
century and enlarged in the 17th and 18th
centuries, the **château** is now the official
country residence of the Presidents of the
Republic. François I died here in 1547,
Louis XV a frequent visitor, Napoleon
spent the night here before leaving for St
Helena, and Charles X signed his
abdication prior to leaving for England in
1830. Much of the rich interior decoration
and furnishings were due to the financier
d'Armenonville who bought the property
in 1700. The **Bergerie Nationale**
(national sheep farm) in the grounds was
founded by Louis XVI who was fond of
farming. The **forest** of Rambouillet, a
royal and, later, presidential hunting
ground, is almost as extensive in area as
Fontainebleau. Parisians love to walk here
and to picnic on the edges of the lakes.
SNCF Gare Montparnasse. Road N10.

Royaumont, Abbaye de

Oise (34km/21mi) Lying south of Chantilly, and founded in 1228 by St Louis who
was also married here a few years later, this
Cistercian abbey was one of the most
powerful in northern France until its
secularization, in 1791, during the Revolution. Considerable parts of the abbey
remain, including the church tower, the
vaulted refectory, kitchens and cloister.
SNCF Gare du Nord to Luzarches, then
bus. Road N16, direction Chantilly.

St Germain-en-Laye

Yvelines (21km/13mi) Except for the
12th-century keep, the castle of St
Germain-en-Laye as it stands today was
built by François I during the last ten years
of his reign, in the middle of the 16th
century. It was enlarged by Hardouin-
Mansart in the 17th century. The castle
houses the **Museum of National Antiquities** whose exhibits include prehistoric
remains, silver articles and jewellery from
the Roman and Merovingian periods. On
the north-east side, the Terrasse de St
Germain, laid out by Le Nôtre, leads to
the Grille Royale and the forest.
Métro RER.

Senlis

Oise (51km/31½mi) Hugues Capet was
elected Duke of France in this ancient royal
residence, in 987. Traces of the ramparts
surrounding the old town and a good many
old houses, dating from the 14th and 15th
centuries, still remain. The 12th-century
cathedral contains a beautiful gallery and
a 16th-century vault in the east chapel of
the south transept. To the south west of the
town are remains of a Gallo-Roman arena.
SNCF Gare du Nord. Road Autoroute A1.

Thoiry

Yvelines (46km/28mi) The grounds of the
16th-century château are now an African
animal reserve and zoo, with bears,
giraffes and lions. The castle has a fine collection of furniture and tapestries.
RER C5 to Versailles Rive Gauche then
bus. Check bus departures (tel: 3054
2772).

Vaux-le-Vicomte

Seine et Marne (50km/31mi) This very
beautiful 17th-century château was built
by Fouquet, superintendent of finances
under Mazarin. Three supreme artists
were employed – Le Vau, architect, Le
Brun, decorator and Le Nôtre to landscape
the gardens in French classic style. In
1661, Fouquet gave a lavish reception for
Louis XIV, who was so displeased at this
show of extravagance that Fouquet was
sentenced to life imprisonment. Louis
then engaged Le Vau, Le Brun and Le
Nôtre to build the château de Versailles.
Check visiting times (tel: 066 97 09):
SNCF Gare de Lyon to Melun, then bus or
taxi.

INDEX

All place names, buildings and monuments which have a main entry are printed in heavy type. Map references also appear in heavy type and refer to Central Paris Maps between pages 40–57.